What The Hell Was I Thinking?!!

'What The Hell Was I Thinking?!!'
Confessions of the World's Most Controversial Sex Symbol

Published in the USA by:
BearManor Media
PO Box 1129
Duncan, Oklahoma 73534-1129
www.bearmanormedia.com

ISBN 978-1-59393-604-4

Printed in the United States of America.
Book design by Brian Pearce | Red Jacket Press.
Cover photo by Robin Perine, Seeing Red Studio. *www.robinperine.com*

MaryJane Clements – Hair & Makeup

What The Hell Was I Thinking?!!

Confessions of the World's Most Controversial Sex Symbol

Jasmine St. Claire
WITH JAKE BROWN

Table of Contents

ACKNOWLEDGMENTS

First, a few words from Jasmin...

WOW!!!!!!!!!! I cannot believe that this book is actually done. Writing this book has been the most therapeutic experience ever and I got to relive so many great moments and many heartbreaking memories. When my ex husband threatened to divorce me if I wrote the book, it took a back burner for a few years...divorcing me was the biggest favor he did for me. I have had an amazing and brilliant life full of joy, tears, travels, fearlessness, laughter, adventure, heartaches and most of all filled with love from my close friends. If certain events did not happen in my life, I may never have had many of the adventures that I did and sure as hell never would have met some of the great people that are in my life now. I am so glad that I was never one of the "lucky ones" who got married right after school and had kids. If I did that, there would be no book or great experiences to share with others.

Since the last chapter of this book, a major change took place in my life. I was, once again, hurt terribly and had my heart broken more than ever. This came in the form of the true love of my life. I will always remember the warm Summer afternoon that he left me in a hotel in NY so he could go and eat with his family. Upon his insecure sister's request, he left me back at the hotel. By his own admittance his sister was jealous, had a lot of issues in her own relationship and never liked me from the second she met me (she claimed I was cheap and trashy looking and he had given up on love thats why he was with me), despite how much I was nice to his family. I do understand that racism also played a role in this. He had no character and should have addressed this issue with his family before taking nearly two years of my life. Thats what I get for standing by someone I had the most perfect and happy relationship with. I was the one who respected him more than his own family for the man he was no matter what. I would have lived with him anywhere in the world and he knew that. True loyalty and unconditional love are hard to find. I doubt he will ever see truth behind his family, their controlling ways, jealousies, disrespect towards him and most of all taking away his chance to move forward in his career in California. The last thing my true love said was for me to do something about my eyebrows because they were very "negative looking." It's okay, because my life goes on and I will never shut my heart down and always be the loyal one who stands by someone no matter how good or bad they have it and most of all, I know who I am and am proud of that. At least I live my life for myself and make my own choices sans influence.

I will never ever complain about anything that I have done or anywhere I have been. Everything you are about to read in this book is real...you couldn't make this stuff up. I am not apologizing to anyone in advance for any feelings that may be hurt..you dance with the devil ; you have to pay the price.

The thank yous are the hardest part of this book and I don't know where to start.

I must thank Jake Brown for being so patient when we started working together on this, Paul Heyman (Ex ECW owner) for giving me first chance to work for a major wrestling company...ECW was a great place, my dear friend Amy for always being there for me no matter when, where and what time...you are the sister I never had and am so lucky to have you in my life Pookie bear, Bill Hudson for being the kid brother I never had and also being there during the worst heartbreak ever, I gotta thank every band that I have ever tortured..oops I mean interviewed.. it was great getting to know the human sides of everyone and I will always respect and support the metal scene, my lawyer Raymond R Granger for being the best damn lawyer in NYC...or actually in the whole country (look him up if you need a damn good lawyer), our agent Albert Longden for your tirelessly hard work getting this book to the finish line, our publisher Ben Ohmart and BearManor Media, Robin Perine for the amazing cover photo, Ron Estrada for always being a great friend, Rebecca (Viva Rebecca) for the killer jewelry on the book cover and most of all for the friendship and creativity over the years, BP at Cleopatra records, Howard Stern, Charlie Frey, Fred Sherman for being a great friend and helping out with the book shoot, Lemmy just for being you, pumpkin and socks the cats for all that you do, Matt Larsen, everyone who helped with the guitars, my mom for giving birth to me and raising me to be humble, respectful and independent, my dad for everything...not a day goes by that I don't cry for you...I will never get over your death, my family at Stay Heavy TV, my friends and fans for the love and devotion over the years and most of all the ex boyfriends from hell for derailing my life and breaking my heart...without you people I never would have half the adventures and wild times in my life...OBRIGADA!!!!!!

INTRODUCTION

America's Most Controversial Sex Symbol

When I got into the business in 1995, the adult film industry was at a crossroads, to put it gently. More roughly — which is what I'm known for in that world — the business was in midst of a mid-life crisis. Traci Lords and Samantha Fox had gone legitimate, and there was a void that clearly needed filling, by 300 men in 24 hours to be exact. That was one of the records I set anyway, during my years dominating adult film. It was time for a new ecstasy; men were tired of the ordinary white trash and looking for something a little more exotic. That's where I came in, and within a year I had become known as ' America's Most Controversial Sex Symbol.' I had always turned the tongues out of men's mouths, like that sexy little porn star in the school girl's uniform you boys always seem to be fantasizing about. Except I really have the Ivy League education. I also speak four languages fluently, which means four times the tongue action I've got working for me around the world. My friend recently went into a small mom-and-pop adult film shop in the heart of Chicago, and asked if they had anything by me, just out of curiosity, and the clerk told him I was still their best selling star. I've been out of the adult film business for over ten years, but as far as most men in America are concerned in their fantasies, I've never left their bedrooms, let alone their fantasies.

I pushed the boundaries of porn to where they needed to be re-adjusted at that time, and really treated it like a business. Men obviously responded to something about my sexuality, so I worked hard to make it my very own brand. I went through some horrific times on my way to the top, but I never looked at myself like a victim. I had a choice, and used it to make sure that men didn't from the first time they laid eyes on me. The aftermath was a multi-million dollar mini-industry that grew out of my desire to please my fans in a way that they'd never seen before me, and couldn't ever forget afterward. I've gotten thousands of letters from fans telling me I was the greatest sexual experience of their life, and most of them never laid more than eyes on me. The point is the indelible place I hold in their memories, and this is the chronicle of my own. Come with me behind the legendary lust, beyond the fantasies, past any borders or boundaries into easily one of the wildest world of fantasies the world of adult film has ever known. This world is mine, and I'm finally ready to share every one of its naked truths with you...

PART I

Paradise Lost

I was born in St. Croix, the U.S. Virgin Islands on October 23rd. My father owned the biggest distribution company on the island that dealt with cigarettes, chips, soda, beer, and so on to all the stores on the island. His company carried just about everything you needed. When I was 4, my parents divorced and I moved to New York City with my mother. Though I was raised day-to-day by my mother, my parents remained very civil to each other for my sake, and so I never felt my father was absent from my life. I would visit him in the summers, and talk on the phone regularly. He would also come up in the spring, and eventually relocated back to the city. Back in New York, I lived with my mom and grandmother, who helped raise me for the better part of my childhood. My spring and part of my summers were usually spent in London or Brazil where I had family.

When we first moved to the Big Apple, we lived across the bridge in the Midwood section of the neighboring borough of Brooklyn, in a two-story Brownstone, which had a nice pretty flower-garden in the back. Many times when I would fall to sleep at night I would feel like I wasn't alone in my room. I would wake up in the morning and find all the furniture re-arranged in the Dollhouse. Other times the T.V. would turn off involuntarily. Another time, when my cousin was over, we were sitting at the kitchen table waiting for lunch, and that day, my cousin was wearing corduroy pants and snow boots. Well, at one point, a pair of feet started kicking me under the table, and when I looked down, I saw a pair of white ballerina stockings, with white ballerina slippers, all colored pasty white. I kept looking up and down at the floor, my cousin finally asked me what was wrong, and I explained what I was seeing. Both my cousin and my mom thought it was just my imagination that time. It wasn't until one night a couple of weeks later when I awoke throwing up little white chunks that my mother started to believe me. No one — doctors my mom took me to see — could determine the cause of this. When my mother did a little research into the background of the house, it turned out a little girl my age had been poisoned there by her parents and had died in same spot my bed sat; in the very room I called mine. We moved shortly after that, which is when we moved to Manhattan, but I kept going to private school in Brooklyn.

I went to a private Montessori School for the first year of my scholastic life. For most of my adolescent years, Brooklyn Friends School, which had very small class sizes, was a great way to learn. My mom liked the Quaker philosophy, which is very non-competitive, and I was happy there. I was a very quiet student who got very good grades. Though I kept attending the Quaker school, at age 7, my family moved to the West Side of Manhattan by Central Park. It was really a good place to be raised, because you're in the middle of everything cultural — all the plays, museums, all the great restaurants, it was just awesome. I think my mom did a great thing raising me as a single parent because from a very young age, it taught me the importance of independence. The flipside of that came with the fact that both she and my grandmother were also very protective of me too, so as a child, I did pretty much everything with one or the other of them. My grandmother would take me to Central Park every day, and because I lived in Manhattan and went to school in Brooklyn, I didn't really have many close friends as a younger child. I was picked on at times by these fat kids at my school, one fat bitch in particular named Sidney Silver. She looked like a fat, Jewish pig; if Miss Piggy was Jewish and miserable that's what she'd look like. So I had to go to see a child psychologist for about a year, but I eventually learned to speak up for myself.

My best friend in grade school was an African-American girl named Njeri and we'd go shopping for Barbies every week — she'd get the black one, I'd get the white one, we were very close. I was accelerated twice in my life between 4th and 5th grade, and 7th and 8th grade, so I was used to dealing with older people all my life. I was still very quiet though, I think because I skipped grades; it made my mom a bit more protective, so I wasn't allowed to go out nearly as much as the kids around me in school were. I felt really comfortable at home, and didn't like sleepovers as I didn't like being around other kids as much. I liked it at Friends School; that's where I went most of my academic career before college. The atmosphere was very supportive of learning, and less about stupid JAP social scenes, everyone was all about helping one another, and weren't there to cut your throat. So at that school, I was around really good people.

In my younger years, I'd travel a lot to Europe and Brazil to see my extended family. I didn't know what it felt like to have siblings, but I'd have to say the closest thing I had to that were my cousins Cindy and Patrick, who lived in London. Patrick would pick on us like you wouldn't believe, like a big brother might, and it scared me at first like you wouldn't believe because I was so non-confrontational as a child. He would pretend to be a ghost, move the furniture around, and just fuck with us all the time like he was scaring his little sisters. Back in New York, my cultural education was very important to my mother, and so she and I went to a play and to a museum exhibit every weekend. I remember once my mother had tickets to the King Tut exhibit, and I could tell her all the exhibits. I would go with a friend every weekend, which was really cool. I think the museums and plays molded me quite a bit, I was spoiled by all the different foods, and I would say traveling overseas every summer was a great thing because not many kids had an opportunity to do that. Being exposed to different cultures, going on summer trips to Europe and Brazil, it was all amazing because its very normal for kids growing up in New York to never leave Brooklyn, or Queens, or even Manhattan.

When I was younger, up until about 10 when my dad moved back to New York, I would go to the U.S. Virgin Islands in the spring to visit him. I felt privileged, and had a lot of kids that were jealous of me for it. I remember once my mom picked me up on my seventh birthday from school and took me straight to Florida, to Disney, and it was a total surprise. So some kids were jealous, which is part of why I didn't have as many friends as other kids did back then. I don't regret it though; it was one of the best things in the world. If I have a child of my own some day, I want them to travel, I'd insist on it. Being around everything as a child was like an amazing Carnival ride — Central Park, Manhattan, the theatres, going to see a play every weekend with my mom — it was great. There weren't a lot of kids who had that luxury. My mom was definitely my best friend then, and to her credit she never said anything fucked up about my father, because he never did anything fucked up. They didn't have a nasty split; I just think she basically pushed him away. It wasn't abnormal too for me to grow up in a single-parent home, because my best friend was raised by a single mother, and in Manhattan, so it didn't feel like anything uncommon or out of the ordinary. My parents never bickered or fought in front of me.

I looked up to my mom back then, and as I mentioned before, she remained my best friend throughout those early years, her and my first cat, a little gray tabby I got from the ASPCA that I named Scooter. I really like animals. I always had a soft spot for them. Once in a while, my mom would let me have a day off from school, just for being good, and would take me shopping. My mom was definitely the closest one to me back then, because she was really the only other person I had around me that whole time. Every single weekend, for instance, we had a routine where we'd go see a matinee movie or play, then go to Howard Johnson's in Times Square, and I'd always have the clam strips and a milk shake. From seeing all the theatre I did when I was a kid too, it might surprise you, but I never had an interest in acting that stemmed from that. In fact, when I was a little kid, I wanted to be a Veterinarian when I grew up. I had no interest in acting, though I did take ballet classes as a child. I never wanted to do acting, because I was always smart, and thought I didn't need it. In fact, I did drama one year and didn't like it, I didn't like the people I worked with, and this was at the Anglo-American school. It was ironic, because I went to summer school and different classes after my regular school day was over all during my formative years, and NOT because I needed to catch up, but because I was ahead. I was taking AP language classes, and different courses too advanced to be offered at the school I was at. I never liked the social scenes at most of the schools I attended. I hated the petty cliques, and was always more interested in excelling, or going to France for the summer to learn in French.

Most people who know me today wouldn't believe that, but I was very quiet as a kid. I was a nerd — a HOT nerd, but a nerd for sure. I played recorder and guitar in junior high, but I wanted to play drums because I loved the Go Go's back then. Mainly, I liked Heavy Metal — it represented the dark side of things, which I was really attracted to. My first two concerts were Black Sabbath and Carcass, but Iron Maiden was hands-down my favorite band back then — Eddie was my icon. My mom thought it was weird, but didn't see it as a hostile thing until I started hanging out with these longhaired guys. She never knew I went to rock shows, I had to sneak out. My dating life was even more pathetic at first, because my mom watched me like a hawk, and I really didn't start seriously dating till I was 16, I was too concerned during those years in-between with sneaking out to go to concerts. My best friend in high school was a girl named Penny, and we were both disciples of metal. We had French together, and had met in a study group. She was Greek-American, very pretty with long black hair, and I knew she smoked pot, which intrigued me. One day after school she invited me to go home with her and I tried pot with her. We looked like twins, and both wore black, matching Bowler hats, which were the 'in' thing back then. We both loved metal competitively, and would go to see everyone together. We saw Carcass, Morbid Angel, Suffocation, Warlock, Iron Maiden, Anthrax, Cannibal Corpse, Megadeth and others. We would sneak off to the Garden, Irving Plaza, the Beacon Theatre, and CBGB where they had matinee shows. Because we spent so much of high school going out to rock and metal shows, our routine was: I would tell my mom I was at her house, and we'd sneak out instead. Looking back, it was typical teenage stuff to me. Naturally my mother would have seen it differently, as evinced by the MUCH harder time she gave where dating guys was concerned. Because of that, I definitely discovered guys well before I was publicly dating them. I loved metal heads from the get-go. I felt they were much better looking than any stupid pop star. I liked the music, the guitars; the harshness — everything there was to like about heavy metal. I dug the anger in the music, I thought it was awesome, and I related to it as well but who didn't as a kid. The first guys I really flirted with dating at that age were the guys at the metal shows, even though I was still too shy to speak to anyone. I thought a lot of the guys who went to metal shows were cute, but I was also scared of them because many of them were fucked up. I would hang out in places like Hell's Kitchen, later on in high school, but I was always at the shows — and believe it or not, always went straight home afterwards.

In terms of my shyness, it got better as I got later into my teens because I took a non-matriculated Public Speaking course independently at Columbia University while I was still in high school. That definitely helped me to learn to speak up for myself. I focused pretty heavily on languages in high school, and thought at one point about teaching. While I was still in high school, I had also taught in an after-school program called '*Art Without Walls*,' which I really liked, and was a really great non-profit organization. My best friend's mother ran that whole program, so I taught French to under-privileged kids whose parents were in prison. At Friends School, you had to put in X amount of hours of community service for graduation, and it was a really good experience. I also went to the New School for Social Research, in another after-school capacity, to study accounting, and some other fucking Poindexter courses. That was distracting, but I really enjoyed the French, and had a way with languages. I spoke four languages — Portuguese, French, German, and Spanish — which I excelled at. Another thing I tried to excel at during this period was sneaking away to Washington Square Park, which wasn't far from the New School, and to Sheep's Meadow, which was the first place I ever had an acid trip. My friend Penny and I were off the rest of that day from school, and it was nice out, so I figured what the fuck? We were about 10 blocks away from my friend's house, which was across from the 57th Street Playhouse. So I remember calling my mom to tell her I was going to sleep over at Penny's and I was just flipping out. She wasn't buying it, and by the time we got back to Penny's house, my mom was already downstairs at the restaurant Penny's mom owned and operated — which incidentally was across from her house — giving her mom reasons why I shouldn't sleep over. It was like debating, and thankfully I was in the debate club, so we won her over and thank God I got to sleep it off at Penny's house.

Then I dropped acid a second time a few weeks later, this time two hits of Clown-Face acid, and went to Laser Floyd, and then Laser Zeppelin shows both in the same day. The next day I had my driver's test and I was still tripping, so needless to say I failed. At one point in the test, I thought a tree was moving while I was driving and in trying to drive around the tree, ended up running right into it. I think I eventually passed the second or third time I took the test. It hardly mattered in the end since growing up in New York with the subways, you hardly drove. Anyway, I didn't do hard drugs in high school, just weed here and there, and of course the acid. Aside from the mind-altering, I was always into the mind-opening, and I had always been in a pretty open environment culturally growing up in New York, where I was encouraged to take everything around me in, but it had always been under my mom's protective wing. So when I got a bit older, and I started growing physically into a woman, and wanted to continue with that same routine of exploring, my mom took on an entirely different attitude, and the tone changed completely between us on the subject. That changed my focus too because I was so baffled by some of the things my mother would say to me about going out. For instance, I wanted to walk around the Village one weekend with a friend of mine, and my mom took the attitude of 'Well, you have to let me know where you're going and I have to be there.' It was just the way she would say it.

When I entered my last couple years of high school, her tone changed radically toward me, because she made it seem like I wanted to go out in the street and do drugs and get laid, that's the way she made it seem. But that wasn't ever what I was trying to do, and because she's an attorney, she was very good at arguing, so there was always an argument about something. Mind you this was in the daytime too, not at night. She used to check my answering machine when I wasn't home to keep track of who I was talking to and get any dirt she could on me.

For as close as my mom and I were in my younger years, as I blossomed into a teenager, we couldn't have found ourselves more far apart from one another. Take, for instance, the topic of Sex Ed. When it was time for my mom and I to have that talk, I didn't hear about the birds and the bees from my mom's mouth: instead it came from her therapist Judy Detrik! She never had any discussions with me about sex, or even a woman having her period — it was all done through a therapist, which I thought was weird to say the least. I don't think it made her a bad mother, just green in a way. I had my first therapy session at 14. It inspired me out of my interest in going to a movie with a guy who was a year older than me. That must have set all sorts of wild fire alarms off in my mom's head — sirens and all — because she rushed me right in to see this woman to have the whole sex talk. I think my mom's hope was that the therapist would talk me out of the date, and men altogether? I still don't have that one completely figured out to this day. Anyway, when we got there, my mother told the therapist she wanted to control me, and asked the therapist to instruct her on how to do so. She had told the therapist all of this before I'd gotten there, and by the look on her face when I walked in, she was clearly expecting someone who had tattoos all over her body, wearing some slut uniform, and I couldn't have looked more demure. So after talking briefly with me, the therapist told my mother, ' Look, I can't tell you how to control your child, because she's not out of control in my opinion. She seems demure, quiet and sensible, like she can make her own judgment calls.' We got nowhere because there was nothing going on! It was fucking ridiculous, so much so that she made me see a second therapist, Barry Frankowitz. That was even more pathetic, because he just sat there pumping me for information on whether I was doing drugs, and having wild sex, and all this silly shit to be asking me given how shy I was, and for my age. I never did anything to deserve to sit there in an office for an hour on nice, spring day with these doctors denying that I was out '*prostituting*.' That became my mother's favorite word very early on. I remember how wild she reacted concerning the very first date I was ever going on, the one that landed me with the therapist to begin with. The boy was a year older than I. We were going to see the Talking Heads movie. She ended up calling up the boy's parents, and just ranting on and on, ' Do you know your son is going to a movie with my daughter?' And of course, his parents had no idea why she was reacting so wildly, and said YES, they did know we were going out. So my mom ended up chaperoning us to the movie, sat in a seat a few rows behind us, then trailed us to McDonald's and sat at another booth while we ate. I didn't understand what was so abnormal about that. What really freaked me out though was a few months later, when another boy asked me to my first high school dance, which is chaperoned by both parents and teachers, and my mom forbade me to attend that as well. She really ruled my life with an iron fist back then.

Then when I had just turned 16, my mom made me go with her back to Barry's and that shit lasted for almost a full year. It's hard enough as a teenager trying to fit in with your peers and develop any sort of confidence as a young woman when your mother is constantly trying to keep you 10 years old forever. On top of that, most of the children I attended school with got massive freedom in exchange for the type of grades I routinely brought home. But my reward was even more scrutiny. Occasionally, she'd buy me things to compensate for the freedom I wouldn't get, like a diamond necklace from Cartier. Tell me what fifteen year old has diamonds. It was obvious a reflection of the extent of her guilt. Other times, my mom would take me to ride my scooter sometimes after school. She'd leave work early to take care of me, which I thought was important in spite of her overall nutty approach to raising and disciplining me.

One of my mom's favorite surveillance tactics was to sit and listen in on my phone conversations, with boys or girls. As you can imagine it used to make me feel uncomfortable. Of course I knew she was on the other line, and it was very embarrassing. Among my mother's more absurd episodes was sending me away to England for the weekend because she didn't want me attending the Halloween Day Parade. Part of why I had so little experience dating, which led me to get involved with Dick 'The Pelicanose' later on because of that lack of confidence, was that even years earlier, she always did everything she could do break up any dating scenario I was ever in. In the New York private school system, it was hard enough to make friends because everyone is so cliquish, especially if you're a metal head like I was, so you can imagine it was that much harder to meet guys. One of my first boyfriends, for example, dumped me because my mom never gave me the freedom to go out and spend any time with him. It was always an issue for her, and she always came between relationships. His name was Damien, and we dated when I was 15 1/2. He was Jewish, very quiet, had long, curly black hair, was really good looking, shared my love of Heavy Metal — Carcass and Suffocation specifically, and went to school with me. He was my first love as it were, and we shared some very special moments together, from our clandestine afternoons together after school to sharing the loss of virginity together — he was very special to me. My best friend at the time, Penny, had introduced me to Damien. At the time, he was attending a rehab center called Phoenix House, and I think was in recovery for marijuana. Anyway, he went to our school and I was — of course — too shy to speak to him, so my best friend Penny spoke to him for me. On Valentine's Day I sent him a flower, and eventually we were introduced.

In this same time, I was a member of a French language institute called FIAT, on the Upper East Side in Manhattan, on 66th between Madison and Park Avenues. I went there every day after school; it just happened that FIAT was located in near Damien's Apartment. I'd go there to watch movies in French or read French newspapers, so I used it as an excuse to go and spend time with him. Technically speaking too, I was doing what I said I would be doing, I just had Damien along with me when I was at FIAT. Eventually, we exchanged phone numbers and started talking on the phone, and of course, my mom got curious. I remember on one of our few dates, we went to see *Platoon,* and out for a burger at the Silver Square Diner afterward. I called my mom to tell her where we were heading, but even that wasn't cool with her because I was raised a vegetarian, and if she'd caught me eating a burger that would have been another battle. What annoyed me about my mom always hawking on me with guys was her inconsistency: on the one hand, she'd always tell me, 'If you want to stay out later, just call me.' So then I'd do exactly what she asked, and get yelled at anyway. So it was really a no-win situation. So no matter the fact that I'd done what she'd asked, given her all the details of where I was going, she sill demanded that I 'get home now!' Well I'm sorry, but I wasn't going to GET HOME NOW! I decided to take a stand for once, blew her off, and went to dinner anyway. Well, afterward, needless to say, I was rushing home from the East Side of Manhattan to the West, which for those of you unfamiliar with the island geographically, takes some time. So it was getting a little chilly. I'm running like an idiot and all of a sudden I stopped myself and thought. 'Wait a minute, I get straight A's; all my homework is already done for the weekend. We had a perfectly innocent time out, why am I in the wrong here?' I got home by 6:30 or 7:00 on a Saturday night (Late, right?) and my mom is standing there on the stoop in her robe with arms crossed. She goes, 'It's dark out, only prostitutes are out this late. What are you doing out at 7 in the evening?' Then she wanted every detail on this guy, and wanted his home phone number, which really freaked me out. Of course, she ended up calling his parents to tell them about our top-secret conspiracy to go out on a date, and they had the same reaction of every parent she called over the course of my high school years, 'Yeah, we know; what's the big deal?' Honestly, when I use the term conspiracy, it's not that far removed in context of how paranoid my mother was. You may think for a minute, 'But Jasmin, try to see it from her side, she was just being a concerned parent, like any other.' Let me shut that shit down for you right now and tell you about the time my mother went so overboard with her paranoia that she hired a PRIVATE INVESTIGATOR to follow me!

This story could almost be a scene out of a satirical movie, but it really happened. I was between the ages of 16 and 17 when she had the P.I. following me. On one occasion, after I'd found out about it, I saw a picture of myself hanging out with some Hell's Angels, and one of them had come to my rescue one day when some nasty dude grabbed my ass on the street. I was out in the summer selling my friendship bracelets at my usual spot on 6th Avenue and 8th Street, and this biker came to my aid when this dude groped me. Another of my mom's private little surveillance collage of me was at the beach hanging out with some friends from school, listening to a boom box. God forbid I go to the beach, right? Another time, she had a photo of me waiting at a bus stop to go to that same beach and she accused me of heading off to Atlantic City to prostitute. Her routine was to have me followed, then confront me with whatever her latest batch of evidence was in our weekly therapy session. It happened to have been the Queens Bus line that I was taking to the beach, so whenever our next session with Barry was, she whipped out her evidence, and his reaction was the same as mine: to tell her how out of control *she* was acting! I was heading to the Rockaways to go to the beach, so that's why I was at the Queens Bus line stop, and the Hell's Angels were local to the block where I sold my friendship bracelets. She thought they were my pimps! Only someone as paranoid of my mom could have put that into her own head. After that, I just got used to assuming that I was being followed by a Private Eye at any given time for a while, a very normal thing for your average teen to expect, no? My mother gave me no right of privacy whatsoever, be it her monitoring of my phone calls, checking my answering machine messages, etc.

I remember another time, I had WON tickets to see my favorite band, Iron Maiden, which she had ok'd and knew all week prior to the show that I was planning for it. Come the night of the concert, of course suddenly it became an issue, and she wouldn't let me go. Well, for all her bullshit that I did put up with, I was 16, got straight As, and this was one thing I wasn't going to miss, both because I'd earned the right to go, and because she'd already okayed it. So naturally, when she sent me to my room early, I climbed right out the window and went to the concert anyway. Well, sneaking out, no matter how normal a routine for most teenagers, is not as simple as slipping out a suburban bedroom window when you live in MANHATTAN. Our apartment was on the second floor, so when I got home from the concert to my building, I had to climb back into my window through the fire escape. Well, I made it up the first fire escape okay, but as I got to the second, the neighbors saw me and called the cops thinking I was a burglar. Well, while the police are busy rushing over to respond to Jasmin the burglar, I gave up trying to get in the second fire escape, knocked on my first floor neighbors' window and told them I'd gotten locked out. That was fine, but by the time I got up to my own floor, I walked in my apartment to find two of New York's Finest had already arrived, and were standing in the living room with my mom and grandmother. Needless to say, I was in trouble: my mom and grandmother weren't happy at all that I'd snuck out and the cops weren't pleased about being called over on what had turned out to be a waste of their time. Now I could see my mom having gotten pissed and grounded me, but she actually told the police that I was a runaway and had been out prostituting. Being an attorney, she fucking knew what the police procedure was for such a claim, and to no one's surprise by mine and my grandmother's, the cops wanted to haul me off to some juvenile detention center! My grandmother was horrified, she was crying, and trying to come to my defense, but my mom still persisted with her insane claim. What made it worse was when I first walked in, I saw my mom talking to the cops and filling out some paperwork, and thought naturally it was a Missing Persons Report. To my horrified surprise, it turned out she was filing some sort of arrest report telling them her child was out selling drugs and prostituting. It made me feel so awful about myself that she would ever think that, let alone try to have me arrested for it without any proof whatsoever. Thank GOD I had proof that I was at the concert in the form of concert tickets, so the NYPD saw I was scared shitless, and could tell I guess by my body language that I wasn't lying. So they basically interrogated me for a bit about what I'd been doing at the concert, could tell I hadn't been high or anything, they turned their attention from me to my mother — who didn't want to let it drop. She was actually still persisting in trying to get them to file what would have amounted to a False Arrest Report. So once they explained that to her, and actually scolded her for the fact that she should know better being an attorney, then left. So then my mom yelled at me, and slapped me in my face, which was the first time I'd been hit in my life. That upset my grandmother, but things were so out of control at that point that they eventually fizzled out. I went to bed crying, as did my grandmother, and my mom probably went to conference call with my therapist Barry and her P.I. about what my next big conspiracy might be. Needless to say, after that, I never snuck out again.

I did get in trouble again though for seeing Damien when we WENT away one Saturday to Port Jefferson, Long Island. And in my mom's defense, I told her I was going to be somewhere else with Penny, and ended up taking the Long Island Railroad out there. When we got in Damien and I hitched a ride out to the sand dunes and it was a really gloomy overcast day. So I felt like I was lost away in some fantasy where I didn't have to check with my mom to go to the bathroom or worry about her wire tapping my phone line for a day. It really felt like an escape for us, and I didn't feel like leaving, and almost didn't for a minute. Damien and I actually contemplated for a few magical moments running away, but we were old enough to know the idea was silly. Kids run away to New York City, not *from* New York City, and when we finally decided to head back in, to no surprise, my mother was angrily waiting for me at the train station. We had one of our usual fights and I really had to hold my tongue because if I had told her of my intention to run away that day, she would have locked me away in a dungeon somewhere. She still would have interrogated me about the imaginary guys she suspected me of prostituting with. Eventually, my mother's overbearing ways broke up the relationship, because Damien had a freedom I couldn't be compatible with, given the restrictions of my home life. He was very patient with me, but after a while, he got tired of waiting for my mom to loosen the reigns, and at one point, he even spoke with her to try and reassure her that she could trust me with him. He broke up with me in the spring of my senior year, and it wasn't Damien who broke my heart in the end, it was my mom. He was one of the nicest people I'd met in that chapter of my life, and I still remember him fondly to this day.

In high school, I had a head for being organized and being in control. I got a challenge out of being industrious, and remember I used to make these friendship bracelets, and sit out on 8th Street and 6th Avenue and sell them. I would make $800 to $1000 selling them because I would go buy a huge plastic thing full of ones that were already made. Then I would sit on the street and make my own, in addition, and people passing by would think I'd made all of them, and be that much more compelled to buy one from me. I'd get all the Jersey people and tourists — the B&T (Bridge and Tunnel) crowd. I could sell quite a few in a given sitting. When I got to the end of my senior year, it was hard to figure out what direction I wanted to head in as far as college because my mother had always wanted me to become a lawyer. She preached at me so much about it that it almost convinced me that was what I wanted. Usually, if a parent says something loud enough times, the kid comes to believe it and she filled my head with enough of that about becoming an attorney that I started out with that in mind. She was also so busy putting me down socially, like saying the only people who carried pagers were prostitutes and drug dealers that I didn't know what I wanted. No matter what I did at that point, it wasn't ever good enough for my mom, so maybe I was motivated on some level to become an attorney to try and please her? I don't know, but I headed off into my first year of college without a fucking clue personally as to what I wanted to study. On top of that, my freshman year was spent at Schiller International University in London, where my mom sent me to get away from New York.

She didn't want me to be around boys with the kind of freedom that college can provide. To her credit, there weren't many metal-heads at Schiller — so I started using Hit Parader Magazine's Penpal section to write back and forth with guys. In London, I lived with my mom's sister, so I was still under a pretty watchful eye anyway. Schiller University was an international university, with campuses in Germany, France, and so forth. I really liked it, and did really well in my classes, and liked everyone, but it was kind of weird for me because there weren't any Americans, and definitely weren't any long haired men. So I just stayed in school for the most part. My best friends were these girls named Nasrin and Rosita, the latter of whom was from the Fiji Islands. I also eventually met these two headbangers Patrick and Michael, two brothers from New York. Anyway, it was not your average freshman year — there were no sororities, no keg parties, and because I stayed with my aunt, I was pretty much under constant surveillance. She wasn't as protective as my mom, but it was still restrictive. After a while, I got homesick for New York and knew I belonged back there, and wanted to travel to Brazil (every experience there was the BEST) as well. I think the event that finally sent me back to NY was my mother coming to England to visit me and staying for a month, and going as far as to escort me to class each day. She would ride to school with me on the trolley, sit in the back of class basically chaperone me. I figured I had a better chance of avoiding that kind of thing repeating itself if I went to school back in the States.

After my freshman year, I came back to New York and enrolled in Columbia University, where I finished out my undergraduate degree. I wanted to go to an Ivy League school, figuring it might shut my mom up, which it didn't, but I had no regrets about the school. I had already taken some AP courses at Columbia while I was still in high school, so it was a pretty comfortable environment for me already. So when I got settled in, I made my major Business and my minor French. I had some really nerdy classes — Philosophy, French and German, and International Politics. I was there 3 ½ years, and despite rumors, I didn't blow anyone for my grades. I probably didn't fit in very well with the traditional Columbia mold because they didn't have very many headbangers and by that time, I was a big-time rocker. My best friend there was another headbanger named Elise Carter, who was a film student. My first acting job actually was doing an independent film for her that we shot in the middle of freezing winter in Times Square wearing a mini-skirt, which was a lot of fun. Of course, my mother insisted I stay living at home while I went to college, which considering I enrolled at 17, and was a sophomore by 18 I guess wasn't that hard to understand in one light. So I took the train to school every day, and you'd be on crack to think my mom backed off while I was in college. I guess she wanted to keep more an eye on me than ever because she was intent on molding me into what she was professionally, so at first I thought about majoring in Business Law, but didn't want to.

On the side, I started modeling, did some small ads for Benetton, some catalog work, but my main focus was always school. I wanted to run a business, but my mom really didn't like anything I had to say about that idea. So in a minor way, modeling was an escape of sorts for me, because it also gave me what money I had since my mom kept most of my money from me at that time in an obvious attempt to limit my freedom even further. Another escape of mine was going to art museums, which dated back to when I was a child. My favorite artists are Van Gogh, Monet, and Pissarro, and I would always be making things — be it jewelry, or those friendship bracelets — whatever, as a creative outlet, which I would also sell for extra money. At one point I bought these Pennaflax Water Color pencils, and drew things that blended into others, I guess trying to imitate my heroes. It never turned into anything more than fun, but I wasn't really raised to be competitive, I was raised to be a shark. My mom had raised me to always reserve my comments toward other people's feelings, for instance, someone's musical tastes. If they disagree with yours, you don't tell them that, you just say it's not for me. She also raised me to always be independent, never to rely on a man for anything, to always have independence financially. Basically my mom brought me up to never rely on anyone for anything. In spite of her Nazi teenage parenting dictatorship, I admired her as a woman for being very independent, strong, smart and beautiful; she kept herself in really great shape, and was a lot of fun to do things with. She really took me to cool places as a kid, be it Connecticut, or the Hamptons, or museums, plays, and so forth. I was pretty sheltered in terms of men, which gave me a dangerous naivety when I got involved with Dick Pelicanose, but I was very enlightened from a young age on all things cultural, which drove me to experience every artistic thing I could throughout my formative years. Some of them I tried to turn commercial, or into little businesses — for instance my aforementioned friendship bracelet business — but others were just in the spirit of the whole idea.

All throughout college, even after I was enrolled at Columbia, I still traveled, such that I still went to London, Paris, Brazil — everywhere. I was still very shy in college though, at least on campus, because I didn't fit in with the typical Columbia mold; they were mostly corn-fed pieces of shit who think they are hot because of where they go to school. Also, I hated the school's campus because I felt it was a totally artificial environment in relation what New York was really about, and for example, where NYU's campus, by contrast, was basically the East Village, Columbia had a very model-like design to theirs. You don't get to see what's out there, so I gravitated toward the headbangers and the odd ball students who were clearly feeling the way I was about the campus, and believe me, we all stood out. One of my best friends in college, for example, was in the Russian Mafia, but was a really cool person. Going to college in New York I would say was a healthy thing overall as opposed to doing it all in Europe. I definitely found myself in New York, but I also didn't in many ways because my mother worked so hard to define me in her terms. Thankfully, even at that age, I was determined to live life on my own.

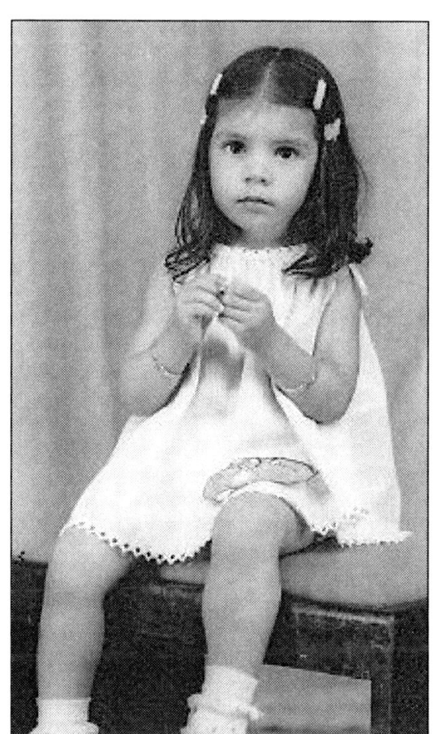

CLOCKWISE FROM TOP LEFT: Jasmin and her Grandfather; Jasmin as a baby on the beach in St Croix US Virgin Islands; Jasmin as an infant with her favorite stuffed animal; Jasmin as a baby.

CLOCKWISE FROM TOP LEFT: Jasmin as a small child; Jasmin with her mother as a little girl; Jasmin in early school years; Jasmin in grade school.

TOP: Jasmin with her Brooklyn Friends grade school class *(top row, far left)*; BOTTOM: Jasmin with her 9th Grade Class *(plaid shirt, 3rd right, 2nd row from top)*.

Jasmin as a Metal Head Teen.

PART II

The Toys!! The Toys!!! My Painful Descent Into Hell. . .

While I was still in college, I met the aforementioned asshole, Dick, who worked in a store called It's Only Rock n' Roll in the Village (he was the first of many dysfunctional relationships) which was like a record/collectibles store. The owners were Mark and Debbie Zacharin, and they seemed pretty cool. I would pass by there every day on my way to and from my job at the *Jersey Journal* in Jersey City, New Jersey, where I took classified ads over the phone. I was 18 at this point and one day I went into the store and we actually started talking more personally, beyond just hello and 'How are you?' kind of stuff. For whatever reason, I thought he was cute. He had black, curly (poofy,) long hair, and a LONG, rail-thin nose, like a Pelican or a coke-addict's (although I didn't know one way or the other if he did that shit at the time.) He wasn't a bad boy, but thought he was. His mother was deaf, and was a Jehovah's Witness, and he lived with her in Cliffside Park, New Jersey. Anyway, Dick worked directly for Mark in various capacities, one being he was driving errands for him for Mark's side business, which was dealing marijuana. That was a back-of-the-store operation, so Dick did a mix of things — legal and otherwise — for Mark. Anyway, I would go into that store every day after work because I was hanging out in the Village a lot at that point — it was a hip, happening place, where Heavy Metal was king. It was maybe the closest thing you would have found at the time to the Sunset Strip in L.A. but nowhere near as exclusively themed around hair metal. Still, for New York, it was a very cool place to hang out.

Once Dick started talking to me and gave me his number, I saw the (201) area code, and should have seen that as my first red flag, because

New York people try not to mix with Bridge and Tunnel people (i.e. those from New Jersey and Long Island.) So one day, he asked me if I wanted to go out to lunch and 'hang out,' so he had a pretty cool Pontiac Firebird at the time, so I thought that was cool enough to hang out for a day, and the dick ALMOST ended up standing me up. He claimed he'd gotten home late from work, and after waiting on him for about an hour, I was ready to leave the store when he called, and begged me to wait for him. Having no self-esteem at that point in my life because of my inexperience with men, I — like a jackass — agreed to wait some more for him. Finally, when he showed up another hour later, he showed up with a flower and then we went to some Howard Johnson's-type shithole to eat. So that was our first date. So we started hanging out after that, and I think on our second date, basically went from the store straight back to Fort Lee, New Jersey to his friend's house, had sex, and that was it. He wasn't my first sexual experience, but only the second guy I had been involved with physically up to that point. Anyway, he seemed more into hanging out with his friends at that point than anything else and this became a running theme in our relationship in time. His friends were scum bags, and basically after we'd finished having sex that day, he drove me almost immediately back to Manhattan and left me there feeling like total shit about myself.

Our next date was basically the same routine — I'd meet him late at night after work or somewhere late on a Saturday, but I put up with it because I thought he was the best I could do for myself at that time. There really wasn't ever much for us to do, we usually went back to New Jersey, hung out, had sex and listened to records. It was really boring, and though I hadn't done an extensive amount of dating up to that point, the guys I had dated were much more exciting than he was. What was more frustrating as time went on was finding out that he regularly cheated on me with all these slutty, trashy women — and I don't say that out of some lingering bitterness over it — they were truly ground hogs. These were all girls he had dated before me, but he would keep their numbers and photos around, in open, plain view of me. It was truly pathetic, on his part to do it, and mine in that I tolerated it. So for the first two months we were dating, this was our routine. Then I met this Westie named Tommy, an Irish Mafia member, who I started seeing on the side because Dick wasn't giving me enough attention. He'd only see me on the weekends and Tommy was an authentic bad boy, which I was very attracted to, but also wanted to spend every waking minute with me. He had long, brown hair and tattoos, very cute, and he basically beat people's asses for a living for the Irish Mob. I remember one day I had to stitch him up right on 5th Avenue after some fight. He had some nasty gash in his chest, and told me to meet him with Butterfly stitches, but I was very attracted to that bad boy aspect. Anyway, I started dating Tommy on the side in July and did so while seeing Dick for 3 or 4 months into the fall. During this period, things only got worse with Dick. He got me pregnant at one point, made me go get an abortion *(I HAD NO OBJECTIONS,)* and then that same night, made me go with him to some trashy Jersey bar and openly flirted with other women in front of me. He was a real piece of shit. That was probably one of the shittiest feelings I'd ever had in my life and I obviously couldn't tell my mom about it, because she would have disowned me.

Between she and Dick constantly criticizing me, I rarely got a break, which I guess is one of the reasons I kept seeing Tommy because he was my escape from all that. For a 19 year old girl who was pretty naïve to the world to begin with, even growing up in New York, trying to carry a full load at Columbia, juggling two men, dodging my mom whenever possible, (in terms of keeping tabs on my life) plus keep a job, I definitely had my hands full. Dick and I over the summer had started the bizarre pastime of attending a lot of antique/collectible conventions, where every item you could possibly imagine was sold or traded. In our case, it was usually rarity pop culture items — be they Barbie or Kiss Dolls, and I learned quickly that there was quite a market for this business. It's one thing to see it in a Village specialty store, but these shows went on every weekend all over the East Coast, and Dick regularly dragged me along to them. Anyway, since I was being dragged along to these without a choice, I figured I'd express a genuine interest to see if it would help our relationship improve — maybe thinking Dick would take more of an interest in me? I don't know, but he was still his regular old piece-of-CRAP self, flirting with other girls at Kiss Conventions in front of me, you name it. I did like going to work the Kiss Conventions because I loved the atmosphere, there were a lot of cute guys with long hair there, which was a nice distraction from asshole. He never let me talk to anyone though, other than when I was making sales. I remember one convention, in particular, when Dick had disappeared as usual, and at some point in the day, I wound up playing pinball with this little nerdy kid who had bought a bunch of stuff from us. It was funny to me, because the kid was a zit-faced teenager who could have been my kid brother. He was 15 at the oldest, and our crime was playing a Kiss Pinball game. Well, needless to say, when Dick saw this he yelled at me for it in front of everybody. I also got hit in the face two days later. Dick called me a whore because the kid had to give me the 50 cents to play the pinball game because my asshole boyfriend wouldn't give me any of the $7000 he had on him from the convention earnings. That one really confounded me, even looking back at it now. It wouldn't be ridiculous to say that there were times where if I breathed wrong, he would get upset at me.

That summer was when the physical abuse began in our relationship. One particularly vicious incident came during a convention weekend when I'd gone out to lunch with a friend of mine named Andy, who dressed like Paul Stanley, and was a local at the Kiss conventions while Dick was out of town. I got busted on that one, and the irony was two-fold in that. First, Andy HAD A GIRLFRIEND, and second, my mom was the one who busted me instead of Dick, but ended up telling him about it anyway. It was nice to know where her loyalties were. It may as well have been Dick though the way she tore Andy's head off on the phone, accusing us of sleeping together and all sorts of nonsense, telling him I had a boyfriend, and in essence, defending Dick in the process. The worse part was that she told Dick about it when he got back from Chicago and concocted some paranoid story that I was sleeping with Andy, and Dick beat the LIVING SHIT out of me for that one. I ended up spending the night in the hospital, and I still blame my mother to this day for that, because I'd told her Andy was gay, and she still saw fit to let Dick know anyway. Of all the guys I dated, Dick was the worst, and yet he was the only one my mother accepted. After a while, it even seemed like she and he were conspiring together to keep me under one large thumb. If he wasn't keeping his eye on me, my mom was, and would report back to him from time to time if she imagined something was up. And that's just what it was, IMAGINATION.

It's still ironic to me that Dick was the only guy my mom was ever really cool with me dating, who turned out to be the worst guy she could have picked to endorse my going out with. He was the first guy she ever trusted me with, be it the TOY conventions we went away on, or even a trip to Cancun. While we were there, my mom even went as far as to take a day off of work, get on the bus, go into New Jersey, and enroll Dick in Community College classes he'd forgotten to register for. I think the fact that I thought she was actually going to accept a guy I brought home for once was among the reasons why I deemed it necessary to stay with Dick for as long as I did. My mom's acceptance was very important to me, and in time, Dick's was as well, in spite of how shitty both of them were to me for my efforts. I thought, perhaps if my mom approved of Dick, maybe she'd finally approve of me in the process. Unfortunately, for the most part, that hasn't happened to this day. If my mother is reading this book, this will be the first time she learns about the nightmare that Dick Pelicanose put me through, and even then, I fear her reaction would be to criticize my judgment in men, not hers. The irony of that is she's responsible for my lack of judgment where men were concerned when I started dating Dick because she'd never allowed me any room as a teenager to develop that skill like normal girls my age would have. It came to plague me in my relationship with Dick, and while I don't blame her for it, that's a luxury I don't have to afford her. I choose to spare her that guilt, but hope in time she understands the role that lack of experience played in other decisions I've made in my life that have disappointed her.

Anyway, during this same summer, I was still seeing a lot of Tommy, who didn't know about Dick, and after a while, started to get a little suspicious as to why I wouldn't go out with him exclusively. So I told him I was seeing someone. I can't, to date, honestly say why I didn't leave Dick for Tommy, who treated me worlds better. I guess deep down I was afraid of what Dick might have done to me physically, but more afraid of what Tommy might have done to Dick had he found out. Dick by this point was going out to go-go bars, drinking with his friends, and as I found out later, just fucking anything that he could get his hands on. Still, on the other hand, Dick and I would take a lot of trips to upstate New York together to the Catskills, going to a lot of these collectible conventions. Then I made the worst mistake I could have and moved in together after a few months into this shitty garden-level apartment in Union City, New Jersey. At that point, Dick also coaxed me into investing $2000, which I borrowed from my father, into this antiques business together, so I thought in some warped part of my mind that the relationship still might have hope. It pissed my mom off when I moved out of the house, even though she didn't know it was with Dick! Even after moving in with Dick, I was still seeing Tommy, which got that much more complicated. But he was very sweet to me, always paid for everything; bought me all these little gifts. He was very nice, and it was nice to be treated that way for a change.

Back on the Dick front, we'd started an antiques business together that basically consisted of buying vintage toys and collectibles, character collectibles, model kits, and stuff like that. We made most of our money at these conventions we'd travel to on the weekends, and during the week I was commuting into New York to attend Columbia, which almost felt to me like leading two lives. And as time went on with Dick and my living together, things just worsened. He kept this odd hole in his closet where he displayed all the girls he'd gone out with before, which was really fucking insulting. Then one night, he didn't come home at all, till 11 the next morning. He lied about it at the time, but I learned later he'd gone home with some slut named Ginger from this bar called the Naval Base. Why I didn't leave him I don't know to this day, I didn't know any better, and he really took advantage of my lack of self-esteem. Plus I had just invested this money with him in the antiques business, which turned out to be just another situation for him to take advantage of me in. In truth, our 'running' a business together meant me doing virtually all the set-up at our booth, then him leaving me at the table alone *ALL DAY*, while he walked around and flirted with girls in front of me. When he did stop by to check on things, it was usually only to take whatever money we'd made selling our items and then to disappear again. He gave me no spending money, and got only that much more controlling as time went on. I wasn't allowed to speak to anyone other than customers buying things, and he'd regularly yell at me in front of everyone when I didn't set something up the right way or the way he wanted to, or didn't know the price. I guess that made him look cool in front of his fellow grease balls too, because no one ever came to my defense among his friends. Anyway, as I suspected, when I finally told Tommy about him, Tommy wanted to take a knife to his throat while he slept which of course I didn't allow to happen. Dick definitely was starting to deserve it by that point though.

I guess looking back on it now in hindsight, I continued to try and believe in Dick, reasoning that if I put more effort into the relationship things might work out, which is why I had invested with him in the antiques business to begin with. Anyway, another stupid decision on my part along these lines was to co-sign the loans for him to go to Bergen Community College; loans that he eventually defaulted on and fucked up my credit. Around this time, we moved from the shithole in Union City to a place that was a little nicer in North Bergen, New Jersey. At this point though, I was going broke, because he wasn't giving me any of the money from the antique shows and my mom paid my tuition at Columbia. So in some desperate attempt at an escape or maybe just to have something for myself, that was mine and that Dick or my mom (or anyone for that matter) couldn't touch, I got a job dancing at the Kit Kat Club in Manhattan twice a week. I got the job obviously for the money, but equally as importantly, because I felt attractive, which I really needed as a woman at that point in my life. I danced under the stage name Karen, and hid my dance costumes in my dresser. I told Dick I'd gotten a part-time job working for a bridal company, selling merchandise to their stores. When I'd get home after shifts with a lot of money, I would hide it from him naturally — which felt good — but it didn't buy my way out of any of the many problems between us. So for every self-esteem boost I might feel coming off a dancing shift, when I got home: this chauvinistic asshole was waiting like Archie Bunker, saying shit to me like, 'You need to learn how to cook.'

On top of that, aside from my dancing earnings, we never had any money, which was hard to believe because we'd make an average of $3000.00 from a given antique show and on a bad day, at least $1000.00. Of course, he never gave me any of it, so on my own, at one point, I started collecting vintage Barbies from the 1950s through the 1970s, which was a lot of fun. I bought most of that collection with dancing money, and honestly, they were better company at that point than Dick was, because every night he'd go out with his friends drinking and leave me at home alone. I felt like he didn't want to have anything to do with me. In the meanwhile, Tommy was doing everything he could to get me to leave Dick for him. He was a very sweet and sensitive guy for being such a bad ass, and would pick me up every night after work to make sure I got home safely. He was always begging me to move in with him so he could take care of me. I couldn't cut loose of Dick for one simple reason that only another battered woman reading this would understand. The fear that is beaten into you as a victim of domestic violence is what leaves the most permanent mark — not the bruises.

By that point, Dick's physical abuse had deteriorated slowly but surely from his yelling at me to just hitting me when he felt I hadn't done something right. Every day, he'd come home, go out to the strip clubs with his friends, or sneak out of the house when he was home to make calls to girls from payphones. And of course, whenever I attempted to call him on it, he'd smack me or slam my head into something. I still have a mark on the back of my head from one time when he slammed me into a closet door. At that point, in addition to being scared to leave him, didn't understand why he was doing this to me, and on some sad level a lot of women reach,

I felt it was my fault in some way what he was doing to me. I just wanted to have a normal relationship with my boyfriend — wanted to be loved by someone outside of my family. Even though I did all the right things, it never worked. So as the months rolled on, our dysfunctional routine continued with Dick going to strip clubs every night with his friends, hitting me whenever I made noise about it and making me feel so shitty about myself that I kept dancing to cling to any basic sense of self-esteem. The Kit Kat Club had become Flash Dancers by this point, and they had started doing features, which sounded interesting to me, and honestly, I was in need of the money going broke between paying for his student loans and my one, which I'd taken over from my mom.

After a while of this vicious down cycle, I guess Dick slammed me hard enough in the head to finally see clearly that if I didn't leave him, he might honestly have killed me.

It's sad that I had to feel my life was in danger before I was willing to try and change it, but I finally did, moving out of his apartment and back in with my mom, and he moved back in with his own. I still to this day don't know where it was okay for me to tolerate that kind of treatment by him because no one in my family did that. He was very controlling, sort of like my mom, and never paid any attention to me, and I guess the fact that he really used to beat the shit out of me was so surreal I didn't accept it as reality until I'd left him. Being home was at least a relief from that to some degree but then I had my mom on my ass. On top of it, Dick had taken my entire Casper the Ghost collection and anything else he could steal of mine and moved it all back into his mother's. I was afraid of ghosts growing up. It may sound stupid to some of you, but collecting Casper memorabilia — which included board games, bobbing heads, wooden pull toy from the 1940s, hand puppets, the talking dolls, comic books, puzzles, costumes, and all types of odd items — helped me overcome my fear of ghosts. It was an odd form of therapy, but also the only escape and thing I'd had for myself while I'd been under Dick's vicious thumb.

Thankfully, I got my Barbie collection out, but he just kept driving me deeper and deeper into debt in one form or another. So I started doing this Robin Byrd show in New York, and dancing at Flash Dancers because I really enjoyed the attention a lot. I don't know to date if my mom ever knew explicitly what I was doing in terms of dancing, but I do remember once she threw out one of my $500 costume gowns, which I had to replace while saying nothing about it. Don't ask me why, but after a few weeks, I started seeing Dick and trying to make that work thinking the distance might have helped. I remember he called me one night and said he'd been mugged and beaten up, which I still to this day think Tommy was behind, so I broke things off with him as a result. Tommy was very sweet to me, but I think that scared me a little, knowing Tommy would have been capable of that with Dick. Anyway, it was very sad. Tommy was in tears when we broke up. It was upsetting for me because he made my life happy at that time, but I guess I thought I had more invested with Dick, and needed to see that out to what turned out to be its bitter end. Tommy was the perfect guy for me at that time and I will always cherish the time we had.

After breaking things off with Tommy, I kept working at Flash Dancers, and was looking into feature dancing at this point. So I would hide my gowns from my mom, and my schedule during the week usually involved working a 12-8 shift after I got out of Germany or Philosophy class at Columbia, or I would work one night shift which ran 4-12, or 8-4 in the morning. I would do a couple of those. For the day shifts, I would usually tell my mom I was studying and I brought home the grades to prove it. For the night shifts, I told her I was out with friends. During the weekend, she was usually gone to North Carolina, where she had a store, so that was easier. It was exciting to me to have such radically contrasting worlds to co-exist within. It honestly was the foundation of my acting career I think, because I had to play two entirely different characters, and the only time I got off from keeping both worlds running full-time was when I slept. Still, I never changed who I was as a person in either, just learned how to let people see what they wanted to see. That was a survival instinct of mine by that point, and one that would serve me greatly in my future career.

When I wasn't working during the weekends, Dick and made slow progress toward a reconciliation. We would take trips to Pennsylvania to do the conventions, and at one, sadly, a toy dealer had allegedly seen me dancing at the club, and that finally got back to Dick. Well, as you can imagine, he didn't take it very well. When I tried to be honest with him about it, explaining it was to help make ends meet, and to feel better about myself, things went right back down the toilet with his reply that I was 'a fucking whore.' Of course, he concluded his reaction by punching me in my mouth, in front of his friends, who were all laughing. After that, I was that much more motivated to keep dancing — and OPENLY — just to spite him, not to mention the money I was making. I would pull down $350 to $400 on a bad day and anywhere from $500 to $800 on a good night although I never did lap dances or anything like that. This was strictly from the stage. After a while, Dick even started to begrudgingly shut the fuck up about my dance gig because I was struggling to keep both of us in school, paying his and my loans. I guess I still felt Dick loved me somewhere in my own twisted view of things.

My one protective mechanism against Dick's temper was that, following our split, I was living at home. On the weekends, Dick and I would go away to do these conventions in Pennsylvania or Chicago, and he'd make me sleep in the van in the freezing cold. When he did wake me up, it was at 3 in the morning to go set up, while he'd either go back to sleep, or go off and smoke a joint and walk around with his friends while I did all our set-up work. Ironically enough, for as much as my mother liked Dick, the whole time we attended these conventions together she would tell me 'You're way too elegant and classy to be doing that with them, traveling around like this.' During this period, Dick tried a couple times to bust me at work too, and fortunately, both times he walked in, I ducked and was able to avoid him because he never knew my exact shifts. Before too long, he was back to his old self, and he'd managed to hook me back in just enough to keep me around. By this point too, when he wasn't beating me or bossing me around, or forcing me under the threat of physical violence to pay his school loans, he spent the rest of what would have been any other normal couple's free time together out cheating on me. When he wasn't cheating on me, he would routinely check out other women in front of me and put me down physically on context of their looks. It got so sewer-like at one point that he came home with some kind of bacteria infection he passed to me, so I was sick from that for a week. Thankfully, it got cleared up, but that fucking infection had more class than he did.

After a while, I cut down my days dancing, and stopped altogether for a while. I was nearing graduation from Columbia at this point, which meant I could start working more regularly. Before graduation, I landed a job working as an investment counselor in the financial district in downtown Manhattan. I did financial consulting for investments. At that point, Dick enrolled full-time in community college, and also expected me to be his in-house tutor, which basically meant doing his homework for him. I remember one day I was trying to help him with his French class, and he wasn't getting it, so he slammed the book, threw at me, and screamed,

'You stupid cunt, you can't even help me with this!' So things kept deteriorating from there, he slowly but surely stopped having sex with me, and was going away more with his buddies and leaving me in the city, so I started finally to lose a little interest. Around this same period, my dad died of lung cancer, I was 20 years old. I had no one to support me through it, because my mother was bitching about everything and my boyfriend went out to a strip club and then to some Korean whore house with his friends the night my dad passed away. It was April 14th to be exact, and probably the worst night of my life, and in general, arguably the most difficult experience of my life. For a brief period, I signed over every single legal right I had in the world to my mother because I was emotionally very unstable for a period. It was very fucked-up how things went down, because my dad had quit smoking for 10 years and he ended up dying of lung cancer anyway. His family were such assholes through the whole thing too that I had to go to probate court at one point and I just hope they all die in hell, and don't care if they read this too. It's sick that while my father was slowly but surely dying on a respirator, none of his family showed up until he was on the verge of death. It turned out that he had a will that had been revised enough times that his Estate, which was left almost entirely to me, was suddenly being challenged left and right. His whole family tried to drag me through court, and the stress finally took such a toll that I signed power of attorney over to my mother to deal with it.

I was trying to deal with my father's death, finish school, deal with Dick, and just trying to have a life in general, so I was in no shape to deal with fucking Probate Court! When she convinced me to sign over Power of Attorney, I was almost relieved, but it put me more in the dark. To date, I don't have any idea what happened with the money. I found out at one point later that summer that I had some loans in my name that had been defaulted on that I had never even taken out, which means my mother had to have set them up having power of attorney. When I called to inquire about it, she called me a 'loose whore' for going on the road to do some toy shows. When I did get back later on that summer and brought it up again with her, she got this extremely strange look on her face that was the equivalent of a bitter piercing glare. I suspected she was trying to fuck up my credit so that I couldn't move out again. On top of that, when my mother took a break from trying to manipulate and control me, Dick picked right up where she left off: convincing me in my vulnerable state to withdraw $10,000 of the money my father had left me to invest in the toy business. Like an idiot, or maybe more like a confused, emotionally drained and vulnerable 20 year old student at an ivy league University who'd just lost her father, I stupidly agreed. Of course, I never saw any of that cash again. Giving money my father had left me away wasn't like losing another part of him, but it did feel like another of the last shreds of dignity I had left had been stripped away by that asshole. I had people coming at me from every side trying to manipulate me. My sociopathic boyfriend, a controlling and paranoid mother who refused to let me grow into a young woman even after I was legally already one, and a bunch of Chicken Hawks who I'd once considered relatives trying to steal my father's money from the Estate.

Before my dad passed, I was lucky to have had a few years to get reacquainted with him. We'd been out of touch some years prior when my mom moved us back to New York, but my dad relocated back from the Virgin Islands when I was a teenager, and we'd gotten reacquainted again very quickly and naturally. I remember one day calling his office and telling his secretary it was his daughter Jasmin calling, and he picked up the phone right away, and it had sounded like whatever call he'd been on prior was fairly important. Anyway, it didn't matter, whatever it was, it could wait when I called. I remember him telling me that day that I'd made him 'the happiest man in the world.' I remember those words exactly coming out of his mouth and that's how he always made me feel. He was very happy to hear from me and we'd started seeing each other again. At first I didn't tell my mother I was seeing him again, and then when I finally did, she threw a fucking fit as expected. My grandmother got really angry with her at that, and it was one of the times I really remember her speaking up to my mom on my behalf, like, 'Why are you yelling at her? It's her father. She needs him. Get over it.' That calmed her down a little bit, but she'd still make fucking sour faces and remarks whenever I said I was going to see my dad. We had this routine where we'd meet for pizza after school and go to the movies. I'd go see him on weekends, and we did all kinds of fun stuff- from going hiking in the Pocono Mountains to horseback riding. I had my own horse named Chief my dad bought for me at Cloverleaf Stables on Staten Island, and every Saturday I'd go to ride him. My dad also taught me how to drive before I was even old enough legally to have a permit. We would do crazy shit like go to the mall together, and we would make these barking sounds sometimes to fuck with people and they wouldn't know where it was coming from. To a little kid, and even thinking back on it now, it was so funny. He was so laid-back and so cool. He had a really good sense of humor. He was on the immature side, but like, when it was right to be immature. He always supported me in what I did, which was really important to me. We had a great relationship in that aspect. I think my fondest memory I have of my dad is when there was a tropical storm. I was there for tropical storm Fredrick and Hurricane Emily, like all of those. I was in St. Croix at that time. I was little girl, and I think my fondest memory is sitting there on the balcony of our house when my dad was smoking a cigarette and he just held me there. And it was like the most amazing thing, the storm. You know all the winds and everything, the gusts; all the leaves blowing all over the place. It was so scary, but it was so cool because I was just watching it there with my dad. I just felt so safe.

When I think back on that time now, the only thing that got me through it was the memories of my father. From the time I was an infant on through to when he passed away, I was always daddy's little girl, I was his princess. I had fun. My dad was awesome. My father was a very, very tall man; he had a couple of tattoos. He was very good looking guy, and very smart. His ethnic background was Russian and a hint of Dutch while my mom's lineage was Brazilian mixed with Portuguese specifically, which I think helps to explain her draconian ideas on child rearing. My father was a friend to me when I really needed one, but also there when I really needed my father in my life. He made me feel very safe, very loved, and very supported in many ways. He was really the perfect father. As such, by the time he got sick, given the kindness I felt in my heart toward him comparatively to the other men in my life during that time, it saved me from being bitter about his dying when I needed him most in my life. If he'd ever known what Dick had been doing to me, he would have killed him, but I couldn't bear for him to know that was going on while he lied dying a little each day in that awful hospital room. I'd come to see him, but a lot of times, I couldn't go because I was black and blue, and makeup wouldn't cover it up. It would have been harder on my dad to have seen me like that and have been too weak physically to do a thing about it. So that kept me from seeing my father as much as I'd have liked to. He knew Dick and I were having problems, and would give me money from time to time to help pay off Dick's debts, but I know he wished he could have done much more. He was just too weak by that point. I got to visit with him one final time before they put him on a respirator, and I remember he couldn't talk much, but seemed really happy to see me. That's all that mattered to me at that point.

Following his death on April 15th, 1992, the funeral was just as much of a fucking mess as I was. My mom kept his family out of the wake and had him cremated. She even made me go with her to watch his body burn — that was extremely devastating. That fucked me up pretty badly, to the point where I became really non-functional for a while. I felt alone...I had nobody to turn to. That made things even worse with my mom, because she had hidden his ashes from me, than convinced me to sign over my Power-Of-Attorney rights because my dad's relatives were suing me in Probate Court over my dad's estate. Whenever I'd try to bring something up about my dad or want to talk about his death, my mom would just bring up something negative about him that just wasn't true. She wasn't the most supportive person during that period, and I don't know if it was her trying to be protective in her own twisted way, but it really made things hard for me. I tried to kill myself. I was alone and without my dad. A big part of me died when he left this world. I sliced my wrist vertically trying to possibly see my dad again and escape my hell. Unfortunately, the nosey neighbor came downstairs and stopped me. I left the door open by accident and she had come to invite me to a movie. I wish she just let me die in peace.

So coming out of that horrible spring, the summer just continued in the dysfunctional pattern it had for the four years prior. We kept going to these conventions, which I tried my hardest to find some enjoyment in, despite the company, but even that was hard when I would put in most of the effort and watch Dick reap the reward from me every time. We would routinely clear $3000 a weekend and Dick would always keep ALL of the money, not the lion share, all of it. During this same period, he decided to make a wise business investment in this crap-blue van that eerily resembled Buffalo Bill's from Silence of the Lambs, or perhaps something you might see a child molester driving around in at 3 in the morning on some dark street. The fucking thing even had one of those cheap murals on the side that looks like some cheap painting from a Chinese Fast Food Take-out Restaurant, or a white-trash art print you'd by at the carnival in Coney Island. Dick made me buy the van in my name since his credit was as shitty as he was. Prior to that, he'd driven this shit-brown station wagon, which I almost lost my life in once. It seemed like each year that went by, Dick got a car that was that much shittier, and symbolically parallel to the level our relationship had sunk to by that point. It was bad enough the way Dick treated me, but that he'd gone from a Firebird to a shitty brown grocery-getter to a child molester van just didn't help from a matter of presentation. Not so much in the way I wanted to be seen, but in terms of how much he thought his shit didn't stink! It was ridiculous the way he and his wanna-be Ramone, white trash Jersey buddies would strut around the toy conventions, acting like High Rollers on the floor of some Vegas casino. They certainly didn't have limos or high line sports cars sitting outside and what was more pathetic than anything was that Dick treated his piece of shit cars better than he ever did me.

A prime example was the before mentioned shit-brown grocery getter station wagon. I almost lost my life in the previous winter. We'd been on the way to a toy show, driving through North Bergen to get to the Jersey Turnpike via Tonelle Avenue, which is the busiest Avenue for traffic in North Bergen. It was very icy out, and Dick had decided to take a shortcut down this really steep hill, and ended up in even worse of a traffic jam than we were already in. So while we were stuck for the moment in a line of cars, he told me to stay with the toys, and got out to check with some cop regarding the traffic situation. When he did, he left the car on, sitting pointed at a steep, downward angle in park, running without the parking break on. So while I was sitting in the station wagon, the cars in front of us began moving, and then some other car started sliding behind us, and Wham!, rear-ended our car, which sent the station wagon racing, slipping and sliding down the hill toward Tonelle Avenue, and all the oncoming traffic. While I'm freaking out watching my life flash before my eyes as we head directly for a major intersection with no cars in front of ME to stop the car, I can hear Dick slipping and sliding behind me yelling 'The toys, the toys!' I didn't know what to do, I was trying to press the emergency brake, it wouldn't work, and I just kept sliding toward the intersection. He clearly didn't give a shit about me, and that's what I was focused on more than anything. Well, thank GOD, about 10 feet before I WAS about to slam into the traffic, the car slid to the left into a curb and then a wall. Now with any other guy, you'd think that when he reached the car, the first thing he'd be doing was checking on his girlfriend who'd almost just lost her life, right? Not Dick, who, upon reaching the car, yanked the door open and franticly asked 'Are the toys okay?' His next comment after seeing his merchandise was intact was to remark, 'Good thing the car is okay.' He never made mention of me once, or showed even the slightest sign of concern about my well being.

When the cop got down to the car, the first thing he did was check on me, and when he heard Dick commenting about the car and the toys, gave him a disgusted look and offered to call me an ambulance. Dick, of course, refused for me, because he had a toy show to get to after all! I couldn't believe the next comment he made, which was 'Well, it's a good thing we got hit now we're past the traffic jam.' For the next hour and a half driving to the show, I was in silent but visible state of panicked shock, which Dick clearly saw but ignored. Even when we got to the show and Dick went around telling everyone about how close his toys had come to getting destroyed, he didn't mention me once. When his friends did make any inquiry into how I was doing, Dick said, 'Oh, she'll be fine. If she says anything else, she's a fucking baby.' I was still so shook up that I was setting up the show a little slower, and he told me 'If you can't set this stuff up, then you're a whiney little *CUNT*, and you shouldn't be here.' I should have seen from that day how out of whack his priorities were, but still I didn't leave him. As bad as that story was, a contender for my worst experience with Dick ever was at a convention in Atlantic City a year later once he had moved from the shitty, brown grocery-getter to the Buffalo Bill Serial Killer/Child Molester crap-blue Van. This was one of the biggest toy conventions of the year, and we were in the hotel room getting ready for the show, and Dick saw a bunch of money I had from dancing. Well, naturally, since he never gave me any, he assumed I had stolen it from him, accused me of stealing from him, and slapped me. He, of course, also accused me of cheating on him. I guess by that point I was starting to get tired of not fighting back, so I slapped him back, and he pulled a knife on me. It wasn't that he carried a knife on him regularly, he just happened to have one for the show. He held it to my throat and told me he was going to 'stick a knife in my *CUNT*' if I ever stole from him, those were his exact words. I was so frightened that time that I actually stood up for myself, kneeing him in the balls, for which he ended up slamming my head against the wall so hard I passed out briefly afterward. After that, I started carrying a switch blade on me.

For as unfortunate as the way Dick treated me at the trade shows, I actually did enjoy them outside of that, namely when Dick was off strutting around the convention floor like Tony Soprano with his Guido, wanna-be Ramone buddies. After a while, I had started collecting vintage Barbies, which I wanted to sell at the shows, but of course Dick wouldn't permit it, so I had to make deals on the side while he was off strutting. I actually met an ok person there, Mike a.k.a. Sickie. The circumstances of that were actually pretty funny, because like many other urban legends, Sickie was born in the back room of a tattoo parlor in the Bronx. Basically,

Barry, another regular at the toy conventions, told me that Sickie was the one who'd told Dick about my dancing, which had earned me one of asshole's famous physical and verbal lashings. Naturally, I was pissed about it, and had been dying for months to know who had ratted me out. I called Sickie pretending to be someone else, which would become our theme in the years to come, and confronted him on why he'd outted me to Dick? Well, he denied it, and told me it was actually Barry who'd seen me there, which meant he was the only one who could have told Dick from that circle. It made sense once I got to know Sickie. Even though I yelled at him pretty hard that first time we spoke, he came up to me at the next toy show and gave me a Casper Bobble-Neck toy as a peace offering and we became fast friends after that. He'd feel very bad for me, because he always used to watch me sitting there like a beat-up dog, so he used to bring me little presents from time to time to cheer me up. What really made us bond though was our fourth or fifth phone chat, when we started making prank calls together. Sickie and I were like a couple of 14-year-olds in terms of our sense of humor, we were both very immature and pranked everyone from his ex-girlfriends to other toy dealers to random strangers, a pastime that we've continued through present day. Socially, we mostly saw each other at the toy shows and he was always by himself. I tried to invite him out with Dick and me to lunch, but Dick didn't think he was cool enough. I think I needed a friend in that business, I felt like such an outcast. I felt like no one wanted to talk to me, and they talked down when they talked to me, because I was Dick's girlfriend. He was more like a friend to hang out with and bum around with. We'd go to different weird toy stores, flea markets, different close-out sales, and he'd teach me about the business: how to pick what merchandise to buy, where to buy stuff from, how to price things, things like that. He was very low profile at the shows, and mostly bought and sold stuff in bulk. We'd go out to lunch at Mumbles, just terrorize the town; we were basically hang-out buddies. Ironically, I spent more quality time with Sickie than I ever did with my own boyfriend, and Sickie certainly took more of an interest in me than Dick ever did at that time.

At the heart of it, Dick was just a bastard who beat on me whenever he had a short coming, or did a bad business deal, I was to blame. I was really afraid to speak back up to him then, both because I thought he was the only man who would love me, and because I feared what he would do to me physically if I had. Thinking back on this now, I'm saying to myself the same thing I bet you're saying, WHAT AN ASSHOLE!! I remember once we went to Tampa to visit friends, and he hit me so hard that he broke my gum, and I had to go to the emergency room. The police came to question me about it, and of course, I covered him like a jackass. I knew we were in this downward spiral, and I knew we'd have to hit rock bottom before I'd be completely free of him. That moment came when he nearly took my life. We were at a convention in Atlantic City, and we were in the hotel room fighting over something. Anyway, I guess I'd gotten to a point where I started to say to myself, 'I'm not going to take this,' and it was a rare thought, because it was one of only a couple times that I hit him back. Well, he responded by pulling a knife from his back pocket and pressing it to my throat. I was scared by the look in his eyes, but I managed to knee him in the balls and get out of the room before he could do anything.

PART III

My Season in Hell

By the time I was 21 years old and worn down to the bone, the battered-woman syndrome had come full-circle in my relationship with Dick. I was working full-time and paying most of his bills, still getting over my father's death, receiving regular beatings by this psychopath, who at this point I was staying with out of fear more than any other motivation. As the holidays approached, the camel's back finally started to crack. First off, when we exchanged gifts on Christmas day, Dick had — in plain view of me — this enormous Victoria's Secret bag that held a Santa's Sack full of lingerie, while his present for me was so small, you could have fit it comfortably in a fucking brown lunch bag. On top of that, when he took me to his family's house, he pretty much ignored or insulted me the whole time in front of his family. He wouldn't even hold my hand. So needless to say, that holiday was awful. My mom wasn't much help, and I didn't have my father, so I felt almost entirely alone. When New Year's Day came, the hell was finally raised. Dick basically blew me off New Year's Eve to go out to some strip club with his friends, ended up hooking up with some gutter-snatch named Barbara, who he ended up leaving me for the very next day. The biggest irony about that one was that for all the shit he gave me for dancing and liking clubs, he met Barbara at a STRIP CLUB! What frustrated me about the whole way the break-up went down was that I had no closure. All he basically said to me was 'Maybe we shouldn't see each other anymore.' So we didn't talk for like a week after that, and finally told me to come over and pick up my things. So stupidly hoping there might be a final chance for things to work out, plus in an attempt to get my things back, I went all the way out to Jersey in a snowstorm, and he wasn't even home. The fucker stood me up, and to top it all off, leaving I had a nasty spill down a steep, icy hill and almost broke my head open. I knew he was home too; he just wasn't answering the door. He left me with nothing, I couldn't even take our little kitten. He was grey with little white paws, for comfort. It was a fitting ending.

I went into his van on my way back, and found all these love notes from Barbara, so it was obvious they'd been seeing one another before New Year's Eve. Looking back on it now, I count myself lucky, because if I had married him, I'd never have lived out the wild adventures I had in my later 20s, and my life would have been horrible. I would have ended up a battered, Jersey housewife. Two weeks after that, my mom and I started getting all these notices in the mail about tickets for his Child Molester van, and I told my mom that I had put the van in my name. So my mom called Dick and demanded he pay the tickets, which he refused to do, so we had his van towed in immediate retaliation since it was in my name — but the satisfaction was only fleeting. He called my mom after that and told her I was dancing, which I was able to refute thankfully — I guess I did have some natural ability as a litigator, because I had to pull off a Perry Mason-sized moment to convince her that he was lying. Dick left me raped financially and emotionally, with my spirit beaten down to a point that I could hardly recognize myself inside anymore. Everything that my mother had raised me to be in terms of toughness, he had beaten out of me — for the moment anyway. In addition to the emotionally shitty shape I was in, the aftermath of our break-up financially was even worse, because he had stopped paying the bills on credit cards he'd made me take out for him in my name, student loans, his van payments, the works. So I was dancing primarily at that time to pay off those debts, and I'm talking about thousands and thousands of dollars. Even still, I was still paying that debt off to this day. We'd been together for 5 years, and they were to date the most hellacious years of my life. I am still earning back my pride in the pages of this book.

That said, I'm not above admitting I've dreamt for years that Dick would die a slow and violent death, and that his soul would burn in some form of eternal hell and damnation, but it never came. Men, by and large, always seem to get away with beating women in this country because the problem is symptomatic. Over 75% of women in prison for murdering their spouses were the victim of domestic battery, and yet congress refuses to pass any sort of shield law regarding sentencing. The system is truly set up as an old-boy network, fearing that if women were given the benefit of a doubt that their violence was retaliatory and justified in context of the larger abuse pattern by their husband. Having been there, I know every one of them were motivated by a cornered sense of helplessness that reduced them to primal defense mechanisms that would typically exist only among wild animals. It would never matter if Dick had been arrested for every time he'd hit me, he still would have been given some probation or fine, or perhaps some joke's worth of jail time. Then he would have gotten out and done it again, because the slap he received on the wrist was never as powerful as the one he gave me regularly across the face. I was never strong enough to slap him back, because it would have made it worse the next time. On top of that, he threatened to kill me if I left him more than once and backed it up with his fists. Men do that by the millions across our country and the courts tolerate it by not sentencing men to more substantial jail time, nor by giving women the proper reprieve or protection under law of justifiable homicide for being driven to that extreme by their abusive partners. Women who kill men who abuse them are reacting and almost every time they were driven there by the savagery of the abuse suffered at the hands of their partner. It's not vigilantism to defend your life and if I'd stayed with Dick, I might very well have been an inmate rather than movie star. You might be thinking right now, 'Wait a minute Jasmin; you're an actress, not an attorney!' That might be true if my mother wasn't an extremely successful shark of a litigator who raised me in a house where there was constant debate. My argument stands on its own. I would challenge anyone to go through what I did and not feel this way. I do NOT believe in karma until something horrible befalls DICK.

If you haven't ever dated a monster like this, consider yourself lucky, and read my story as a warning for your own love life. Many women who come from abusive backgrounds end up dancing, or even getting into adult films, I'd say 80% or more, because their self-esteem is beaten to such a pulp, that they become THAT DESPERATE for attention. I was a Columbia University student who became a FEATURE dancer and ADULT film star, so if I was driven to that sort of desperate extreme of escape, it should tell you how bad it can indiscriminately become for women in domestic violence situations. I've done my best to move on from the hell that Dick put me through and am finally started to believe in love again with my current relationship with Matt, my fiancé when we started writing this book. Not all men are like Dick. All women should take into account that statistically, a woman is hit every 14 seconds, as well as that, women who leave their batterers after staying in an abusive relationship are 75% more likely to be killed by the batterer than those who stay. As such, the only preventative measure is to leave the first time it happens. Period, there are no exceptions to this rule, only to the guy because I have a good one finally. I plan to hold onto mine, even as I try by the day to let go of the long-term pain Dick has caused me. I have never been a victim, and don't want to be read that way. My life has not been cast in this experience, but it is a part of my fabric, and I live with it daily as a survivor of that bastard. I have the utmost respect for those of you who have gone through a similar nightmare, on any scale, and I hope we all move forward together into a time when this sort of shit will no longer be tolerated by society at large.

By this point, things with Dick were completely over and I was close to graduation. It still makes me sad to this day to know my father didn't live to see me move on, but I was trying to make the best of things. Once asshole was out of my life, part of me felt like doing a jig on his ball sack with high heels sharpened into points. But in reality, my self-confidence was crushed. Following my break-up with Dick and my father's passing, my mom sent me away to Brazil to get some air from the whole situation for about a week and then I visited France, Germany, and a few other places. After that, I went back to dancing, but really had no career-direction at that point. My mom kept pushing me to apply to law school, but I really had no interest in following in her footsteps. Then she switched to just pushing me in general to get my Masters, or a PhD, and so forth. My question was always: 'For what?' What good does that really do me if my heart isn't in it, also I know many people who have graduated from law school or any number of other graduate programs who ended up without any grander job prospects, and $50,000 in new debt from the graduate loans. So my spring and early summer were really aimless, I just worked to pay off Dick's debts. If I had any professional aspirations, they were to run or own my own business, because I had seen the money potential in the collectibles business for one example. I just couldn't get out from under my bills long enough to get anything started on my own. I tried to have fun when I could. I'd go to the beach or pool and relax without worrying about Dick becoming paranoid over me saying hi to some guy, or for that matter, wondering if he was off in some motel room fucking some bimbo he'd met on the Casino floor or in a bar. I definitely felt alone in the world, I had some friends from dancing, but none whom I was very close with. One friend, Elise, was there for me, but I was largely alone. In general, I never had anyone there for me growing up, not when my father died, never.

My mom just insulted everything or talked down to me all the time in a very condescending way. She would be nice to everyone around me, be it my friends or whomever, so they would then think I was nuts and lying about everything she'd done. It was very much like Dr. Jekyll and Mr. Hyde with my mom, and it wasn't about a fucking curfew. It was the fact that I never did anything that was good enough for her, and there wasn't ever even a fucking established bar to try and meet or talk, because she always moved it. If I was doing well, she'd set it higher, if I was at a low, she'd make it so high I never felt I had any potential of reaching a point where she'd accept me. Nothing was, or is to this day, ever good enough for her. Personally, I think she's incapable of ever being happy. Her favorite word to describe my clandestine teenage activities: *PROSTITUTING.* I laugh at it now, but that was a fucked up thing for any parent to say to a child. How did she think that was going to make me feel about my self image? As far as I'm concerned, she's as much to blame as I am for anything I've done since that she's disagreed with in terms of my adult life. Frankly, she's as responsible for my choices as I am, right or wrong, and if she'd been even a little more trusting with me as a teenager, I believe things would have turned out very differently. Even when I told her about my wedding plans, she shot that all to shit. I think she honestly wishes I could have stayed a 10 year old girl forever. Dick certainly never treated me any better. If anything he only added to that lack of confidence. Eventually though, if you beat anyone down enough, they either wither away and die off, or lash back out at the world.

My grandmother had died not even a year prior to my father's death, in September of 1992, which was brutally hard on me, losing two people who were that near to me in such close proximity to one another. My grandmother had helped raise me, as a hands-on parent, and from you've read thus far, it's clear I didn't have a conventional parent-daughter relationship with my mother. I found out about sex from a therapist because my mother couldn't have the conversation with me. The same with drugs: through a third party. I got used to that dynamic, as odd as it sounds, and so it made it easier to see my grandmother as sort of a surrogate mother in ways, because she made herself more emotionally available to me at times than my own mother did. My grandmother used to stand up for me when my mom would be off on one of her rants. In some households, grandparents are just that: grandparents. In other households, like mine, they're more directly involved with child rearing, and my grandmother definitely helped to raise me. She was awesome; she always tried to see my side and would always do little things like sneak me cookies that my mom wouldn't allow me to eat. Or she'd take me to Central Park and we'd go to the petting zoo and feed the birds together. I remember once she got me this 'My Buddy' doll that had these two red braids, and a red shirt, and blue pants, and these little black Mary-Jane shoes, and we'd have little tea parties with it. I remember my grandmother even coming to the beach at St. Croix once with my dad and I. I remember another time, I was 18 or 19 and had signed up with a modeling agency in New York, and wanted to get some portfolio pictures done. My mother as usual just started yelling at me, making a huge scene, and my grandmother came to my defense, told her not to yell at me, and in the end, my dad paid for the portfolio pictures. It sounds strange, but I think in a very ODD way, I felt at times more like my grandmother was my mother in terms of being my friend, but she was also a disciplinarian too. Lord knows she'd raised my mother, but I don't even think my grandmother felt she'd been as strict with my mom as she was with me. I think my grandmother felt my mom was excessive a lot of the time, which is why she tried to make up for it with kindness. I miss my grandmother and my father dearly and daily — even as I sit here writing this book. The years since both their passing has given me some perspective and patience, but at the time, I was devastated and feeling aimless of direction or a care in the world.

By the fall of 1992, I was definitely not someone to fuck with. I had so much anger inside me toward men that I was walking around something akin to a ticking time bomb. One such example was the late spring following my break-up with Dick. I was hanging out at a bar on 8th street in the Village, and some scum-fuck came up to try and hit on me, and ended up grabbing me. So I told him to fuck off, and he responded by bringing drunken his friend back over, and they started fucking with me simultaneously. Well, I got scared, and I guess fear translated into me finally standing up for myself to a guy. My ulterior motivation was the fact that I had gotten off of a dancing shift and was carrying around a large wad of cash on me. I figured that if I had put up with Dick pushing me around, no fucking way was I going to take it from some drunken asshole. So basically I asked, 'What's your problem?' to which the first drunken asshole replied, 'Nothing, you just have a fresh mouth.' So not knowing to this day what came over me, I said, 'Do you want to step outside and talk about it?' and I ended up beating the shit out of them! No bullshit, as soon as we got outside, the first guy said, 'So what are you gonna do now?' I replied, 'I don't know, what are you gonna do?' and before he could respond, I broke a beer bottle against the guy's nose and kicked the other guy in the balls. Then I started throwing hands, fists, and elbows at him and when it was over, I was thankfully still standing without a scratch on me. First off, any MALE who would actually be low enough to go outside and be willing to fight a woman my size has it coming, so I guess I had the element of surprise working for me. They're lucky too, because I had a switchblade I carried around on me and was pissed enough to use it. Not to mention how drunk both of them were. When I was done, I just went back into the bar and continued drinking and they both went to the hospital. That's a reflection of how angry I was at that time in my life — at the world — and at anyone who got in my face in even a remotely confrontational way. I was developing a hardened emotional shell to a world I felt at the time was very cruel to me for reasons I couldn't understand. I never felt like a victim, but I definitely felt what I was getting — from Dick, from my mom, from my father dying — was undeserved, and I was truly confused as to why I had that coming. And it kept coming and coming, next up in the form of an asshole named Kurt. We'd started dating late in the next spring of 1993, and I'd met him under the auspice that he was a construction worker. When that veil was eventually pulled back, the truth would expose me to a world that both horrified and fascinated me in the same time…

PART IV

Kurt the Construction Worker a.k.a. Gay Stripper/Porn Actor

Let me state at the outset of this new nightmare that Kurt was an asshole, flat out. I am unfortunately one of those girls who is attracted to bad boys, and even in the beginning — operating under the assumption that he was a construction worker — he still had DICK written all over him — I just had no idea at the time how much so. I'd first met him working at Flash Dancers. Typically I as a rule would NEVER date customers, but we ended up going out for pizza and everything seemed fine on the surface. He told me he was in from California on some sort of big business deal for his family and he had the build and look of a construction worker, so I assumed he worked for some kind of family business along those lines. He had a real muscular, hero build, only he didn't have long hair or like heavy metal, but I was willing to go against type at that point for the chance it might be different with this guy. I felt maybe I would finally bring someone home my mother would accept, and at that point I felt desperate for any kind of approval from her, which also made me additionally vulnerable. The next time we went out, it was at a restaurant in Mid-town called Charley O's, unbeknownst to me also down the block from a GAY STRIP CLUB! The latter will come into play a bit later, but basically in the middle of the meal, Kurt excused himself and told he needed to pick up some money up the block at the Marriott for his father. Technically this was true. But what he failed to mention was that, in reality, he was off picking up the money with his ASS CHEEKS on the stage of a grimy Times Square GAY strip club called The Gaiety, where it turned out he was known by the stage name Scott Randsome. Well, I thought nothing of it at the moment, until that moment turned into more twenty minutes, and then began to wonder. Had something happened to him? Had he ditched me? My self-esteem was at such a low point I would have believed anything, and I did when he returned after almost a half-hour covered in a marathon run's worth of sweat. He gave me some bullshit excuse I was more than happy to believe as I was so relieved he came back at all. Experiences like this were an unfortunate pattern in my life that had first caused me to begin dancing, seeking the attention and approval of men. After Dick, my ego was reduced that much further and my desperation in turn had grown that much greater for the approval of any man I was interested in. In the case of Kurt, I took it to a new low — starting that night when we walked past the Gay Strip Theatre following dinner and a guy asked Kurt 'So how much money did you make?' He blew the guy off, but in hindsight, it was clear the gay bouncer had been speaking to Kurt.

Kurt returned to California a day or so later, and naturally, the distance fueled longing, and built up my hopes that much higher, putting myself in yet again the vulnerable position to have them knocked down that much farther, and with that much harder to fall. My mother apparently wasn't having any of it, disapproving of any dating scenario after what Dick had put us through. I guess I couldn't blame her in a way. She went about it all wrong as usual: he called one night to speak to me, and I happened to be out with some girlfriends at dinner, so naturally my mother answered, and proceeded to tell him I was out with my boyfriend. He was pissed and believed me after I explained her nutty history with men. It was still clear this wasn't going to work living under my mother's roof. I was a grown woman anyway, and it was my life to lead, not my mothers, a concept almost impossible not to agree with. Anyway, I decided it was the perfect opportunity to take a trip to California both to visit Kurt and to check out the West Coast on the possibility I might move there. Well, needless to say, I badly required the break and loved every moment of it, and came back home to New York strongly considering the possibility of relocating. My mind was made up by the time I reached the front door and finding all my shit set out on the front stoop by my mother. I was lucky nothing had been stolen, but my mother had thrown me out. I took that as a sign that it was time for a major change of some sort...(Who knew how big of a change I would end up making!) Anyway, I stayed in some shithole motel for the next few nights in Jersey. It was just awful. My roommate was a mouse, and the place cost like $100 a week, so I guess I got what I paid for. Anyway, I was basically broke, so Kurt flew me out to L.A. and paid to ship all my belongings out there, and I felt maybe this was fate pointing me in the right direction to some new start. I moved in with Kurt. Almost immediately, he took me with him to Cancun, Mexico for a 'vacation,' which was fine by me. Trouble came quickly into paradise on that trip when he did several of his now infamous and increasingly puzzling disappearing acts, always returning sweaty and strapped with more cash. I almost didn't want to know at the time, so I didn't ask, and he certainly didn't tell.

We lived in a beautiful apartment complex in Huntington Beach and I enjoyed not being under my mother's thumb, but still missed New York. I didn't have a car, so I supported myself by running a friend's antique business out of my living room. I went back to New York in August, trying to make contact with my mother so she at least knew where I was and that I was okay. I took up residence at the Sheraton Hotel on 52nd Street and while I was on the fact-finding mission regarding my mother's feeling toward me, I uncovered an awful truth about Kurt that would rock me to my very foundation. It happened one day walking past one of the dozens of adult video stores that adorned Times Square (this was before Rudy Giuliani cleaned the place up.) I happened by chance (or fate I believe) to see a picture of my LIVE-IN boyfriend on the front of a gay jack-off video called 'Sunsex Boulevard!' I almost immediately flew back to California, and when I confronted Kurt about it, he told me it was none of my business. Then when I tried to leave — a natural reaction I thought at the time — he started ripping my clothes up, so I agreed to stay to get him to calm down. Almost instantly, I found myself back in the abusive-relationship hell I had just gotten out of, and things just got worse from there. After that, every time he left and came home in his nasty-ass sweaty state, I knew he'd been stripping for faggots, and when he wasn't doing that, he was off shooting gay porn videos. If not that, then — as I found out later — he would be running off to Laguna Beach or Palm Springs for the night with older men, doing God knows what. I would soon also discover that he was a strip club fanatic, and since he dated me, I had to give him that he wasn't totally gay. But then was he bisexual I would wonder, and of course, he'd have knocked me across the room if I'd tried to probe him about it. Once things calmed down a little, I went back to New York to again try to re-establish some relationship with my mother and when I returned, I found blonde hairs all over the bedroom pillows. It turned out he'd hooked up with his ex-girlfriend — a fucking CALL GIRL — while I'd been gone, so that added a couple new logs onto the fire that was my latest relationship and ego burning down to fucking shit again. One, the fact that he was cheating on me openly was obviously upsetting, but to boot, the fact that I'd been sleeping regularly with a guy who also had slept with a prostitute just freaked me out on a whole other level. Things got that much more out of control over the next few days when he started calling escort services and bringing girls to our home.

At that point, I took what little self-esteem I had left and decided to make a stand. I confronted him about everything, and of course, it quickly turned nasty and he started smacking me around. The beating culminated with his knocking me out cold with the phone. Then he took all my shit and dumped it on the front porch while I was still lying on the floor in a bloody ball crying. I had no car, no where to go, but I decided to take advantage of the window of opportunity he was giving me to willingly leave. I managed to get to a Comfort Inn down the Pacific Coast Highway a bit, and just tried to get my shit together over the next day or so. Anyway, this was August of 1994, so the O.J. Simpson trial was just starting, which gave me something to watch on TV during the day while I figured everything out. I remember the final thing that convinced me to stay in California. In part just to spite Kurt and show him I could make it without him. It came when I was on the phone with Sickie back in New York and Kurt showed up at my hotel room window, high on drugs with some sign he'd scratched out telling me to go back to New York. We shared a lot of the same friends from the local gym we frequented and a lot of them took my side. I think he felt embarrassed about what he'd done, and knew all our friends knew, and so that burned him on a whole other level. The final straw was one night shortly thereafter when I'd been out to dinner with several of his former friends at a local restaurant, and saw him eating with some she-man steroid bitch, that let me know in my heart it was officially over. It also cemented my decision to stay in California to show him, my mother, and anyone else who I felt like showing up that I could and would be something bigger and brighter than anything they would have ever expected of me.

PART V

The 35% Guy

At this point in my life, for my Ivy League education and all its implied intelligence, I really felt I had no common sense when it came to men. The only thing I had figured out was they liked to have sex with multiple women on account of them all cheating on me, which was probably subconsciously my first lesson in the porn business. I knew a lot about how to please them because I'd been dancing at this point for a couple years, most likely to a bunch of assholes whose wives were at home with no idea they were out paying to watch me. It was escapism at its most basic, and the idea didn't totally bother me as long as the guy I shared my bed with wasn't the star of the show. I knew that there was a market for some massive sort of dissatisfaction in the home life of a lot of the male population in America, but through dancing I'd only flirted with the outskirts of the pleasure they were after. I could tell even from that vantage point that they weren't getting it at home and that confused me even further as to how to please the men in my own personal life. Oddly though, it planted the seed in my head that where I couldn't be happy in my own life, I could possibly find some satisfaction — and potentially stardom in the same time — in making men happy vicariously through the pleasure I gave them onstage (and later onscreen.) The latter hadn't occurred to me yet as an option, though a personality would soon enter my life that would introduce me into the world of pornography, and transform me from Rhea to Jasmin St. Claire.

Heading into 1994, I needed to make some bread fast, so I took the last $400 I had and bought a plane ticket to New Orleans to do some dancing dates that would last a few weeks. My plan after that was to head back to California, but I rented an apartment for the month for $500 through a local realtor as the dates spread over several weeks. I guess at that time in my life I was focused most on survival, rather than thinking ahead on any bigger dreams, but a new man would come into my life around this time that would change it forever. The owner of the club I was dancing for — Charlie Frey — lived in Florida, and was a booking agent and manager for female talent all over the United States. He booked dancing features, arranged photo shoots in adult entertainment magazines like *Penthouse* and *Playboy* among many others, and little did I know at the time, also had the ambition to break into the adult film business. He seemed like a competent agent at the time, and my only interest was in getting work at that point, so we were a good fit. Charlie was the coolest friend/manager, and ironic as it might sound, the kind of male presence I needed in my life at that time because he wanted NOTHING from me personally. He was my friend: he listened to my problems and was comforting. He was also — hands down — the best businessman I have met to this day.

The temporary vacation to New Orleans was a good break for me. I was there for three weeks and during this period, Charlie convinced me and a fellow dancer I'd met from Texas to come down to Florida for a series of extended dates that he said would last about two months. He said he'd put us up at his condominium (very pricey place) and he also gave us a car to drive, and said we could spend our days at the beach or the gym, so that sounded good to me. I just needed a mental break from pressure of any sort. By that point, I was desensitized enough from dancing in my mind to handle work without viewing it as a pressure, and just getting over two fucked-up relationships, was keen on rebuilding my ego from the ashes back up. For better or worse, the attention I got dancing and the money I made helped with that, so I went with it. It was really a good move too, I made really good friends with this girl Jennifer, and the staff at the clubs where we worked, were very nice to us, along with Charlie, who I was building a business rapport with in the same time, so it was cool. I felt I was around some very cool, positive people — just as people — and I needed that at that point in my life. To cement the foundation of my recovery, I found one of Kurt's gay porn videos at a local adult video store, and mailed it to his mother's house.

As far as I was concerned, he more than had it coming. Anyway, once the dates came toward a close, I decided I was ready to return to California. I had decided by this point to sign on with Charlie as my agent, which officially changed his name to the '35 % guy,' because that was the commission he demanded in my contract. Being naive completely to the illegality of it all, I signed his agreement without batting an eye or reading a line.

Charlie Fry, a.k.a. Mr. 35% Guy: I wasn't doing it for free. A large part of why I asked for that percentage had to do with the reality that I knew from experience that within a short period of time — a year to two years usually — we were going to wind up going our separate ways. So to do all the work I had to do, with no budget or backer, to create and help build their brand, for the first 6 months or year of that time I'm not seeing a dime. So I was getting 35% of a very little amount of money starting out, and mind you my commissions from booking them adult feature gigs didn't include a piece of their tips, just their appearance fee from the club. So for instance, if Jasmin at her pinnacle was paid $6000 to feature at a club, and then made another $6000 in tips that I saw none of, I was only seeing 35% of the principle booking fee. To charge any less, I'd have to ask 'What is the point of me doing it?' when I'm putting in thousands of hours of labor, using all my contacts, all my creativity to make nothing. So I feel I earned every penny of that 35% every single time I was paid a commission.

Jasmin: See, I hadn't come out to California with aspirations of stardom like every other girl from the South or Mid-West. I hadn't stepped off the bus — or plane in my case — and immediately started looking for a talent agent. I hadn't desired to pose nude in magazines, let alone movies. I just never had that kind of agenda, my only agenda had been to get 3000 miles away from any type of a rationality my mother had to offer me about men or anything else involved in how I should lead my life. That is the extreme she'd pushed me too, and I honestly felt like I could breathe for the first time in a way. Anyway, where I lacked ambition, Charlie more than made up for it on my behalf, even before I knew it, he'd started building the foundation for what would become my launching pad into stardom in the adult film world. It would turn out the industry wanted me as badly as I could have ever wanted it, because that rise would happen almost overnight, and was as unexpected for me as it could have been for anyone who was involved. It even widened Charlie's eyes.

Charlie Fry: When I met Jasmin, she was a wallflower, a very sweet, subdued personality, but underneath all that was a desire for recognition and fame of some sort, and typically what I was very adept at was saying:

'Okay, you can have it. You can have all the money in the world, and international fame. Here's the price for it. Being not just a porn star — because there were lots of porn stars — but to be the most infamous porn star,' and to be the most infamous porn star in 1995 meant doing anal scenes at a time when it was very uncommon, kind of taboo. Because in the porn industry at that time, it was a big deal for a girl to have to do anal so you wound up watching not the prettiest or most famous stars that did those types of scenes. In the porn industry — like every other, there was a hierarchy. At the top, there were girls who would only do girl-girl scenes, but wouldn't do girl-boy scenes. Then there were girls who would do girl-boy scenes, but you couldn't cum on their faces; then there were girls who would do girl-boy scenes, but only with one guy at a time; so a gang-bang was in that context a horrible thing.

Dominic Accara (Jasmin's Assistant): When I met Jasmin, it was before the gangbang and I was working a lot on John T. Bone's sets as a porn journalist, and I remember her standing out immediately. She seemed like she knew what she wanted to do and had no qualms about doing what she had to do to get it done.

PART VI

California Fun: The birth of Jasmin St. Claire

I want to reiterate that I didn't come out to L.A. to get into show business; I came out with a guy. Really, I came out West for a change of scenery, but it never entered my head that I would become an adult film star, or even start doing magazine and calendar modeling for that matter. I also want to be clear about the fact that my childhood was wonderful — it was filled with education, culture, travel, and love. Despite what Howard Stern may think, what happened to me later in life is what drove me professionally in the direction I eventually headed in getting involved with adult modeling and film. I would say it was the key thing. In terms of that too, there's things I do and don't regret about getting into that business. You have a lot of these young girls who don't know any better. Believe it or not, I can count on both hands and feet three or four times over, the number of girls I have talked out of getting into the adult film business. I don't counsel them too hard, because I can hardly counsel myself on the subject, but I try to tell them there are better things to do with their lives, and no matter how bad it seems it can only get better.

I realize that seems like generic advice, and in many ways it is, because I would estimate only about 10% of the girls who start in adult films ever gain fame on the level I did, or girls like Jenna Jameson, or Vanessa Del Rio, or so forth. Most end up back on the pole dancing, and those who were meant to stand out beyond that usually do. But I do use my story to try and ask the question — what about when you want to move onto other things? That career can come back to haunt you, it certainly has been both negative and positive for me. The biggest negative for me has been the stereotypes and judgment I've gotten. I felt I was driven to that extreme by my experience with Dick just to get away from him, and look at the background I came from educationally, culturally, and financially. That shows you how bad it was for me to be driven in that direction, because it wasn't for a lack of other opportunities. So there is an element of helplessness in it I think, especially for the 80% of those who do porn — they come from the other side of the tracks, certainly not from the background materially and culturally that I did. They either can't do anything better with themselves, or come from abusive households. I'm too smart to be in that business, which is why a lot of people dislike me. It's not that I feel I'm better than anyone, it's just that they look at me that way because I used it as a stepping stone and got out. I was in that business in the moment for the money and the attention, and in the longer term, as a means to the end of doing something larger within the entertainment business. I never discerned between dancing or adult film, or magazine and calendar modeling, or even more mainstream acting from the collectibles or wrestling business I ran, they were all a means to the same end for me: to make money. I was never interested in anything beyond that, but I did pay attention to the fact that my sexuality had something unique about it to others as I started to get more known in the business.

Charlie Fry: With Jasmin and in the case of every other star I handled, they very quickly realized they don't want to be one of the pack — making small money. They quickly realized they want to be a star, because like many girls in the industry, they're dealing with all kinds of negative self-image issues, and inherent character traits that lend themselves to needing and wanting attention. That is what I played on, and Jasmin already had a negative self-image when I started working with her, and what I did was tap into what was causing them pain to essentially exploit it by directing them where to go in the business. Jasmin was definitely emotionally scarred, deep enough that she would do whatever it took to get to the top — no matter how unsavory the image she had to take on.

I found Jasmin to be extremely malleable, extremely responsive to anything that I needed for her to do. She was very motivated in the beginning, and was a natural back then at selling this outrageous image we were building for her as the world's most controversial sex symbol. So starting out, she was very gung-ho, very motivated, she had the attitude of, 'I want it, and I'll do anything to get there.'

Jasmin: Once I was back in California, Charlie had me working almost immediately in a variety of adult entertainment-related avenues that in hindsight were clearly designed to push me toward the eventual goal of film. For all his underhanded business dealings and charging me 35% of every fucking dollar I made in commissions, I will give him that he was good at what he did. One lesson I've learned after this many years in the business is an agent's job is simple: to get you work. Well, Charlie kept me busy right from the beginning. First off, he had me doing feature dance gigs locally and in some cases nationally that brought me between $1800 and $2000 per week. He'd also lined me up with some calendar and magazine shoots in publications like *Penthouse* and *High Society*, which provided me with some great initial exposure. Being entrepreneurial on my own right from the start, I also landed photo layouts independently with *Hustler* and *Gallery*. Charlie got me some little vignette video pieces in a couple Playboy video specials, so it was clear to me that there was some demand for me right off the bat.

Charlie Fry: First of all, most of the girls I dealt with had already had experience being a stripper, and Jasmin had already done some dancing, and with Jasmin, both of our interest at the time was in her becoming a feature. Because just doing porn scenes alone wasn't where the big money was, it was out on the road in strip clubs dancing live for your film audience as a feature. She was a pro right from the jump too. I remember when we first got started I had a feature booked into Ft. Myers. We were in Ft. Lauderdale, and another girl I managed had started the gig Thursday night at the Orenthia, but had been beaten up by her boyfriend Friday during the day, badly enough that she couldn't appear on Friday night. Jasmin at that time had done some stripping, but hadn't danced as a feature before. I decided it would be a perfect opportunity to put Jasmin to the test and gave her a crash-course on what to do. She then borrowed a mini-van I'd let her borrow, drove to Ft. Lauderdale, literally showed up at 8 o'clock, stepped into a borrowed costume and went on stage. She pulled it off too! I think that showed me that she had a mix of talent that blended very naturally with a boldness that she displayed right from the jump. It's this gung-ho/do anything attitude that got her as far as she did in as short a time as she'd had in the business when she became a star.

Jasmin: Because of my ethnic make-up and darker complexion, I also had a unique appeal that made me a bit more exotic to the generic white girls who dominated the business at the time I was beginning to enter that world. As the weeks wore on heading into the end of 1995 and beginning of 1996, the more money I made and the more attention I got, the more I also began to see where I had something unique to offer. Things truly changed when Charlie got me onto the *Jerry Springer Show*, offering me national exposure for the first time and showing me its implied potential. While the magazine shoots and feature dance spots were great, I wasn't able to properly expose (pardon the pun) myself to maximizing my money making potential without the component of video stardom, which was a norm for any high-profile dancer on that circuit. It was just a fact of the business, and I could already see from the differentials in what I could charge versus someone like Tiffany Lords, who Charlie also managed at the time. As a manager, Charlie also had a subtle but ever-present way of controlling every situation he was in that made me afraid to question him. He was very convincing, and he used basic dollars and sense in my case to secure my agreement to give adult film a shot. He didn't appeal to the glamour of it with me, because he knew I was a businesswoman, unlike most of his dim-witted clientele. He also told me he knew he could make me a huge star. I believed him once he explained the demographics of porn and where he thought I would fit in as something different.

Charlie Fry: I would basically just lay out what I called an 'If / Then' statement. Wherein I said, 'If you want to be a big feature star and don't want to spend years building up your reputation, then here are the choices of what you have to do. You can go out and fuck a Senator or Governor and get caught; you can become a major porn star by doing something outrageous; marry or get caught with some celebrity — but those are all flash in the pan type things. If you really want to see the big money — which is really what the premise was in feature dancing, you need to have the infamy.' And from my memory, she was into it: she wanted the money, the fame, to change from an unknown to becoming a name in the business.

Jasmin: To me, that meant that much more money and the catalyst actually came one day when we were discussing features and the fact that they grossed more when the dancer was also an adult film star. They were the ones who could command the most, and he made it sound like that was something to consider. The other porn star he managed at the time, Tiffany Lords at the time, who had co-starred in a John Wayne Bobbit movie, had gotten a good bit of media attention from it, so I saw the exposure factor was naturally much higher. While I had Charlie talking in one ear, I had had Kurt talking in the other prior to our break up about how much the feature dancers made when they also had film going on. Once I'd agreed, he sent me to a company called Blue Coyote Productions, that he'd worked with in the past, and they had me in mind for a single-scene that would pay me $800, plus another $500 for a photo shoot they would do on-site. So it was $1300 for a day's work, which was basically two-thirds of what I was used to making in a week dancing. I also was thinking in my mind about the fact that doing this would raise my feature rates, so I kept my eye on the money, and suffered through whatever inevitable anxiety I was feeling my first day on the set.

My first day on the set of my first scene fell on a spring afternoon in April of 1995. I was supposed to go down the night before and had no car to speak of, so the company had to arrange a ride for me. Anyway, getting down to Palm Springs, I had actually been chauffeured — so to speak — by my actual *CO-STAR*, Peter North, who I had never heard of before. I actually even confused him with another porn star named Randy Spears, so you can imagine the look on my face when he showed up at my apartment to pick me up. My naivety would come back in my face BIG TIME later that day — and I'm not speaking figuratively — but on the drive down, I was just obviously nervous. You could read it on my face like I was wearing a sign that said 'new girl' across my forehead, and in truth, I had only ever seen one porn movie before in my life. Anyway, I was happy we were shooting in Palm Springs, because it's a very relaxed resort town about two hours outside of L.A. and is designed to calm, which I needed badly by the time we pulled up to the Palm Desert Springs Resort. The confusion about my co-star had been shared by the company producing the video and when we arrived, Randy Spears' picture was up on the wall instead of Peter's. To boot, even though we were shooting at a really nice resort hotel, they had put me up at the Motel 6, fulfilling Charlie's 'Deluxe Accommodations' promise! At least Peter took me out to dinner the night before at Tony Roma's, which was nice of him. I guess he could see I was nervous and wanted me to feel more comfortable with him the next day, and soon enough I would see why.

So lying in bed that night, with the next morning and all that was to come hanging over me, I was trying to review any and all advice I'd gotten over the past spring and summer, from dancers who'd done film to Charlie to people who worked at video companies. Later on, the director who I worked for on my rise to stardom, John T. Bone's had the best advice to keep work and business separate, which was more general, a few specifics I had picked up from visiting a couple sets were as follows:

Most of the men who actually fucked on screen weren't that good looking, which had been a big revelation to me until you considered the stamina factor. In that average-looking guys statistically had an easier time keeping it up for the amount of time it took to shoot one of these scenes, which could run several hours at a minimum. Some of the men I worked with even used DICK injections to stay hard. I never helped a guy off-screen to stay hard, because it's his job; he's getting paid to be a performer. Part of his job is to keep a hard-on. So on screen, when the camera's rolling, I did whatever I had to do, but off-camera, never. On top of that, most of the viewers of these movies were average looking men, and John had once explained that from a marketing point of view, we wanted our target audience to feel like they were right there in the room fucking us. The men were ornamental, as most times it was the women who were the focal point — i.e. stars of the movie and fantasy, so those two points added up nicely in my mind because it made me more the star and my male counterpart on screen more like my driver.

The fact that the men I had to work with on screen were average looking made it easier to not be tempted to date them off-set, because they weren't hot. To amplify that point, I had met Ron Jeremy on one of the sets I'd visited, and I noted both that I didn't find him attractive in the least, and he could stay hard forever. He was a very nice guy though, but I never worked with him.

One of the most practical pieces of advice I suppose I got was from another porn star named Misty Rain, who I met at a feature once on the road. I befriended her, and she gave me some simple words of wisdom: Have a glass of wine or two before your scene, because it will help massively to relax you. John was very strict about people not drinking on set, so it had to be discrete, but that definitely helped to relax my nerves a bit. You just had to be careful not to get outright drunk because eventually you'd pass out on set. So with all this swirling through my mind, I felt a little bit woozy and fell thankfully to sleep.

When I got up the next morning, I felt naturally nervous, like I was heading into an audition of some sort even though I already had the part. When I got to the set, there was an extremely cool make-up artist named Steven Ernheart waiting to work with me, and he did a very nice job, which made me feel better, but I still felt really out of my environment. He was also EXTREMELY gay which meant I naturally felt more relaxed around him also. He did my hair up big and bouncy and had dolled me up with all different kinds of face make-up, like dark lids and light lips, so it looked really sexy. So from that, I at least felt the set-up was professional, which also made me feel more at ease. Next, they did my photo-shoot, both to get it out of the way and to transition or ease me into the next phase of the day, which was the actual porn shoot. So the photo shoot went like a breeze, I could do those in my sleep. So a couple of hours later, they ushered me from the photo set onto the movie set, and it immediately disagreed with me because there were an obvious ton of people hanging around who had no direct relevance to the shoot. To me, this was 100% business, not a social hour, and it made me very uncomfortable, but I wasn't established enough yet to just wave them all off the set. I guess they were going for some kind of a 'family environment' where everyone was very friendly with each other, which stood contrary entirely to the impersonal method by which the actual porn scenes were shot. On screen, it was all business, in spite of how we made it look for the viewers at home, and I preferred to stay in that headspace the entire time I was on set. I didn't mix business and pleasure ever if I could avoid it — that went back to my dancing days, and every time I'd broken that rule, I'd ended up with an asshole like Dick or Kurt.

When I'd first signed up with Metro, which at the time was one of the biggest porn video companies in the business, John T. Bone had given me the indispensable piece of advice of keeping my personal life as separated from my professional life as I could. He explained I would have tons of groupies and hangers-on who wanted to be my friend as I became a bigger star over time. He pointed out that the set wasn't for socializing, which was a little funny sounding that day because there were people everywhere hanging around who didn't belong. But in the larger scheme of things, John had the right idea regarding work ethic. I saw quickly that other girls and guys around me who were also acting in these movies would get together on the weekend, party, and have orgies and whatnot living like their whole life was a movie set. It was just not the way I approached things at all, even from that first day. I was all business, I didn't see anyone there as a friend, and tried very hard to maintain a life outside of my shoots that had nothing to do with the business. I was there to make money, not friends. So while I'm sitting there that day, trying to prep myself mentally for all of what was coming, there's all this irrelevant chatter going on around me I was trying to block out. Well, I should have been at least listening a little, because someone asked me if I'd ever worked with Peter North before, and when I replied that I hadn't even known who he was before that day, a bunch of the make-up and hair people started laughing. They had actually been laughing in reaction to an answer I'd given to the question of whether I had ever worked with Peter before. When I had answered not just no, but that I had no idea who he was before that day, they all just erupted.

Anyway, Steve, my make-up artist could clearly see I was NOT getting the joke or laughing along. So he took enough mercy on me to let me in on the fact that Peter came VERY well endowed, such that Steve had to use his curling iron as a visual aid to re-enforce his point! Naturally, my eyes went wide when he held this thing up, but then to boot he went past the size issue when he told me Peter North's nickname on the set- THE DECORATOR. I supposed to a bunch of gay make up people that is funny, but they weren't the target — figuratively or literally — of the joke, I WAS. Anyway, right around the time all this was flooding through my mind, washing away any confidence I had built up for what was about to *CUM*, the director John T. Bone calls for everyone to get prepared to shoot. I felt like I was in a daze of some kind, with television monitors and cameras and lights. I was dizzy and felt a little like someone had spiked my drink or something, which was probably the best mental state for me to be in given it was my first time. A porn star's job isn't like anyone else's where you walk in the first day and someone greets you with a manual on how to perform your job, and someone else trains you in, and picks up the slack when you're a little slow picking up the pace. You have a director, make up people and a co-star, but in essence you're being asked to take the most intimate thing two people share. Not only do it with a room full of people watching, but ultimately with the potential for the whole world to see you nude and being hammered by what turned out to be the largest male member I'd ever seen. Let alone had inside me. The director was a very patient guy. He was telling us what he wanted, what positions and so forth. Anyway, the whole shoot took about 3 hours, and by the end I was in such pain that I was dying for something to cool me off. Well...not exactly the liquid I ended up getting splashed all over my face, but I finally found out what Peter North was famous for, and why he was called THE DECORATOR when he shot a monster load of his cum all over my face and hair. It was arguably the most disgusting thing

I have ever experienced in my life, in spite of how we made it look to you on screen. I felt...well, dirty, and I guess that was emotionally appropriate in context of what we were doing, but it was degrading rather than sexy to me.

I held it together till the director yelled, 'Cut', but once the scene was done Peter could see I was visibly in a state of mild shock. So he was immediately apologetic, and even more so when he found out I had no idea that was his signature thing as a porn star. When he did it, I was flabbergasted and scared and wondered what the fuck I got myself into. I was flipping out inside, even while he was inside me, because I had no idea how big Peter North was. Then when he came all over my face and it got in my hair and shit, that was the scariest thing. I was just devastated, but in the same time I wasn't turned off. In a way, I felt like I was, you know, creating fantasies. I felt glamorous and hot, you know, even from the first time. Anyway, he drove me back to Huntington Beach, and Charlie called once I was home to see how everything had gone. I lied and told him fine, but I was still a little uneasy inside about the whole thing, but at the same time, couldn't help feeling any damage that was coming was already done in a way. My logic there turned into a 'why turn back now' kind of thing, but it isn't like you do one porn shoot one day and the next they have you lined up for something else. You're NOT A WHORE, in spite of what assholes on the religious right might like to think. Half of those fuckers can't get hard without watching one of my videos anyway, which makes them bigger hypocrites if you think about it. Anyway, to fill time until the next shoot, Charlie of course had a bunch of dance dates lined up down in Florida. We had about a week of press to do down there anyway in conjunction with the movie, so I guess in a way I was grateful for the distraction. So while I was down in Florida, Charlie's mental wheels were already turning on how we could kick start me out of the small time and into the big time, because I guess he saw there was this stagnate thing going on in the industry at that time. Something was missing, and it wasn't so much in shock value, or even in how over the top things could be where they were kind of stationary in a way. In sexual terms, it was like everyone was doing this missionary thing and it felt like there was this massive element of excitement missing from the virtual middle-America bedroom our movie sets were supposed to represent an escape from. So while Charlie and I are sitting in his office one day brainstorming, we came up with the idea that would make me a Frat House LEGEND: *The World's Greatest Gang Bang.*

Charlie Fry: Before Jasmin, a star named Annabel Chong had done the gangbang, and she was nice and everything, but she wasn't really as exotic as Jasmin. Starting out, one of our bigger challenges was her ethnicity, because at that time in particular the popular trend among porn stars was to be blonde-haired and blue-eyed, which I saw as something we could use to our advantage to single her out. In terms of things that were unappealing to her, girl-girl scenes come chiefly to mind — she didn't want to do them. She felt that was the wrong image to portray, and wanted to be known as a girl who fucks guys, and had a good mind as to 'what is going to make guys want me.' And were talking about creating a brand-name star from nothing, and where it normally take years and years and years, within a year and a half Jasmin was a known brand name. Most importantly, we were doing this with zero budget for advertising, zero budget for public relations, and I had to count on Jasmin to be a willing participant in whatever crazy idea I might come up with — including what turned out to be *The World's Greatest Gang Bang*.

Jasmin: Charlie and I had both agreed we needed to develop some kind of niche for me to have any chance of pushing the boundaries that would single me out. So this was right prior to a huge round of press we had lined up to more or less introduce me as a new starlet in the world of porn, and the timing was perfect for what we had in mind. Basically, we came up with a strategy wherein whenever an interviewer would ask me a question about my future plans, I would bring it up, the fact that I was going to top the girl who had done 251 guys in 24 hours. So sure enough, starting with *Excitement Magazine* and then with all these other publications, I kept plugging it and plugging it, to the point where we were actually creating a buzz out of nothing. Then to elevate things even further, Charlie arranged for me to go on *Jerry Springer* for a second time, and I announced on the show that I was going for 300 guys in 24 hours. So next we brought the idea to John T. Bone at Metro and they jumped all over it. And Metro had basically signed me up to do 12 movies, so we collectively came up with this strategy wherein we would build up to the main event so to speak later in the year. As we began shaping the direction of my career, add to the extreme nature of my brand of porn, Charlie and John T. Bone both wanted to capitalize on the fact that I was this. As they put it — beautiful and exotic looking girl doing hard core, and at the time, there wasn't any of that going on. I had an instant niche we could build off of, because we were almost inventing the market as we went along. For instance, the fact that I had lost my anal virginity on camera in my next movie lent kind of a purity to my image, as we began building it in the press. I made it sound sexy in print, but in truth, I'd been scared shitless, pardon the pun. So going forth, that became a signature of my scenes, the fact that I did anal, hard core, whatever would push the boundaries a little at a time. By our estimation, in doing so, those boundaries were bound to SNAP and break open a whole new brand of porn when I finally got to the *World's Greatest Gang Bang II*, as John had officially branded it. We looked at it in a sexual metaphor — like a build up leading to a massive climax over 24 hours that would change the modern landscape of porn forever after.

PART VII

Fame at Any Cost

The way we had plotted it, I was under contract with Metro to do 12 films, and we targeted the 8th film as the *Money Shot* so to speak. We were building my public persona in real time with the shooting of these films. So every month that I would shoot a new film, the scene I'd shot a previous month or so back was coming out. There was always a big promotional junket of photo shoots and interviews to accompany its release. The timing couldn't have been more ideal, because with each film's release, I just kept plugging and building hype for the 'World's Greatest Gang Bang' thing, like getting everyone hotter and hotter and more worked up for it. I shot my second film in late October, in a Castle in the Hollywood Hills somewhere, a literal castle like Phil Spector's. This shoot had me especially nervous because I was scheduled (that sounds funny now) to lose my anal virginity on screen that day, and had to undergo an enema prior to starting the scene. It was almost funny, because you walked on set, and there was like this table set up with coffee and donuts, and then someone on the technical side calls me over to get my *enema* done.

Worse still to my having to have anal sex for the first time in my life on screen, the scene was what they refer to in industry jargon as a 'DP' scene, or DOUBLE PENETRATION. So, in the same day, I lost my anal virginity on screen — which was painful to me, but I am sure looked sexy to all the sick fucks that eventually bought the thing — and was scheduled to have two men inside me at the same time to boot. They weren't fucking around when they used the term 'hard core,' and so for my first scene that day, they really threw me into the deep end of the pool. I was working with two actors — Dave Hardman and Rick Masters — and John T. Bone was directing again. I guess that made me feel a little more at ease, but not much. The scene was shot on a yellow Mazda MIATA outside with the Castle as the backdrop, and losing my anal virginity on camera hurt like a bitch, but I didn't just have to act like it didn't, I had to look like I was enjoying it. It was really torturous in a way, looking back on it now. I kept thinking in my head, "This sucks, this sucks,' and I just wanted to get it done and over with, and the feeling was almost confusing. It was almost like one of those movie scenes where the woman is being fucked for the first time and doesn't look exactly sure by her facial expressions how she's feeling about it. It felt like that in my head, but worse, because I wasn't confused at all about how bad it hurt, and I couldn't give any hint in my own facial expressions to that fact.

So getting into the first scene, both of these guys are inside me, and it's the full extreme, everything that you can imagine in terms of hard core, and it fucking hurt. They were as gentle as they could be, but they had to do all these cum shots on my face and by that point I was thinking from the outside in about it, so I knew what to expect. It was still disgusting though, but the best piece of advice I could ever give to a rising porn actress is to desensitize yourself as quickly as possible, because blowing on a girl's face is as common as blowing your nose. It's just a job requirement. It was good that I'd reached that headspace too because on top of it all, there was this fucking adult film media there. They were all covering the girl who was going to eventually break this world record with the Gang Bang thing, so this was just part of the build-up Charlie and John had arranged. So I felt this MASSIVE extra pressure with the media present, but I also thought that helped me as a performer, as well as in terms of the glamorous side of the business, which I really craved at that time in my life in terms of my ego. Anyway, after the first scene finished, I took a HUGE shower and headed home.

Even though I was clean from the dirtiness of the day, emotionally as I was driving home I felt like I'd stepped on all my morals. I was like 'God, okay, what the fuck did I just do?' I mean in terms of how my mother had raised me, and the kind of home I had come from. Many of the girls who work in this business are already desensitized to it all by the time they start shooting because they came from the opposite kind of home I did. In the same time, my mother was so fucked-up with me where it came to men, coupled with what I'd been through first with Dick and then Kurt in terms of the abuse, in a way I was driven toward it to get back at all of them. Mainly at the men who had mistreated me, but it's like I completely gave up my morals in the process. It was funny, but it didn't really hit home with me that I was doing this in part to get back at those guys until I was in Florida a week or so later, doing a shoot for *Playboy*, and once again promoting my forthcoming Gang Bang special. After the shoot, one of the tech guys who'd been listening to me talk to the press about how big and outrageous this was going to be was driving me to the airport, and he said 'Gosh, someone must have really hurt you.' He was 100% correct, and it kind of hit me like a ton of bricks. It was an important realization personally for me to have because you block so much out to get into the right mental headspace to do porn to begin with. A lot of girls who get into this, they don't actually know what they're getting into psychologically, because its very much escapism for them, but at the same time, you're fully conscious of what's going on while you're filming. It can leave a lot to be explained to oneself later on if you're not clear ahead of time with yourself why you're doing it. Knowing I was punishing Dick and Kurt just made me feel in a way that much more ambitious. To me, it was both to become famous, but also for the emotional torture I could inflict on them both in the process. I felt like I had been emotionally raped by both of these assholes, so I was in a pretty cold place where it came to feeling anything toward anyone one way or another.

My personal life around this time was free completely of Kurt, and I had done some dating, but largely had kept my mind focused on work. The previous summer, even before I'd shot *Hell Fire*, I'd hung out with Ron Jeremy a bit socially as friends, which was educational at least. He was basically a walking example of what John T. Bone had been talking about in terms of how people in the business use whoever they can to climb, and I have to admit I was surprised to see it happen with someone of Ron Jeremy's stature. Basically, he would go out and pick up some girl who was new to town, green to the ways of Hollywood, and then introduce her to one of his mainstream director friends. His intention ultimately would be for the girl to sleep with the director and for Ron then in turn to get a mainstream movie part or cameo, which raised his profile that much more. There is a ceiling on porn stardom, and I saw that for the first and last time I needed to see it with Ron Jeremy, who at the time was considered a giant in the business. My grandmother had heard the name Ron Jeremy, so he was famous in the mainstream, but that wasn't enough to keep him relevant. I guess he and I had that ambition in common, in that we were both always looking for ways to advance ourselves outside the box of porn. It also didn't hurt me locally around the L.A. social scene to be seen with a legend like Ron Jeremy. One mainstream 'star' of sorts I met through Ron during that summer was Corey Feldman. Corey liked mainstream girls because they were tested regularly, and I did sleep with him once, and I'm not revealing anything new here because I said it on Stern, but he was AWFUL. On top of that, when I was on the air with Howard, I went onto talk about how small his penis was, which was in retaliation for the fact that he basically blew me off after we went to bed together. Anyway, I feel like I got him back satisfactorily, so it's no big deal to me at this point.

The second day of the shoot for my second movie was something entirely different from the first in that it was an orgy scene. That one scared me more than anal had because it was a different situation entirely, but I was working with one of the two guys I had the day before, so that was cool. Ron Jeremy was there too, and was actually told to stay away from me, which was funny because he kept trying to inject himself into the scene. Anyway, there were 4 people involved in the orgy scene, and I was very uncomfortable with being with a woman sexually, more so than I'd ever felt about being with a strange guy. Most of the scene was improvised too, rather than staged, and I'd insisted on seeing everyone's AIDS tests before shooting started. The whole thing took about two and a half hours to do and of course at the end, the guys all blew in our faces again, which was just fucking vile to me. When you think about it now, it's really fucking vile, and you're supposed to act like you want it. So then when I finished the scene and went to shower, there was already one of the chicks from the scene in there with one of the guys, fucking again! I just showered in a different room, left and went home, and was just happy to be done with the whole thing. Plus I had the box cover shoot the next day, which I really always enjoyed in contrast to the shoots, it was always a lot light fair, and I got paid for everything at the conclusion of the shoot.

My featuring during this time period had started to pick up a lot too, validating Charlie's claim that my exposure — and therein my rates — would skyrocket. When I was home in between dates, I made the stupid mistake of allowing Kurt back into my life. He'd pulled his dick out of a gay dude's ass long enough to think he was straight again, and for a minute actually had me convinced that he had changed. As the fall wore on, I'd started re-engaging my mother in letters as well, telling her I was modeling out West, which I suppose was true in a sense. I was also doing small shoots for this magazine or that, and I was starting to quickly realize what a mistake I had made on one hand agreeing to give Charlie, my manager, 35% of everything I made. That meant if I made $5000, he got $1750, if I made $500, he got $175. His rationale anytime I attempted to bring it up to him was the same old swindler-logic that boxing managers had used on fighters for years, justifying 50% commissions by arguing that '50% of anything is 50% more than you had in your pockets before you signed with me.'

To boot, as my new management would point out to me in later years, there was no back-end for me built into the structure of my deal with Metro for video sales at the time I had first signed, no residual whatsoever. I would build a business out of merchandise sales that has lasted to date, but would never see a dime in royalties from the sale of my movies, no matter how many years they went onto sell beyond my prime. The point of revealing all this is to give you perspective on how hard I had to keep working, outside of the movies that I shot, to maintain any decent standard of living. Much like a musician who makes most of their money touring rather than off album sales, I was on the road arguably half the year, if not more. Every night, every stage I was out sweating on, dancing my ass off for hours at a time, Charlie got a piece of everything — except my tips, of course (*wink, wink.*) That would have been like asking a waitress to declare her tips on a tax form. I worked just as hard, in spite of the glamorous image you might have had in your mind.

Very few porn stars ever attain the national — or even international — mainstream status that stars like Jenna Jameson or I did. Howard Stern helped, but I learned right from the jump off that you had to keep working and working to keep yourself out there and visible, in as many mediums at once as possible. This meant building up a following on the road at club gigs, selling as many signed Polaroid photos as I could after shows and video stock if I had it. In the beginning, because I was still so new, I had to rely primarily on Polaroids for merchandise, but I sold them for $30 a pop, and sometimes I sold hundreds. That was revenue I was also able to keep out of Charlie's greedy clutches, but again I had to hustle twice as hard to sell as many of those as possible to try and make up for the 35% he was taking out of my ass. The whole mountain of bullshit that it seemed women had to go through in that business really pissed me off, and I made sure to mouth off about it at every opportunity in press interviews. I wasn't just mad at the smut merchants that were ripping us off from the management and corporate side. I was equally as pissed at the actors and actresses for accepting this kind of financial rape as a norm. So that there was no one standing up for any kind of change besides myself. I lashed out a lot at the actors because I felt they had a role to play in keeping us down collectively, but I also had to be careful not to piss off the establishment. I had to keep them hot in the same time that I was going off, but my tongue was always sharp.

To boot, as the fall wore on, in every one these same interviews and appearances, I was busy promoting my *World's Greatest Gang Bang* movie coming in the later spring of 1996. One really cool thing that happened for me professionally in the later fall of 1995 was my traveling to San Diego to meet with a comic artist named Dave about a comic book Metro had commissioned him to design — STARRING ME!!! It was a mix of fact and fiction designed around my 'Jasmin St. Claire' persona, but it was definitely the first thing that authentically made me feel like a star. Titled *Porn Star Fantasies*, I was on the cover, and he and I collaboratively created the story and dialogue inside. The girl who drew me for the cover was named FAUVE, and I couldn't have come out looking cooler. She was very talented. I thought it was really cool that I had my own comic book, albeit one that most kids would have to hide under their pillow from Mom and Dad. I'll bet you plenty of those same parents had my videos stuck under their mattresses though. It amused me to think I was playing such an integral part in the carnival that was male adolescence, whether you were reading my comic book or more likely, watching me on screen staring in the first porn you ever watched with your playground friends after school one day. It motivated me to elevate myself to the top of the game as fast as I could, and what would soon become dubbed the *World's Greatest Gang Bang II* was my shot.

PART VIII

The Rated X Files

My third film, *Vortex*, was shot in November of 1995. The process of filming itself was becoming business as usual, which is not meant to cheat you readers of any salacious details, but really — if you want those you should go out and buy the videos. I will say that shooting *Vortex* was nice because it was done in THREE DAYS; EVERYTHING — from the scenes to the box cover. I worked with a fellow adult film star — Annabel Chong and a male lead named Rich O'Shea and another calling himself Jerry who was very well-endowed and nice looking for a change. That movie had a very nice box cover, very sleekly shot, and I had another appearance on *Jerry Springer* scheduled for that month. Much like Howard Stern, the *Springer* show was always a desired appearance for any adult film star or wrestling star. Now that I think about it — because the television show's viewing demographic was almost identical to that which bought our videos, or would come out to the strip clubs to see us on the featuring. I was just reaching a much broader slice of that demographic at once, and I always went out of my way to make the most of it. It turned out that Annabel Chong was also appearing on *Springer* that same day to promote *Vortex*, along with the film's director, John T. Bone. It was a lot of posturing and shit-talking as usual, and as it turned out, the show DID WELL, but it helped me build a rapport with Jerry Springer for future appearances, so that didn't bother me so much. Besides, it became a mutually beneficial relationship in time, because at one point I was Springer's highest rated guest, largely based off my *World's Greatest Gang Bang* press junket, but that wouldn't be till later in the spring of 1996. That fall, I also made another important introduction in meeting Vic Chaney, who handled the mail-order fulfillment for merchandise associated with my films.

As I started getting bigger with each film's release, the demand for not only videos, but also pictures, t-shirts, my comic book, and related merchandise began to roll in. With the advent of the internet just beginning, he also launched an on-line store on my behalf. It's interesting to think on how much the internet helped catapult me into the international realm of porn stardom when it likely would have taken years longer without the web. The internet is like a virtual porno magazine and video all in one, it was amazing how quickly the technology spread into peoples homes, bringing me into thousands more bedrooms overnight than I could have ever reached in just video sales and magazine photo spreads alone. John's people really had their shit together too in adapting the internet model to their promotion of my movies, and Charlie hopped on board with the rest, so I was in good hands in context of promotion.

While they stayed home minding the store, I still was out on the road working my ass off, dancing night after night to crowds that seemed to get larger by the week. I definitely felt for the first time in my life that things were legitimately growing in terms of both my broader popularity nationally, and locally by the number of growing heads as I criss-crossed the country doing my feature dancing. I was home briefly at the end of October for my birthday, which was maybe the only down-note because I spent the day alone, which made me really sad in spite of the climb toward international stardom I'd begun. I took myself out for dinner at the Cheesecake Factory, and actually felt proud of my independence in spite of my loneliness.

Dominic Accara (Jasmin's Roadie): Our routine when she was out on the road was first to check into the hotel, and then I would usually go in before and set up her dressing room, knowing how she wanted it laid out — from costumes to boots, make-up tables, the whole bit. So my job was always to be her shadow and make her life easier as the feature. When you're out on the road, much like a band, and you're with people from the club, you're always trying to be nice, because you want to get re-booked, and to get referrals from other clubs, so its part of the game. Jasmin always usually had a pretty solid crowd as well. With new cities, much as with musicians, if you hit a new town, you're going to draw more because you haven't been there before. Also if you develop a good rapport with the club owner, the local radio station, the gazette, etc, then you have good word of mouth and the radio stations will plug the shit out of you when you come back. But for Jasmin, even in new towns, she would pack a fucking building to where it was not even funny. When the gangbang came out, this was the case almost everywhere.

When you go into clubs, you make your bread and butter on meet and greets. Your dancing salary is a flat base rate, but most performers make their money in promo sales (T-shirts, Polaroids, etc.) So when Jasmin's credit, when she went to work, she went to work, no matter what kind of mood she was in after a long night, or however many people might have been waiting in line. Inside the club, they were fans, and she spent the time meeting every one of them. In some ways it was like any other job in that some days you got the best gig in the world, and other days, you wanted to shoot yourself. When Jasmin was on the road, depending on the region of the country, she might spend 2-3 hours taking pictures and doing signings after dancing all night. It was always more on the East Coast and the West Coast, which had nothing to do with Jasmin personally, because in California you see porn chicks everywhere now, but back then it was better.

She toured more in the winter because it was cold out and people had nothing to do but go in tittie bars, so if you went in between November and February, sometimes March, you cleaned up. I didn't really have any roots in L.A., so I could tour for a month or two months at a time with her, and she worked her ass off during that season so we could be gone that long straight at a clip. The longer you stayed on the road, the less money you spent as well because everything was paid for. We would rent a car and hit the road six days a week, with her doing four shows a night, and then we'd fly out Sunday to the next big city. If we did have time off, we'd go home to L.A. for a few days, but she was out a lot. To me, it was more fun on the East Coast because there were more hard core fans. You had patches on the West Coast. Like Sacramento is big for porn fans, but overall the East Coast was it, it was just crazy. The other thing was if you went to Al's Diamond Cabaret in Redding, Pennsylvania. Al's was notorious for being considered the equivalent to playing Madison Square Garden, or making it in the big time in the world of adult features. You did 30 shows a week there, and 30 shows might sound like a lot, but the way the routines were set up, it was a piece of cake, and you made money-money. If she had a 4 show evening at 6, 8, 10 and 12, we'd probably arrive at 5:15. Depending on how far the club was from the hotel, if it was across the street, she'd do her show, then go back to the hotel and relax until the next show. If you were working a gig that was a drive away from the hotel, you were stuck in the club all evening and how that went depended on what city you were in. In some cities, things were very relaxed; others were a pain in the ass, especially if you had to deal with local laws that could affect everything too.

Jasmin was one of those stars on the road who, because of her reputation, never really had a problem worrying about people fucking with her, although sometimes people would expect this really hard core personality to show up, and she was much nicer. She played that feisty side up to the media, so that was largely how she was perceived, but it worked for her in terms of club owners playing it straight with her. Because she got on with them, the clubs also let her slide with rules, because they let features slide in general more than house girls. So for instance, there's a rule that when you're dancing on stage, the customer has to be six feet away, or when the feature's on stage, once they take off their top, let's pretend there's a rail around the stage, no part of her body can pass that. She can't lean forward with boobs and stick them in a man's face, when she's naked she has to stay in a certain part of the stage and can't go past, even the features. There's a club in California in Anaheim, where they literally have a triangle on the stage, and the house dancers — when they get topless — can't leave the triangle, it's the most fucked-up thing you ever saw. In Chicago, they have these weird stage rules where if you're throwing posters off the stage, you can only throw them so far into the audience (how are you supposed to judge that distance from the stage?) If you sit down to do a Polaroid, you have to keep your legs closed. Just stupid rules like that.

The other part of being a featured star is you bring more attention, which, in some places, meant more police into the club. If the city had an issue with the club, they would use the feature to try and bust the club on some violation, so there were times where Jasmin had to adapt and work within these 'six foot' type rules. Other times they were more liberal with stars like Jasmin, it just depended. In other clubs, they had rules on what kind of music you were allowed to play — heavy metal vs. rap music — but if you were a feature, you could get away with pretty much whatever you wanted as far as the music they played. Sometimes, EVERYONE there was a fan of Jasmin's, and in those cases, she got to do whatever the fuck she wanted on stage. A good example of that was San Francisco, which granted had more liberal club laws anyway, but still, she was featuring at a club on Market Street, in an anything goes type of club, and she was on stage doing a Dildo show. And I remember she's up there, doing her thing, looks up, and sees two cops standing at the end of the runway with their arms crossed, right in the middle of her act! She finished her routine, came off stage, and immediately went up to them and asked, 'What did I do wrong?' because that was Jasmin, and they surprisingly said, 'You didn't do nothing wrong, we're fans,' and after that show, she posed with them for pictures, etc.

People were very respectful of the features, and the club had trained their audience very well, which you didn't get a lot. In Jasmin's case, we tried to mix it up and start off with lighter shows, say a nurse routine and a little girl routine for instance, and then as the night went on and the audience got drunker, she'd start blasting Metallica and Motorhead and the dance routines got wilder. It was almost always Metal that Jasmin would dance to, she was always a true metal-head. As far as her racier, later-night routines, if she could get nude, she got totally nude, but that was totally up to the club. She'd do whipped-cream dances, a candle-wax routine where she would pour hot candle wax all over her body, and even did fire shows, where she put fire sticks on her boobs and shot fire out of her mouth. She was a better feature in that she put money into buying costumes, the music matched her routines, so if she was doing the fire routine, we'd play metal songs like 'Fire Woman' by the Cult, etc. That turned into a funny story one time. We were flying out from a dance gig to a wrestling gig. I had all the pyro stuff in my carry-on bag. I'd passed okay through security but then when the plane had pulled out about 10 feet away from the gate, and was about to turn onto the runway, it was called back, and I was escorted off the plane by airport security. They spent the better part of 2 hours interrogating me about the contents of my bag, which included all her different stripping costumes. They finally get to this little can of kerosene, and were asking me all this crazy shit about what I had planned for this stuff on the plane. Eventually they let me go, but they also pulled Jasmin aside when her plane landed and questioned her about it too. We both laughed about it when it was over.

Jasmin: Heading into November, John T. Bone and others who I worked with, including my merchandise manager Vic Chaney, were all trying to convince me to move out of Huntington Beach over toward the Santa Monica area. I ended up settling on Marina Del Rey area on the Venice Canals, in a nice little one bedroom for $900.00 a month. I had just a Futon when I moved in, so I went out and got a line of credit for like $1000 at an IKEA-type store, and furnished my whole apartment. I grabbed up some little things from a Pick & Save type place, but it was my first apartment that was fully furnished by the time I was done and I was proud of that. I liked living in my new complex much better than Huntington Beach because the tenants for the most part were either old people or working professionals as opposed to Huntington Beach where they'd all been surfers, burn-outs and body building morons. Or the Valley for that matter where all of my colleagues in the business lived, wanna-be actors and actresses and groupies galore. I liked the environment I lived in because it was consistent with my philosophy of keeping the business and personal parts of my life separate — and living among my co-workers wouldn't have helped that. That same month, I bought my first car, a beautiful little Mazda Miata, which made me really proud of myself. I was giving myself a lot of pats on the back at that point, because I was really working my ass off, and starting to see the rewards.

I did between 15 and 18 shows a month, and was netting maybe $2500 a week, before Charlie's ass-rape commission, so that knocked me back to $1625 after he took $825 a week from me. That seems unbelievable to me reading it back to myself now, but my hands were tied at the time. I didn't know how to stand up to Charlie at the time, and it took me seeing that it would cost me till I did to truly understand the importance of that courage. For instance, when I flew out to my feature gigs, at first my travel expenses only included my hotel room, and not my airfare, which should have been covered as well. That's just standard, but it took me paying for a few tickets out of my own pocket before I finally got pissed enough to rip into him about it. After that, he got me a $200 plane allowance per feature, so that helped a little, but not much, because I was still dealing with cheap tickets. As I finished out the fall, I also shot my third film, titled *Just Jasmin*. It felt good to have top billing in the title, and it was a big shoot: 3 scenes, shot up in Sun Valley, all in one day. It had become routine to me by then, one scene had me dressed up in a Cheerleader outfit to satisfy that part of my viewing demographic whose glory days were playing high school football. The second one was for the straight-up freaks, as John had me dressed like Pocahontas. The movie had four male stars: Rick Masters, Rick O'Shea, Dave Hardman, and Steve Hatcher. That wasn't a walk in the park either, because they were all stars of hard core movies — I'll leave it to your imagination to imply what that meant in terms of making it *HARDER* and *ROUGHER* for me. Given what I had coming up in April with the *Gang Bang* movie, I looked at movies like

Just Jasmin more or less training camp for me, because double penetration was involved in each scene. I also had the routine psychological worry about my co-star pulling out at the right time, which was never actually a problem because it was part of their job to make sure that didn't happen. Also, I was on birth control at the time, so I wasn't really in danger of that even if. It was just something you always wanted to avoid, even with STD tests being required.

It was a weird time for me in a way because this huge transition was happening as a result of the nature of what I did professionally — and everything I was able to do for myself personally was an extension of that. I had never imagined doing this in a million years. I am not trying to sound arrogant, but I had an Ivy-league education and spoke four languages. I really went a little bit against type in terms of the typical co-star of mine — a white-trash bitch with no class and more semen than brains in her head at any given time we were working on the same movies. While I was always looking ahead of the moment, these girls could never escape it, and that's what made them a dime a dozen. My value, on the other hand, kept going up month after month and movie after movie, because it felt like the natural direction of things. If I hadn't been meant to become a star, then the world wouldn't have ever embraced me in the first place, the media would never have cared. I had something special to offer that business, a more cultured light to project onto the metaphorical screen in context of how people saw porn stars in general terms. I changed that perception in every press junket I did leading up to the World's Greatest Gang Bang which would give me my own universe of stars in how it knocked everyone out. They woke up to a new day for porn after that, because I was doing some otherworldly shit in how exotic it was. So heading into the end of 1995, I had to look back a little dazed and dazzled myself, because it had truly been a hell of a year. My entire life had begun to change, and I'd watched it pivot in real time, so that I wasn't just looking back at myself in the mirror anymore, but others around me were starting to recognize me as something special. At that point, my self-esteem badly needed the adulations, so I couldn't fight it. I became an ally, talking as much shit as I could in any interview to be as exotically over-the-top as my movies and image were. I think I worked well with my handlers, and there wasn't much 'shaping' needed, I set the tone most times naturally with what came out of my mouth. My strategy was to be as shocking as my videos; it was that simple. Once I saw things starting to take public shape, I treated my time in porn like a business plan in my own mind. With projections on everything from how popular I could become in the business to how long I would have to be involved in porn before I could use that popularity to transition out of that genre and cross over into others that were ideally more mainstream. I wasn't operating under any illusions though in terms of how long it would take me, I knew I was still at the very beginning of what would be a long road out of hell.

That Christmas, I went home to visit my mother. It was really nice being back in a place I knew as well as New York. I had missed sleeping in my own bed, and I enjoyed getting to see my dolls, my little doll house, just all the relics from my childhood. My old books — I was such a bookworm in high school that it would never have matched up with your typical porn star's bookshelf in a million years. I read everything from J.D. Salinger and Jean Paul Sarte to Albert Camus, and anything and everything by Kurt Vonnegut Jr. My mother was happy to see me, but she kept prying about my life out in California, and I kept with my modeling story. My mother was so removed from that world that there was truly an almost 0% chance of her ever discovering what I was doing. Even if she had, she would have been in such denial that she wouldn't have believed it anyway if she'd watched it on television. For the moment, things were good though between us, and she was obviously happy to see her only daughter.

For me, it was also nice to just enjoy New York. It was just the greatest thing going to Central Park, seeing the trees, and it reminded me of my grandmother, who used to take me there as a child. Anyway, I spent New Year's in L.A., and resolved to begin the New Year out with a *bang* (pardon the pun) as far as my career went. That began with shooting the box cover for my fourth movie, *Possessed*, which I'd shot back in December. My first couple box covers had looked okay, but my third had looked like shit, and so I wanted something a little higher-grade for my fourth movie. That was really the first one I liked, it was just higher class than the others had been. The movie shoot itself had been messy with the male stars beginning the scene by throwing mud at me. It was awful. I was playing a mental patient chained to the gates of a Mental Institution, and we shot both scenes in one day, so it was exhausting. Plus I was in some kind of weird pain all day from the mud mixing with everything else because by the time I got home that night, I was urinating blood. When I went to the doctor the next day, it turned out I had developed a tract infection from the mud. It hurt all week, plus it was a $250 hospital bill that I had to pay out of my own pocket, because porn stars don't get any health insurance benefits. It's really a shitty business, and that's an example right there: I shouldn't have had to pay medical bills from a condition I got on the job. It was wrong, and I had no one to stand up for me, Charlie certainly didn't try.

As January 1996 progressed, I went to Las Vegas for my first Consumer Electronics show, which was old hat for me given my background in the collectibles business from my years with Dick. Still, I wasn't used to being the product, so it was still selling, but different because I was there on behalf of Metro to encourage retail buyers to order my movies. It went well beyond that for me. It was more like a circus atmosphere because we were simultaneously promoting the coming *World's Greatest Gang Bang II* movie with buyers in the hopes of generating pre-orders for Metro. John T. Bone also had me sitting at the company table passing out applications to men who wanted to be in the gang bang — as my SEX PARTNERS. The big movie they were also pushing for me that was already out at that time was *Hellfire*, so that was cool, and I was paid $500 a day to be there so I was making money as well. My expenses were also paid, and in all, the convention was a great success in terms of our goals in being there- to introduce me as John T. Bone's big new find, and to promote *Gang Bang II.*

Of course I enjoyed the attention, and though we weren't really there to socialize, I did run into an old Playgirl model friend of mine and I sneaked him into my room one night while everyone was out, got my rocks off, and kicked him out. John would have killed me if he and his wife had walked in on me, because we were sharing a room with 2 king size beds. He was almost like a father figure at those things, so I felt like a little girl being naughty, it was fun. In sum, it was a crazy weekend that I really needed, both in terms of the attention and the realization that I was starting to become recognizable, which I loved! Metro had been pushing me and another new star Shyla at that convention because we were sort of the company's poster-girls for naughty; we were doing the most hard core porn. Shyla didn't last long. She was part of the turnover ratio common to porn stars with less ultimately to offer the business than I did. On top of that, I had a much higher stamina than she did, which meant she NEVER could have pulled off something like the *World's Greatest Gang Bang II*. She wanted to do softer core stuff, and that put her in competition with a lot of clones and copycat fly-by-night bitches. I got a lot of press from the convention, including a write-up in *Esquire*, and a feature interview on *FOCUS Magazine* among others.

My 5th movie, which started shooting in February, co-starred Shyla — not only in the same movie, but in the same SCENE, which was a first for me. The movie was even titled *Two Much*, so I knew what John had in mind going into the shoot. Naturally, I was the stand out, but I was just biding my time till April, when we started shooting *Gang Bang II*. I had been schedule to go on the *Howard Stern Show* for the first time that month too, but my flight had been cancelled the day before due to some kind of incident with the plane and some guy with a gun. Anyway, Charlie lost his shit over that, calling me a 'stupid cunt' and whatnot, on the phone. He was a true asshole in every sense of the word. In his defense, he kept me working, but I didn't deserve the abuse that came with it. Charlie got me so stressed over it that I ended up in the Emergency Room with an IV in my arm for dehydration. That also caused me to miss a booking for the first time, so Charlie used his three magic words over that one too. I ended up staying off the road for a couple weeks to recuperate, which upset Charlie because he was losing commissions, but he could fuck himself as far as I was concerned. Even while I was at home resting, I was still working though, doing interview after interview on the phone promoting the *Gang Bang*. I did a publicity photo shoot with this big photographer Brad Willis. John Bone planned to run a campaign in all of the adult magazines. He was a host at the AVN Award show too, which was officially the porn industry's Grammys or Oscars, but was in my opinion mainly an excuse for trailer park white trash to dress up in gowns and get drunk.

To me it was 'White Trash Night Out.' It could have honestly been like a Springer Pay-Per-View, just totally classless. Metro, like every other porn studio, has their own table where all the talent and producers and directors sit, and they give out awards for like 'Best Cock' and 'Best Girl on Girl Sex Scene,' shit like that. I presented one, but this company called 'Vivid Video' swept that year. It was just fucking stupid, people crying over winning awards for the most deviant behavior and sexual acts you can imagine recorded on screen. Oh, but wait, it's an 'ART FORM!' That made me fucking laugh, how some fucking bronzed statue suddenly legitimized what we were doing, it was silly to me. I won a few of those fucking things over the years, and immediately turned around and auctioned them off. How is that something to be fucking proud of? You sucked the best cock? It's the most degrading thing they could give a woman in terms of a label, and I realize we brought it on ourselves somewhat by starring in those movies to begin with, but to rub our noses in it afterward was just wrong. I know a lot of readers are not going to like me saying that- or think me hypocritical — but they can fuck themselves.

I won 'Best Selling Movie' a couple years in a row, and by that time, February of 1996, my first couple movies had come out, and both were selling very well, exceeding projections and so forth. So that at least made me feel good about the fact that I was getting out to that many homes around the world, not to mention the seemingly endless press junket I was doing to promote the coming *Gang Bang II* movie. Even when I was shooting other films, it all seemed like steps toward the climax that the latter movie would bring the porn world to in April. My movie that February was titled *Delirium*, and, pleasantly enough was my first time doing a one on one girl/guy scene. My co-star was John Decker, who I'd never worked with before. He had a huge cock, and of course the scene involved anal, so that was excruciatingly painful. It was a price I was paying for stardom, which was starting to blossom around me. People would recognize me on the street or guys would yell something from a car if they drove by in reference to my movies. Sometimes it was a frat guy, usually it was a frat guy, because more mature men wouldn't have taken that tact to compliment me on my performance. Still, whether you disagreed with the means to the end I was achieving, I was intent on having my fame one way or another.

February was a thankfully short month, because I found myself legitimately excited for March, which would mark my first appearance on *The Howard Stern Show* to promote — of course — the *World's Greatest Gang Bang II*. For any porn star to gain even a shred of credibility they had to appear on the *Stern* show, it was like a right of passage into mainstream success in the porn world. I had grown up listening to Howard Stern, so to me it wasn't quite as cool as meeting Bruce Dickinson from Iron Maiden would have been, but it was up there. To boot, I was a star on the show, rather than just a nobody. I was there to promote the *Gang Bang* by way of a contest with his listeners, such that the general public could actually come down to the station and sign up to star with me in the movie. It was a publicity stunt, but a big crowd of fucking dudes showed up nonetheless. I remember leaving the station and being mobbed for autographs and photos, which was weird, but pretty cool. Its different from a convention booth signing where you're signing blindly for retailers who don't in many cases have the slightest idea who you are, they're just there for free shit or to place orders for the product. Being that young in my career, it felt good to get that kind of reaction from the public, especially Stern fans, because in many cases we shared the same selling demographic.

As a result, his listeners likely turned off their radio and turned on my videos in the same day, so it was very much one hand washing the other. One important thing for me was to not let it get to my head, to believe my own hype, because I knew I was a long, long way from where I wanted to be in terms of long-term stardom. Also, the E Channel — which filmed Howard Stern's show, and specifically the one I was on — announced shortly after that they were using the footage from my appearance as part of the television show, so that was exciting. It was a pretty quick turn around, because that episode was scheduled to air sometime in April, coinciding nicely with the *Gang Bang* movie. Looking back now, it was a pretty big deal that I was becoming that popular that quickly given that I only had 4 movies shot and out at that point. I think I filled a void in that business. Something it was lacking in terms of quality, because it certainly had plenty of quantity in terms of generic, 15-minute famers who shriveled up soon enough due to catching AIDS from fucking their co-stars unprotected on the weekend and wilted away from the spotlight. I mean, filled to the fucking brim, if not overflowing. I knew I was better than they were too because other people validated that instinct — Howard Stern for instance, being one who specifically took me aside and said, 'You shouldn't be doing this, you're too beautiful and too smart.' And you could tell he meant it because it wasn't something he said on air, it was a personal moment between us, and given the number of porn stars he'd made his bread and butter with on the air over the years, I appreciated the observation. Still, as much as I agreed with him, I knew that very distinction gave me my edge over my competitors in the business.

My movie that March was called *Compulsion* which co-starred Tom Byron. That movie shoot stands out in my mind not because of anything other than the fact that Tommy boy couldn't get it up, and then once he did, he had trouble keeping it up. I remember they had to stop shooting at one point to help him, because I certainly wasn't going to, that was his responsibility. Anyway, I remember having to make that point to John T. Bone because I was calling to make a nail appointment while they were injecting Tom with whatever hard-on assistance drug they had to get him up to par for the scene to continue. While this was going on, John made some comment to me about the fact that he was trying to shoot a movie and I was on the phone, as though that was somehow the thing holding him up instead of Tom's inability to get it up. Naturally, I shot back at him that 'It's not my fault he doesn't have his shit together,' and they really couldn't argue with me, but I still found it funny. I think that's important to underscore in context of my larger attitude about the business, that it was just that, a business, and nothing more. There was nothing personal going on between Tom and I that would have compelled me to be sympathetic to his impotence, and there would have needed to be for me to even consider helping him stay hard. I guess I took it a little personal from John that I got shit about it when I was not the cause for the hold up, but somehow it was in my job description to be a fucking hooker or something and help get him hard. It's not like he was my fucking trick or something. That just really offended me underneath the surface, but I kept it professional on the face of things and eventually we got back to work. It has always bothered me though that those in the porn business — particularly men — fail as often as they do to draw the distinction between us being porn stars and hookers. Granted we're both being paid to have sex, but one is doing it in the fucking street, and the other is doing it on screen for thousands of people to watch. One is making $40 for their time, the other is making $1750, and there is a defined difference. The public can make that mistake, but not professionals who work in the business. It's important that the line between the two be finely defined and followed, and I just felt really strongly that it wasn't that day.

No matter, I let it go once the shoot was over, and moved on, but incidents like that got spread around the porn rumor mill as gossip, and that helped to spawn the whole 'Jasmin's a bitch' label because I kept it strictly business on and off the set. No matter what they thought or wrote though, my movies sold well, and the press couldn't get enough of me. John couldn't really say shit to me either because I was his company's bread and butter at that point, and we already had talked too much shit about *Gang Bang II* for either of us to back out. He needed me and I needed him I suppose, so John came quickly to respect my rule and didn't slip up again. On a personal front, I found out through friends back East that Dick had found out what I was into and was actually rather passive in his reaction to it, taking the attitude that 'If it makes her happy, she should do it.' Dick cared so little about anyone or anything beyond himself that he wouldn't have been capable of being worried for me, where on the other hand, Kurt found out and actually went about trying to talk me into quitting. It was comical to me that he had originally told me I wasn't good enough to be in the business. I didn't know what his true motive was in trying to talk me into quitting, because he used Stern's tact of telling me how I was 'too good for it,' and so forth. I took that genuinely from Howard because he had no possible ulterior motive in telling me, where Kurt had several. He was married by then and I was well over him but at least it felt a little like closure between us.

On the other hand, with Dick, I felt no sense of closure *because* he didn't seem to care one way or the other. I had also started talking to Sickie again, we'd lost touch for a while, and then he'd heard me on the Stern show and called to congratulate me. He'd had some jealous, crazy bitch girlfriend who wouldn't let him talk to me because I was a porn star, so he hadn't really seen me become one, and we'd lost touch shortly before I signed to Metro. Anyway, it was nice for me to re-establish that friendship because we got along on so many levels as people, and he wasn't anything like most of the shallow fucks I encountered out in L.A. I didn't make my sentiment on that a secret in the press either, my feeling that everyone I worked with on the star side was as light in the brain as their scenes were of any real action. I was a hard core porn star for a reason, because I took it to the next level every time action was called and the camera was rolling. When I did interviews, I wore honesty on my sleeve as naked as I was in my films. I put it all out there for the press and public to sort through, and no one can deny me my 'Queen of Controversy' crown, or I wouldn't have been dubbed by the press as the 'World's Most Controversial Sex Symbol.' I held the line on consistency with everything I did that had directly to do with porn, or rooted out from it. That was the only way to establish any kind of long-term reputation foundationally, and I worked my ass off to make sure I got the maximum exposure possible. Most of the girls — in the context of exposure — extended the boundaries of that word's definition only to include when they had their clothes off on screen. They didn't understand the game of promotion, and the fact that life imitates art in the porn business, so that if you play up an on-screen persona, much like a rapper, the media will eat it up. They love it because it causes controversy, and therein consistently gives them something to write about, to report if you want to call that journalism. My bottom line was: any press is good press, whether I was being positively reviewed for a performance in one of my movies or being negative by trashing everyone I had to put up with in the process of making my climb to the top. My biggest bang was yet to come, but right around the bend of my sexy ass, and I honestly couldn't wait because I knew it would put me over the top! Ironically, the night before the big day, Lemmy attempted to talk me out of it!

Lemmy Kilmister: I had seen all this advanced publicity about the biggest gang bang in the world, and I'd tried to talk her out if doing it. I remember I actually saw her out at the Rainbow the night before. She came back to my house and again I tried to talk her out of it and persuade her NOT to do it, and she wouldn't have it. I tried my best, but she wouldn't listen unfortunately and it changed and spoiled her personality a bit, where she got very bad-tempered for a long time — quite abrasive. She changed quite a bit after that, I felt like it disillusioned her a bit. That bubbly personality went on holiday after that gang bang thing, she became very angry.

I think she wanted the notoriety, she was aiming on becoming a big porn star, but she didn't realize how it would change her emotionally. She's a really nice person, and she's really taken a beating, and it's kind of her own fault, but all the same, I don't think she realized quite what it was going to be like. For a long time she was really uptight, and I think it's why she didn't do porn after 2000. It set her back a few years, and it has taken her 10 years to get this far from it.

Excerpt taken from *The L.A. Weekly,* 'Scenes from My Life in Porn' by Evan Wright, April, 1996:

'In 1996, an unknown named Jasmin St. Claire set out to have sex with 300 men in a XXX video titled *The World's Biggest Gang-Bang II*, thereby breaking an alleged record of 251 men set a year earlier by Annabel Chong. By the mid '90s, gang bang films had become a hot product in the industry. They not only created overnight stars — worthy of *Howard Stern* and *Jerry Springer* — but added a new dimension to celebrity worship. Whereas at one time an autograph served as a hallowed connection with a famous person, now fans, invited to participate in these spectacles, could actually fuck a star.

'Late one Sunday morning on the second floor of a decrepit Hollywood sound stage, Jasmin held a press conference prior to the shoot. Reporters and photographers from such esteemed publications as *Club*, *Screw* and, of course, *Hustler* packed the room. Champagne was served. Jasmin, 23, entered in skintight red latex. She moved imperiously, with her head held high and her surgically augmented D-cups thrust forward. Jasmin's ethnic origins were a mystery. Her skin was coppery brown, like a glass of tea in sunlight. She told people her dark complexion came from Brazilian blood, and there were rumors that she was the granddaughter of a New York mobster. She denied those, and claimed to have been raised by an international-financier father, to have been educated in Continental boarding schools and to have an undergraduate degree from Columbia. At the press conference, Jasmin responded in French, German and Spanish to questions from European porn-magazine stringers. As cameras flashed and the room filled with the staccato sound of 20 reporters calling her name, the scene took on the air of an old-fashioned Hollywood movie premiere. I asked Jasmin why she was having sex with 300 men, and she answered, "To achieve my dreams."

'The event began on a set decorated with paper palm trees and tiki lamps. Perhaps 50 men showed. They were authentic amateurs, a cross section of humanity that might have been culled from an unemployment line: old, young, fat, bald, and skinny. They wore tennis shoes and work boots, but no pants or underwear, as they were herded into groups of five along lines taped onto the concrete floor. A half a dozen fluffers knelt by the taped lines and prepared the men for their encounter with Jasmin. She lay on a low stage and could barely be glimpsed through the clutches of hairy asses flexing around her. Jasmin's hands grasped at erections as the men circled her, copulating with her mouth, vagina and ass. The teams of gangbangers were given five or 10 minutes with Jasmin. They wore condoms when they penetrated her. They removed their condoms to ejaculate on her stomach, thighs, breasts, face, or in her thick, wavy brown hair. When the men finished, they sat in bleachers at the edge of the sound stage or milled around and lamely jacked off, trying to nurse fresh hard-ons for another go.

'I experienced a sense of numbness on Jasmin's set — as I would on many others — that I can only compare to accounts I have read of combat. It was the sense of being in a group of people deliberately and methodically engaged in acts of insanity. Unlike in combat, I was not overwhelmed by the horror of it, but by the grand-scale stupidity, which crystallized that day as I stood by the craft-services cart. Boiled hot dogs on cold, white buns were being dispensed. A man next to me politely passed the mustard. The bottle was sticky with K-Y Jelly. I never attempted to eat on a porn shoot again.

'It was during Jasmin's bid for the title of world's biggest gangbang queen that she acquired her reputation as a bitch. One of the men I spoke to, 40-ish, with the tan and physique of a lifelong desk worker summed up his experience as a star-fucker. 'Jasmin is cold,' he said, then compared her to Annabel Chong, whom he'd met a year earlier when he'd participated in her *World's Biggest Gang-Bang*. "She's not friendly like Annabel was."'

Jasmin Metal Heads Only modeling shot.

TOP: Jasmin partying in Brazil.
BOTTOM: Jenna Jameson and Jasmin St Claire.

Jasmin posing for calendar back in the day.

Jasmin on the movie set of *Communication Breakdown.*

Jasmin in the bubbles.

TOP: Jasmin at red carpet for Toxic Vision clothing company fashion show.
BOTTOM: Jasmin from Adult Film Heyday at In Store Appearance.

Jasmin in the waves.

Jasmin in BC Rich Coffin Guitar Case.

TOP: Jasmin Modeling BC Rich Guitar.
BOTTOM: Jasmin modeling Krank Guitar Pedals

Jasmin Modelling the BC Rich Black Warlock Guitar.

TOP: Jasmin on starring float at Brazil's annual Carnaval Sao Paulo VAi Vai.
BOTTOM: Jasmin on the set of *Swamp Zombies* with ZOMBIE!!

Jasmin Modelling Shot from late 1990s heyday.

TOP: Jasmin with best friend Amy.
BOTTOM: Starring Float at Brazil's annual Carnaval Sao Paulo VAi Vai.

Jasmin Modelling a White BC Rich Coffin-shaped Guitar Case.

TOP: Jasmin modeling Brazilian coffin guitar case. BOTTOM: Jasmin signing autographs.

PART VIIII

The Big (Gang) Bang Theory

The funniest thing to me now looking back on that movie and the phenomenon that followed its release was that the public were the ones who took the biggest fuck, not me. I am not sure of the legal ramifications that accompany what I am about to pull the curtain back on — but here it goes (sorry, guys.) *The World's Greatest Gang Bang* was NOT 300 guys as advertised on Stern and a million other media markets, but rather perhaps among the biggest cons ever pulled off in the porn business. It was a true house of smoke and mirrors and in a sense a testament to the talent of John T. Bone's skill as a legitimate film director. Because 300 wasn't even 50 guys, but rather THIRTY GUYS strategically placed and filmed over a very brutal day of shooting for me (20 OF THEM WHO COULD NOT EVEN GET AN ERECTION.) There it is, and here are some witnesses to corroborate my revelation, as well as offer some additional behind-the-scenes details of how it was all pulled off:

Charlie Fry: Absolutely in reality it was about spectacle rather than Jasmin actually fucking 300 guys. This was a movie, and like any movie, when you go watch *Star Wars,* there's not really spaceships zooming around lasering everybody — a porn movie is no different. In reality, there were only 65 guys that showed up, and yes she had sex with 300 guys. If you look at the title of the movie, it didn't say 300 different guys, so essentially, if the same guy penetrated her four times, even within a few minutes, that is: four individual acts of sex. So did it technically justify the numbers, yes, but was it real? Absolutely not. If 300 guys had shown up, absolutely, but it was hard to even get as many guys as we did to show up. They're paying their own way out from all over the country to L.A., paying for their own hotel, not getting paid, not to mention how intimidated they were when it came time to perform.

Dominic Accara (Jasmin's Assistant): It was clear from the start that the gang bang was not about sex, it was about spectacle, and the bigger the spectacle, the more the sales. That shoot was done at a studio at Santa Monica and Vine, and the day of the shoot, first they brought in Annabel Chong, and she explained what she'd done and kind of officially passed the torch to Jasmin. Then they set up to start shooting, and while they promoted it as though Jasmin was going to be fucked by 300 guys, in reality, it was FAR less. John was such a talented director that he was able to manipulate the camera through a lot of creatively-angled shots to make it look like there were A LOT more guys having sex with her than actually were. I was there and saw the whole thing, and it wasn't EVEN CLOSE to 300 guys. The way the whole thing worked was this. Basically 5 guys would go up. She'd be laying on a table and the guys would all be surrounding her. If one of the guy's dicks literally touched her leg, they would count it as a fuck, and in theory, and would inflate and jack it up 5, 10, 15 numbers per every one real sexual encounter. I would say MAYBE 50 guys fucked her that day, and that would be high, and those that did fuck her — assuming they could keep it hard — were inside her for 15-30 seconds, a minute if you were lucky. You had people stepping up to the table and they'd go limp, and they'd count them, so the idea again was more about the spectacle than about the sex. The impression I got from Jasmin was that's why she did it anyway — I don't think she was ever into having sex with that many people.

When it came to keeping everyone in on the plan, including media people who were on set the day of the gang bang, John made sure they were all taken care of any way they wanted to be taken care of. In other words, there were fluffers on set whose job was to blow male actors to get their dicks hard before a scene. Let's pretend for a minute you're a journalist, he would ask you if you wanted to do a private interview with a fluffer in a private room. And however in depth your interview went, your interview went if I'm making sense. By the time all of that was said and done John had everyone in his back pocket, and no one was going to say shit except along the lines of the script he wrote for us. In other words, as far as we were concerned, she fucked 800 people.

Jasmin: I knew it would make me an instant star, so I went along with the MASS charade that was *The World's Greatest Gang Bang II.* The atmosphere that day was very much as the *L.A. Weekly* described it in the article above, and the week leading up to the shoot I didn't know if

I could go through with it. I was freaking out, until my director John T. Bone let me in on a little secret that came as a mass relief to me: that we'd be fudging the numbers. On set, there would in fact be a couple hundred men there, but I would only be having sex with a fraction of that. The *LA Weekly* was correct in reporting that hordes of men surrounded me in a circle, but the reality is only a handful were actually having intercourse with me. The rest were there to obscure the view of the onslaught of press watching. Charlie even flew out — ON MY DIME — to grace us with his slimy presence.

Anyway, leading into the day, I had this horrible anxiety going on about the whole thing, and couldn't help thinking to myself like 'I can't believe I'm doing this, holy shit.' I was scared too, because the whole thing had been so built up in the press that we almost had to go through with it. If I didn't, it would certainly have killed off any credibility I had built up to that point as a rising star, and if I went through with it, I would be an overnight celebrity. They had Annabel Chong, the girl who at that time held the record for the first Gang Bang with 251 men on set, just to add authenticity, but she was strictly an observer. If only those in the press watching had known that she had fucked FAR LESS than the purported number for the first movie. But for the moment, it remained a trade secret. In fact, I think I'm the first to out both she and I, but anything less than the number of men I'd boasted I would sleep with was a relief to me. On the outside though, I had to look as excited, exotic, and eager as I could about the prospect of having 300 men penetrating and ejaculating in every available ORFICES I had to offer. I'd had multiple penetration scenes before, but this was just filthy to me. It was disgusting, and probably the lowest I have ever felt in my life next to when Dick beat me. It reduced me back down to nothing in my own head, shattering me into the same number of pieces as the men who were supposedly fucking me that day. I felt like I was truly acting that day, so anyone who says there is no talent involved in the porn business can fuck themselves, because the truth is all I wanted to do was go home and kill myself after this.

Charlie Fry: With any of the movies Jasmin was in, I always emphasized she would be acting — in porn in general — including the sex part of it, because you're ACTING as if you like the sex. That was true with the gang bang as well; it was much more about acting than about sex, so whenever Jasmin was on, Rhea shut off. Jasmin was absolutely a sexual dynamo. That was her role. It was her job to portray that she liked what she was doing, that she wanted the sex she was having, that she was really into it. The more you did that, the more they hyped you up in the industry, and the bigger of a star you became. So from day one something I always taught Jasmin was you need to let them think you're absolutely the wildest chick around. So with the gang bang, for instance, nothing was taboo or too much, to the point that in her media interviews she said that she preferred anal sex in her movies to girl/boy, and wouldn't do girl-girl because that was too boring.

Dominic Accara (Jasmin's Assistant): She would take breaks for smokes or lunch, and Jasmin stayed in character the entire day. John had told her, 'You're going to be Jasmin the entire day,' and to her credit she lived up to it. I got the impression with most of her movies that she was acting; it was all business all the time. By the end of the day of the *Gang Bang* shoot, she was tired, beaten up. I got the impression it was a long day with a lot of different emotions for her. I thought she handled the amount of insanity that was dropped on her all at once pretty well, all things considering.

Jasmin: Though I wasn't delivering any lines, I was absolutely acting- and in a more personal way than I would argue most professional mainstream actresses could- because I had to make this look as authentic as people believed it really was in the end of the day took talent. On top of that, I had to look like I was enjoying it, and truthfully, it was horrible. The question from people that used to bug me the most in the aftermath was 'what kind of physical training did you do to prep for it?' As though it was the World Olympics of fucking sex, I guess it looked like that to them, but it used to annoy me. Even after it was over in terms of the physical shoot, it was a long way from over. It was several more months before it would come out in stores, and that whole time, I had to do press lying about what went on, building it up, and promoting a lie. Then when the actual release happened later in that summer, I had to do it all over again. I even went on Stern again and lied about them having to ice me down in-between takes. The whole thing was just ridiculous to me, but it's the trade off I had to make to become a star, that was the way I looked at it.

Anyway, we certainly sent everyone home happy that day, even the guys who had shown up in the hopes of getting their turn. We sent them all home with a free t-shirt with a really cool looking image of me on it and some copy about the fact that they'd been part of the *World's Greatest Gang Bang II* and what number they'd supposedly been out of 300 to fuck me.

In reality, only about 30, maybe 35 men had been there circled around me. Probably 7 of the 10 that I actually had sexual contact with were actually PORN ACTORS, not regular Joes off the street. That had been one of the pitching points in the first place on shows like Stern and at the conventions where we'd had anybody who wanted to sign up. During the shoot, they'd had this counter board that was supposed to keep track of people who had successfully 'banged' me, and John's people kept cheating the numbers that were on the board. We did it in increments of 5 people every 5 minutes, but most of them couldn't get their dicks hard, but their backs were very strategically turned from the eyes of the watching press.

A lot of it was simulation where they could get it hard, and John kept cutting it from 5 minutes to 2 or 3 minutes tops after a while, so by the time the 3 minute mark approached, some of these guys were just getting hard. He would also always have one or two of the real male porn stars mixed in, but so that you couldn't tell from outside the circle and strategically placed camera angles. They also had these fluff girls who were supposed to be helping people to get hard while they were waiting, but they also were there to distract attention from the main event. I would say 80% of the men there couldn't get it up, so the 7 or 8 pros — John would just keep moving them and positioning them so that you could never clearly see any one actor's face. As a result, it was very often the same guy fucking me from different positions because he was the only one who could keep it up, or even get it up at all. Given that most people focus on the woman during a porn movie, who really was ever watching the cock that closely? We counted on that, and it worked. John was a very talented director to pull that off. Then part of my job was to appear to be in pain while I was being fucked, to be really over the top with the dramatics, and I think I did a good job of acting. At one point, I even asked for someone to get me some ice, but it was total bullshit, all of it, or SHOW BUSINESS.

It took about a day to shoot the whole thing, and it was just mayhem on the set. Ron Jeremy was there, photographers and journalists from every trade publication you can name from *Hustler* to *Penthouse*, and it aided us greatly to have that kind of distraction going on to pull off what we did. It's a lot like the end of *True Romance*, when Clarence and Alabama just calmly walk out of the hotel because the police focus in on the general mayhem. They got away with it, and so did we. Once it was all over, I was fine. I'd spent more time actually HAVING SEX on some of my past shoots, if you count the physical time spent shooting a typical scene. This was more fractured, hit or miss in terms of who in the groups could perform, and B.) In terms of the number of minutes I spent having sex, it actually added up to less than I would have spent with just one or two guys who were pros in the course of a normal shoot. Truthfully, the ones who did most the work were the fluff girls, because we never normally had to have them on set, because its part of a male porn star's job description that he's able to keep it up. Anyway, everybody afterward was very excited about the 'record' we'd broke. The one reward I did feel going home that night from the whole thing was the fact that — given the number of regular, average John Q. Publics who'd showed up to be part of the shoot — people actually did desire me. They wanted me, because I was the star, and they'd known that going in, and the fact that they wanted me was something that neither Dick nor Kurt had ever legitimately shown me. Anyway, at the time we all looked at it as a success that we'd pulled this mass con off, but looking back now — a decade later — I can see where it was wrong, and would like to apologize to fans. I hope no one feels cheated, but I had a confidentiality clause that kept me silent for years afterward, tied by legal ramifications if I'd spoken out about it. So I'm sorry to anyone who has bought that, and I personally and publicly want to say I'm sorry for participating in it. It was a very successful movie, it won 'Video of the Year' at the porn awards show the next year, and brought me international stardom, but part of me still wishes I'd never done it. It left a very nasty taste in my mouth, and I hope it does in everyone else's who was involved now that the public knows the truth. I'm happy to have gotten it off my chest anyway.

PART X

Picking Up The Pieces

May 1996 began as a busy month press-wise, and put to rest for me any illusion that the *Gang Bang II* circus was behind me just because the shoot itself was over. Now everyone who interviewed me expected me to recall and recount it in as explicit detail as possible, especially on the *Howard Stern Show*, which I did for the second time at the beginning of the month. Howard definitely rose to the occasion — as did I'm sure the dicks of his millions of male listeners — because he was dirtier than the shoot itself was with his questions, and plays on my answers. I mean, I was honestly shocked by some of what he asked, and I went along with it all like a seasoned veteran, which this movie would make me overnight in the eyes of millions of porn fans even though I wasn't even a year into my career yet. That didn't matter, what mattered was how outrageous my genre of porn was — hard core — and my biggest challenge honestly in pulling off the whole charade to the public was selling it to Howard. He was truly skeptical going in, which probably explained the depth of his questioning. I mean, I've listened to him interview a thousand porn stars, and he took it to the extreme with me, not just in terms of the nature of my style of porn, but in terms of how thoroughly he probed. He just really didn't seem to believe it at first, and he's very smart, so he was really like a porn prosecutor, grilling me on the stand, i.e. except a national radio audience was my jury. I guess I pulled it off, probably sealing the deal when I threw in that they had had to ice me down between takes because of the pain.

Charlie Fry: An important measure in those days of the difference in popularity at that time was the number of times a star had appeared on Howard Stern's radio show was a direct measure of their notoriety, and Jasmin had more appearances, which reflected her having more notoriety, popularity and recognition than Jenna did at the time. Howard being a shock jock, Jasmin had what's called star quality, and had the ability to turn on the charm and magnetism when she wanted to. Star quality is not something you can teach to somebody, they have to have it within themselves and Jasmin had it. She could turn it on and be very magnetic, and Howard liked that she was willing to say anything, and willing to go in whatever direction he wanted them to lead them in. Howard doesn't book shows based necessarily on what we called and pitched, there was a lot of times they'd call me and say, 'We're doing this type of show, who do you got that can meet it?' If they knew Jasmin would fit a certain criteria, they would call us because they could count on Jasmin to deliver on being as wild and crazy as the show called for and that Howard loved. She was a star, and knew how to be a star.

Jasmin: That put me over the top, got me off with his jury of listeners, and probably got them off too in the process. That was the desired effect anyway. It amazed me how fascinated the world truly was with porn, I mean, Howard Stern's listeners were the every-dayers, the John Q. Auto Mechanics and Cab Drivers and Construction Workers of the world. They were the ones who made up much of our viewing audience, so that immediately gave me mainstream validation, albeit in an after-hours light. When I got through, Howard seemed happy and convinced which made me believe the whole world would buy my story, and the tape. It's all hype till people lay their drooling eyes on it, and it was my job to tease and tantalize them up until the movie's release, which wasn't scheduled till late summer. When I got outside of the radio studio, there were hundreds of horny men waiting for me down on the street, holding everything from magazines I'd posed in to movie cover boxes to shit they'd downloaded off the internet, clamoring for my signature. It was my first true mob, and I loved every second of it. My asshole manager Charlie was in New York with me for the appearance and told me shortly afterward that I would have a poster in Times Square in the window of one of main adult film stores, which was huge. The only concern I had was that a family member would be listening and might possibly recognize my voice on the radio. The only one who ever caught wind of what was involved in was my cousin Penny, and she lived in England, and for some reason, kept her mouth shut to my mother, so I didn't really care. My ex-boyfriend Tommy even discovered I was a porn star that way, and would actually call in on one of my next couple appearances on Stern to talk to me, but Howard didn't let him on the air. All that was behind me now, that was one positive that came out of *Gang Bang II*, I felt it liberated me from any remaining need to spite any of the men who had hurt me in my life. I had gone as low as I could go, and the only place to head after an experience like that was up. And higher I would climb indeed.

It should have been a detriment to me that I sounded smart on the air. Society thrives on dumb women, and it comes as almost a requisite assumption that porn stars are stupid. I guess I was trying to defy that whole stereotype in some way, but anytime I would call an interviewer on his shit with a stupid or chauvinist question, I was labeled a *bitch*. Once they saw they couldn't pigeonhole me, I guess journalists started trying to see how far they could get me to go in terms of saying extreme things. I indulged most often to be both consistent with the nature of my hard core porn movies/image and because fans seemed to respond to it. I do think people misunderstood me quite a bit though, which is fine, but I wasn't trying to be snotty or come across as stuck-up when I talked about other stars in the business or in wrestling or whatever topically came up at different points in my career. I was just being honest most times. In terms of labeling me snotty, right out of the gate, I disputed in the press that all porn stars were friends off screen, because it wasn't at all cozy and chummy like that! It pissed me off that I was expected to play along in that lie, because most of those bitches were just beneath me intelligence-wise, and in the end of the day *WERE* my competition. This was a business, and I wasn't talking shit, I was being honest, and usually responding to questions, not instigating the attack. That probably hurt me a little bit in the media, but it did succeed in distinguishing me from that pack of whores, which was the desired effect. Besides, at that time heading into the summer of 1996, I was still building my reputation, and Charlie told me to be as outrageous as possible to raise the hype-level surrounding *Gang Bang*'s release.

Beyond that even, I don't know if it hurt me fan-wise to be as candid as I was about how things really were off-screen. I think me telling the truth about the infighting and discord that did go on between porn stars turns fans on because they probably translated it to mean *CAT FIGHT*—which turns all men on. It certainly didn't seem to hurt me with fans in terms of sales. I think I did more damage amongst people in that community because they treated it as such a tight community as friends and family and to me that's not what a family is. My definition of family is decidedly different. My definition of family is someone you're related to by blood or someone that's maybe been a long-time friend that knows everything about you in and out, and I found very few people in that community who I could trust enough to call a close friend, let alone family. Also to me — and this might sound silly to read — but to think of those people who I worked with as family literally, which some of them did, felt like a form of incest to me. Some went home together and fucked off screen and weren't even involved and then the next day fucked someone different, and had no line separating the professional from personal, they were just whores.

There are a lot of industry people who will read this book, and will definitely hate me for saying what I just did, but it's true. I wouldn't have socialized with most of those people outside of an industry event if you paid me, and usually you had to pay me to hang out with any of them off-screen. I'm not saying I was better than any of them, but above them in at least that I wouldn't do it. What did I have in common with any of them outside of porn? I can understand why a lot of them gravitated toward their co-workers socially, because of the way the mainstream world viewed people who worked in that business, looked down on them, and judged them. Socializing with people who were doing the same thing immediately eliminated that, but what they didn't ever see was the fact that the only way to move beyond that scarlet letter was to do so literally. By letting the public know this wasn't something I planned to do forever, it made them more eager to buy up anything I did for the simple fact that it wouldn't last forever.

On top of that, it allowed me to network with other entertainment mediums while still in the business. I didn't just want to hang out with mainstream stars; I wanted to be one of them, because I had enough talent to be. To me, it was that simple, and if it wasn't, I wouldn't have been able to move so smoothly into wrestling and then into mainstream acting in a fucking National Lampoon movie among some of the other non-porn films I have done. I always kept the bigger picture in mind, even years ahead of getting there — it was a dream, a goal, and I always kept my eye on the ball in that respect while most of my fellow porn actresses were busy licking those of their male co-stars on the weekends. While they stayed home and fucked each other, I was out on the road featuring, or doing interviews, or photo shoots, or media and convention appearances- anything I could do to set myself apart from the norm. I feel it's an important distinction that I treated it like a business and nothing more when almost everyone I saw around me was taking their work home with them.

Dominic Accara: After the gang bang thing and she really, really started taking off, it was a golden time in porn. The days of stars of Jasmin and Jenna Jamison's caliber are gone. And I don't know whether she did it intentionally or not, but Jasmin understood marketing, what it meant to do interviews with both porn and mainstream media like Howard Stern. So when Jasmin was on the scene, she was a big fish in a little pond, and while she did help to create her reconcilability, but when she was on Rhea time, and fans couldn't differentiate, it did bother her. In the grand scheme of things, she came to understand that when you're a celebrity, there is no distinction for most fans. When you step out in public, you're on, love it or hate it, for better or worse, its just part of the turf. When you've done the gig, your meet and greets, etc inside the club, and in theory, she wasn't playing Jasmin anymore, she wanted to mentally shut down and go back to being Rhea, which her fans wouldn't let her do.

So even as she became more and more recognizable, a lot of times when I traveled with her, she never seemed to be really happy, even though she was one of the biggest drawing features on the road. She had one of the highest profiles because the woman busted her ass the whole way through. Here we were staying at the best hotels in the country, she was making top dollar, and she didn't really seem to want to deal with it. I got the impression that she never wanted to be recognized as Jasmin the Porn Star offstage. Most of the times when you meet fans on the road, they're terrified of you, because for whatever reason, whenever men meet woman who have sex for a living, they're intimidated. Today, with the internet, it's not such a big deal, but back then we were still taboo, so to see someone like Jasmin in person was a big deal. Because of the gang bang and everything else she was doing, she had a higher profile.

I'm not sure if she intentionally pissed people off as a defense mechanism or to make a name for herself, but whenever someone would come up to her in a hotel lobby or outside of a club and ask for a picture or autograph, she'd say, ' Leave me alone.' I can't totally blame her, there were times when it was very inappropriate on her fans' part; for instance, from the vantage point that some of her fans would get REALLY into her scenes. So we'd be sitting in Denny's at 2 in the morning after she'd been on her feet for 8 hours, because a lot of times when you did club features, in addition to the dancing, there were bookstore signings and radio and whatever else. I remember a great example of this being one time when we were in Sacramento, and at a Denny's after a long day, and some fans of hers recognized her, walked up to our table, and just started engaging her, 'You remember that scene you did with such and such?' These guys would know how long the scenes were, the different positions, everything. I could see that it both annoyed her and in some ways, it creeped her out a little with their weird fascination.

Charlie Fry: As a sex symbol, that doesn't end when the scene's over, she had to be on, and she got tired of that after a while to the point where she developed a hostility that came through to fans, and anybody she worked with. It's one thing to be a diva on the set, it's another to be one with fans, and that's part of what hurt her. After she became a star, she got this 'Fuck You, I can do anything I want' attitude, which eventually bled into me as well, where we both I think big heads because she was such a big star. Unfortunately, that 'I can do whatever I please' attitude can lead people to be irresponsible. For the first 40% of her career, she would pretty much listen to my recommendations and behave appropriately. As she became more and more a victim of her own success, she lost site of that she had to be polite to her fans, and essentially what she felt was probably being funny, was actually abrasive.

Jasmin: Some people don't understand that being a porn star — in terms of the fucking — starts when the director yells action, and stops when he yells cut. It's a character we play on screen, not who we are in real life — ideally anyway. When I answer my door at home, I'm wearing jeans and Metal band T-Shirts, not a fucking G-string. When I went rollerblading at Venice Beach, I was wearing shorts and a t-shirt, not a fucking nightie. It was vitally important to me — given the psychological rigor of the work I did onscreen — to maintain that distinction in identity between Rhea and Jasmin. How else could I ever have had a regular boyfriend? The sex I have onscreen is very different from the love I make to my man, believe it or not. To me, that should just be common sense.

Obviously when I would do meet and greets, there is a certain expectation among fans that you'll be as sexy in person as you are on screen in terms of overall persona, and that is one thing. But when I go into the fucking grocery store to buy fruit, you don't find me sucking on a banana like a dick in the fruit aisle. I know a lot of people wish that were the case, and maybe fantasize it is when they see me out and about in my personal life, but I have NEVER had one of them come up to me and do more than ask for an autograph. I never had an issue getting that respect from my fans, it was always within the industry that I had my battles in the press, or was dubbed as controversial because I was the first to call the business and its slutty-bitch-whore-'stars' like Jenna on their shit. Even when I did features, I never did lap dances or danced for dollar-bills. I had a much shorter set, usually 20 minutes, and it was a pre-set fee the club put up in deposit ahead of time to secure my appearance. I would sign stuff afterward, and sell Polaroids for $20 a pop, but it was fucking business to me. I never went out back with some sweaty dude who was willing to pay me $1000 to fuck him, and A LOT of the girls I worked with did JUST THAT. That is the point I am making, I called a lot of them sluts because they were, and drew no distinction for themselves on and off screen. I won't name any names on the advice of my lawyer, although when I call someone a slut in the press maybe now you have a little better idea of what I'm possibly implying. Anyway, heading into the summer, I had a lot of features scheduled, and had also started to feel the affects of my stardom taking hold in the public's perception, namely in that I was getting recognized around Los Angeles and on the road a lot more, which I LOVED. One thing I will readily admit I LOVED about the porn business was the stardom it brought me. My ego craved that, and I have no problem admitting that. Any woman who tells you she doesn't like being desired by thousands of men is lying to both you and to herself. Who wouldn't? I think this new rapper who just came out recently, Kanye West, said in one of his songs, 'The people highest up have the lowest self ESTEEM.' That explains it in a nutshell, so I didn't mind the glamour at all, because my ego and confidence was still re-building itself after Dick and Kurt.

The only thing I felt ill about — talking on Stern about the details of the *Gang Bang* — was that I was lying to everyone, from Howard to the public, and it just didn't sit right with me. I've honestly felt bad about it since that day. I just don't like lying to people, especially when, in every other facet of my public persona, I was known for saying exactly and explicitly what was on my mind. It was like I was violating my own standard — and I'd certainly already lowered it enough. But I was on national radio lying to sell something, and that worried me always too, that I might be opening myself to some legal exposure. But I had signed a confidentiality agreement with Metro, so I couldn't talk about ANY of the truth, the only thing I could talk about were the LIES I was telling on the air that day. I would come to tell it so many times, in so many interviews, that I should have probably come to believe it myself. I was certainly convincing.

Charlie tried to make me feel like it was part of being an actress, which I never bought, that bullshit they tried to feed into porn stars' heads that they're somehow also legitimate actresses. I knew what I did, I knew how people saw it, and I never diluted myself with that illusion. One thing I will give myself props for though, as an actress, was pulling that shit off, because everyone grilled me on it, starting with Howard. I had to be as convincing as a fucking Oscar winner as far as I was concerned. It also made me HIGHLY anticipate the release of the movie myself on one level: to see if John T. Bone actually successfully pulled off the con I had been busy selling to everyone on screen. This might seem small to some of you in the grand scheme of things. I grant you it's not the same as rigging a ball game or a boxing match but in the circles I traveled and promoted in, it was a big deal to pull off what we did. For me personally, that movie made me too. That whole scam made me the 'World's Most Controversial Sex Symbol,' and selling that image was part of the whole package, bundled with the gang bang movie.

One immediate benefit was my stock shot way up on the feature circuit, even if club owners were billing me as Jasmin St. Claire 'from the forthcoming' *Gang Bang* movie, in other words, my fee went up a few months before the movie's release. I really can't say how much for legal reasons, but it was A LOT. The buzz over the movie also did a lot to shoot my stock up with in the film side of the business, in terms of the BIG male stars who now wanted to work with me. I was getting better at doing one-on-one scenes by that point — which they build to incrementally with porn because many girls are visibly nervous on screen, so they throw in two guys or another girl to distract the focus off of just you. So it meant I was getting more close-ups and had developed longer stamina to keep the sex scene going, so everything just felt like it was naturally elevating — on every level. On the other hand, that meant that certain other 'name' female stars, a lot of the time from then on, didn't want to work with me because they felt I would take attention from them. To be truthful, I didn't want to work with most of them either, A) because I wasn't into women, and B) because I didn't want contact with nasty bitches like Annabel Chong, for instance. Anyway, that was never a problem with my male co-stars, so for my May movie, *Degenerate*, I worked with Tom Byron, and this new comer named Mila, a Russian who Metro had just signed. I didn't mind working with her. She was very sweet. She was actually probably the first friend I made among my co-workers, to where I went to her house in West Hollywood a few times, went to a picnic there with her family once. We had the same kind of cars, little red Miatas and we used to go hang out together. We lost touch in time, but I have fond memories of her. Anyway, that movie also had scenes with Rick Masters and Dave Hardman — basically who had become the usual suspects in our circle. In June, once I was back off the road from featuring, I went and did the *Madcow Morning Show* to promote *Gang Bang*, which was my first negative media experience. Basically, the asshole kept trying to talk down to me, and expected me to dumb down for his audience I guess, but I wouldn't play along. I hate being condescended, and I had no problem letting anyone know that I had to — on air or off. I was setting a new standard anyway with the kind of porn I was doing, and in terms of my look, which was more exotic than 90% of my competitors because of my natural ethnic mix, I figured I had nothing to lose speaking my mind. Every time I'd heard a porn star on Stern, they would play up the whole sexy, pool side 'Howard, I wanna fuck you' image, and he treated me different right off the bat, and he was definitely qualified to judge.

The summer began with another movie. I also attended the VSDA Convention, which was held in L.A. that year, so I didn't have to travel and worry about sharing my hotel room with some slut. I signed at our booth all day, and hung out with celebrities like Drew Carey. I also saw Corey Feldman there for the first time since I went on the air talking about his under-sized unit, so the tone between he and I was more business than anything else. We also had another stupid awards show to attend, called 'Night of the Stars,' which was similar to the Vegas AVN Awards, but on a smaller level. I traveled up to Las Vegas for that, and I also had a signing at the Metro Booth every day promoting my movie, which had been released that July. Anyway, the awards show was as lame as any other; people were winning awards for like 'Best Anal Scene' and 'Best Boy/Girl Scene,' shit that was just really stupid. I don't remember what I was nominated for, but I remember presenting that year. When I got back to L.A., we shot yet another movie and another one in August. The whole affair was routine by that point, professionally speaking. Personally, I hadn't really been dating anyone, I was really too busy between all the travel I did featuring, but I had made a friend in Lemmy Kilmister from Motorhead, who I was hanging out with quite a bit at that point. I remember one night I passed out on his couch after we'd been out drinking at the Rainbow, and I woke up to see this huge Nazi memorabilia collection in his living room.

Lemmy Kilmister: I first met Jasmin at the Rainbow. I knew her as a porn star first starting out in L.A., and we exchanged numbers some night and became friends. I remember she actually called me, which was unusual, even for me. Most guys would love to have this beautiful, young chick come over and hang out, and we'd hang out and get naked. She was really cute, and of course, I loved to see Jasmin always, you know. We remained friends throughout her years in and out of porn, but I wasn't going out with her. She used to come up to my house a few times, and it was really fun, we'd listen to metal. I had a great time with Jasmin, and I really have a soft spot for her.

Jasmin: We would hang out a lot at his apartment after that, watch movies; just shit like that. He didn't drive either, so whenever we went out, I was the designated driver, for better or worse. It was a fun and odd relationship, because I had been a huge Motorhead fan all my life, and it was relieving to hang out with a rock star who for once wasn't trying to fuck me. That September, with my *Gang Bang II* movie release fast approaching, I went back on Jerry Springer for the 3rd time, which went well enough. The audience loved me, and John T. Bone went on with me to help hype the thing. That kind of filth is right up Jerry's audience's alley, so I suppose we all felt like bums hanging out behind the same dumpster together. That analogy isn't totally off either, because in 'show business' terms; his 'set is like a shithole.' You don't even have your own dressing room, and you get like a $250 stipend for the whole 2 days it takes to shoot the thing, which I made in an hour featuring. On the other hand, as John continually reminded me, the publicity was priceless.

Heading into the fall, I got on this big feature tour for the Déjà vu Club. It ran all over their chain of clubs in the Midwest and ended in California — 2 clubs a week for 5 weeks. That was grueling, and really took a personal tool on me because I was traveling by myself at that time. Typically, you have a roadie of sorts who travels with you when your tour runs that long, drives, handles your luggage, acts as sort of a personal bodyguard, all of that. Also, I would have to deal at times with DICK club owners, like this one prick at a club in Michigan who wouldn't pay me or let me leave unless I did another set. Had I had the Blue Meanie with me then, believe me he never would have pulled that shit. I would fly from gig to gig, but the crowds at these clubs were just a frightening flock — straight out of the backwoods from *Deliverance*. I tolerated the clientele because of the money I was pulling down and took them with a grain of salt, but it was very lonely, and had no one to talk to being on the road all the time. This was back before cell phones, so it was just really lonely. That's the specific word I'd choose to describe that time in my life. Plus I was suspicious that Charlie was stealing some of my deposits, because I would be shorted a little at this club or that one, but it was nothing I could prove conclusively at the time.

On top of that, I had a couple checks from Metro bounce, which were reconciled shortly afterward, but it just made me realize in ways how unstable a business it was in the long-term. That really sharpened my focus on getting out of it as soon as possible, but also gave me resolve to make sure I didn't leave with nothing. I got home from the tour in mid-October, and spent my birthday alone. I took myself out to the Cheesecake Factory, and I think saw Lemmy, but he was really my only friend to speak of at the time. It's hard to get close to people when you travel as much as I did, and he and I had that in common as he also toured a lot with his band Motorhead, so that commonality helped us frame our friendship accordingly. Many people in the entertainment business, at least in my estimation, are shallow and insecure, and therein clingy, and by nature in constant need of attention, both on and off screen. I was the opposite, maybe coming from my background in New York and being more naturally independent, but I didn't really require that. As such, while I got lonely on the road, I also knew better than to try and form any close bonds when I couldn't give the time and attention it took to maintain those relationships — be they romantic or just platonic. That stance would make me enemies within the business, one example being this cunt named Christy Canyon, who said in some interview my pussy was as big as a Mack Truck. She's lucky I never ran into her, or I would have ended up in jail for the night and she in the hospital. Most of the shit-talking people did about me happened behind my back, but it was to the press, which is the only reason I heard about it. Why would I then try to go make nice with any of those bitches? Perhaps my initial disinterest in befriending them fueled their standoffish attitude toward me, but I think a lot of it was jealousy too. I was getting a lot of attention during this period. We still all had to play nice at the conventions and Award shows, but that was about it. In November, *Gang Bang II* was finally scheduled to be released, we had the Comdex Convention at the Sahara in Las Vegas, which ended up being the genesis of my and Jenna Jameson's rivalry.

Basically, because of all the hype we'd built behind *Gang Bang II*'s release over the past few months — I was a big deal that year for the show, to the point where Ron Jeremy and I shared a billboard along Las Vegas blvd. I went on *Howard Stern* that weekend to promote the whole thing and Stuttering John made a comment that I was their highest rated porn star guest. Robin Quivers followed-up that I had beat out Jenna Jameson in their ratings. Anyway, that made me feel good, but I guess Jenna heard it and got really pissed as a result because they'd said it on air. To boot, when I was signing later that day on the convention floor, my booth was drawing more of a crowd than Jenna's. Finally, later that night, while I was out at some nightclub with a friend, a friend of Jenna's, some cunt named Felicia, came over to a guy I was speaking with and told him if he kept talking to me he'd catch Hepatitis B or some such shit. Well, my friend Angel Hart took umbrage to that, drug her by her hair out of the club. Well, as it happened, the next night, I was co-hosting this show at another club called 'All NUDE Triple X Review' with Ron Jeremy, which explained our Billboard.

Jenna had a show down the street that was drawing no heads because everyone was down checking us out. So at one point in the night, I guess she had to come down and see what all the hype was about, and in the process, she started to pick a fight with me, and was escorted out of the club by its owner! It was priceless. I think the club owner even told her in reply to some comment that he wouldn't fuck her with a dildo. Jenna's a very competitive person, BUT my mother raised me to be a shark, so she was out of her league in that department. At that point, she was still just starting out, and I was clearly the bigger star, and that just couldn't bother her enough. I mean, we'd both basically gotten into the business around the same time, and here, nine months into my career, I was starring with Ron Jeremy — the male giant of porn — on a Billboard along Las Vegas Blvd. Jenna clearly felt she deserved to be on that Billboard and I give her props that she's lasted in the business a long time, but I can't help but also point out that she started getting bigger after I retired. That's just a fact if you look at our numbers. The funny thing is I only became competitive about the whole thing after she started it, she began that rivalry. You might think it was the other way given how outspoken I was in general, but I never called anyone out specifically in my press interviews, just spoke generally of the people I worked with. Jenna was the first girl I spoke out on personally — lashed out on is probably a more accurate way to say it — but she had it coming. That was a big month for me with *Gang Bang*'s release, to the point where heading into December, my Brazilian distributor told John they wanted to fly me down there for some kind of a promotional tour. That wouldn't happen till January of 97, but December certainly wasn't by any means lacking in excitement. First, I met a guy named Keith at the Rainbow one night who would go on to become my next serious boyfriend, and my mother came out to visit me in Los Angeles for the first time.

Thankfully, by the time my mother arrived it was the week before Christmas, and I was done with everything business-wise for the month, so that she had no opportunity to become suspicious, still she found ways to spy on me. I remember one day I went to the grocery store, and upon my return, found my mother standing on my balcony talking to my neighbor, asking a whole bunch of questions like fucking *Cagney and Lacey*. My neighbor called me on the phone and said my mom was asking shit like what kind of people come over, if I had guys over, what time I came in, and of course, my neighbor covered me, but it was still very embarrassing. She liked Los Angeles in general, and we had a nice Christmas, we ate at this really cool seafood restaurant in Santa Monica, exchanged gifts, and did all the normal stuff families do at Christmas. She tried her best to be accepting of my decision to live in L.A., and my 'modeling' career, but she did give me shit about my Mazda Miata. She didn't think it was safe, normal mother shit. I kept her away from most all of my friends, but we did eat with one of my friends Mila, who ironically was also a porn star, but as far as my mother was concerned was also a 'model.' She was very sweet and polite around my mom, kept it very clean, in spite of the nasty things we both did on screen, this is again an example of the fact that NOT ALL porn stars have to take their work home with them. She was very different off-screen, and my mother picked up on nothing, and would have with many of my other co-workers because of the latter fact that they couldn't separate their business and personal lives.

On the subject of my own personal life at that point, following my mother's return to New York, I decided it was time to take a chance and start dating again. I craved the male company- both romantically and sexually, because again guys — there's a pronounced DIFFERENCE between the nature of the sex we have on screen and off. Well, the guy was Keith, who I'd met earlier that month through his brother, and our first date was New Year's Eve of 1996. We went out to the Universal City Citywalk, had dinner at Wolfgang Puck's Café; went dancing afterward and just hung out. Nothing happened the first night, in part, because it was important to me he understood I wasn't a fucking slut or anything.

It plays to the larger importance of a guy understanding — and more importantly, accepting the difference I pointed out above — that it's just work when the camera is on. It also helped me that Keith's brother, T.T. Boy was also an actor in the business (and no guys, we never worked together in case you were wondering. I never would have BEEN dating his brother.) Anyway, my occupation was just something he had to accept, and not get jealous of, and not take personally. I grant you that it's a tall order, but he seemed to be up to the task. We had a really nice time, which gave me something to be hopeful for personally, heading into 1997.

PART XI

1997: The Year of Living Dangerously

Heading into January of 1997, we had another AVN Awards Show to attend in Vegas, and the whole circus began again. I did Howard Stern's radio show again, along with a new one that Kevin Du Brow was hosting, and we got off on the wrong foot, because we were both kind of standoffish with each other on the air. That can never really hurt me, because it only breeds controversy, which built buzz heading into the awards show that evening. Not surprisingly, at the awards I won 'Best Selling Tape of the Year' for the *Gang Bang II* movie, which had sold extremely well and put me on the map officially as an international porn star. It was really kind of funny to me, winning the award given the sham we'd pulled off in filming it, but I played along.

I guess I was having a bad radio weekend, because another show I did was Kevin Dubrow's from *Quiet Riot*, who attempted to be funny by calling me 'Jasmin E'claire.' I'll let you figure that one out for yourselves, but my retort put him back in his place when I asked him on air, 'How do you have a full head of hair when you were bald back in the early 80s?' We hooked up a few months later for a one-night thing and I discovered he like Corey Feldman — also had a tiny penis, so I guess if I'm Jasmin E'claire, he was packing a mini-pastry. Anyway, preceding that encounter, I called him on-the-air during an interview, and we left on good enough terms to hook up later on that year. I didn't really care about anyone but Howard Stern, and he was nice to me, he didn't ask me to flash my tits, so I took that as a good sign he had earned some twisted form of respect for me after seeing my movie. He also didn't quiz me on that again, so maybe as silly as I felt that award was, it did work to further legitimize me in his eyes. In the grand scheme of things, Stern's show was the only one that mattered. Anyway, as the month went on, Keith and I started dating regularly. It was nice; we just did basic boyfriend/girlfriend stuff: went to dinner, hung out at his house, watched TV; went to the beach, HAD SEX, which was nice for a change. I have to admit, in spite of the stardom, it felt really nice to have just a normal relationship on a personal level for all the other sacrifices that line of work naturally brought you if you kept the two worlds separate. I still had to travel for features and what not, which was hard because I missed Keith, but it also fueled our romance because distance naturally does that to anyone.

One big trip I did have to take for work heading into February was a promotional trip to Brazil, paid for in full by Metro's distributor. I almost didn't go because I wasn't feeling well at all. I had just done a gig in Miami preceding the trip in that shape, but Charlie threatened that they wouldn't carry any of my videos down there if I didn't do the trip, so I agreed to go in the end. It was smart on Charlie's part to force me to go at that point because I also subconsciously didn't want to leave Keith for that long. He brought out a different side of his personality then too that I hadn't seen before. He was really cruel with the way he guilted me about it, but he was so cute and nice to me overall and everything that I just kind of dealt with it at first. Okay, he had a big dick too, which was also an incentive. He'd even modeled for Playgirl at one point. Once I got down to Brazil, I was happy Charlie talked me into going, because it was truly A LOT of fun in spite of the fact that I was working. It was the first time I really felt like a star, because I was in a foreign country, and people knew who I was.

I did Brazil's equivalent of the Tonight Show, called *Jo Suarez,* and the show's host and audience were really nice to me, it made me feel good to be appreciated for once in my fucking life. There were a lot of photo shoots and magazine interviews too, which I could understand because I spoke Portuguese, so I answered questions in their native language, which impressed everyone as well. We also did Brazil's version of our own video convention, but it was much nicer because you didn't have every single piece of fucking trailer park trash there trying to talk shit to me with their two teeth. The Brazilians knew how to treat their stars. They had wine at the booth where I was signing, and put me up in my OWN ROOM at a beautiful, 5-star hotel for a week. The fan appreciation there was just really cool. When I got back from Brazil, things with

Keith started to get strained, especially in that he became more and more possessive, which is a REAL turn off to any woman, that one's just for you guys reading this. The more you try to pull a woman close to you through that, the more then push away, many times in the case of my girlfriends to where they do what I ended up doing to escape: have an affair. In my case, the fling was with the Scorpions bass player, Ralph Rickermann. We met at the Rainbow Bar and Grill one night, and things just went from there. He invited my friends and me back to his house to listen to some of his band's new stuff. He had a really awesome house up in the hills too. Nothing happened between us that first night, but I knew it would sooner or later. The attraction was clearly there, and we hooked up a few days later. I kept both Ralph and Keith in the dark about each other, which I knew couldn't last forever. One reason for that was Ralph constantly had people over at his house, and was always out and about when we were together and weren't in the bedroom. It was really annoying after a while, because he loved groupies, and you can't really date someone if you always have people around because alone time is just a requisite component to any successful relationship working — in my opinion at least. He was a social butterfly, and wasn't really dating material because of that. I figured it was just a matter of time before word got back to Keith. I wasn't happy, and at that point, neither had enough to really satisfy me singularly, so I guess a rationalized in a way that by dating both guys at once, they would somehow make up for one another's deficiencies. Naturally, that strategy did NOT work in the long run, but it made for an amusing spring of dating.

In April, I shot another movie, but the next big to-do professionally came with a lunch between John T. Bone and I where he pitched me on a brilliant idea for a movie he had called *Fuck Jasmin*, where I would fuck my fans on-screen. It was similar to *Gang Bang II* in some ways, with the difference being that for this movie, now that I was established, the men having sex with me knew who I was, and it would be like I was fulfilling their personal fantasy. Naturally, I was too weak to stand up to the idea, so I went along with it, saying something like 'Yeah sure, I guess if that's what it takes.' Looking back, I felt like he was treating me like a fucking hooker, but at the time, I was already so settled in that mind frame that it didn't occur to me to say anything about whatever objections I did have at the time in my own head. We would end up doing a couple movies like that; neither film was very enjoyable, because, again, having sex with regular Joes as opposed to pros on-screen is just a different type of pressure.

No one knew what they were doing, and the whole thing was just kind of thrown together. There's just basics that a professional porn star knows — placement, stamina, how to position their faces, blocking, knowing how to fake orgasms and make it look real, etc. By the way, anyone who tells you they have real orgasms onscreen is fucking lying. Anyway, with an average fan, they get nervous because of all the lighting and direction, and it turns out to be a lot harder than they thought. Plus they are trying to act like a porn star, which makes it even funnier, because they look like total morons, and have no idea because no one has the heart to tell them. The first thing they'd lose is their confidence, and then their hard-on, and then we'd have had to start all over again with another guy. It was just a bad idea all around, and I give them all the credit in the world for trying because it was any red blooded American's dream come true, but it was really just a waste of my time, and the audience's ultimately.

We were scheduled to shoot the first one in May of 1997, and another was shot later that summer. Thankfully neither sold very well; so they cut it out. But sitting back at that lunch in April, I felt really sleazy agreeing to it at all. He convinced me it was the best way to keep things fresh with my image, so I went along with it. One change professionally for me at this point was my decision to leave Metro when my contract was up to go with John T. Bone over to a new company he was starting with my manager Charlie Frey called Cream Productions. Talk about a conflict of interest: my manager being a co-owner of a company who employed me and made money off my video sales, and then in the same time also taking 35% of the pittance they did pay me. It was bullshit, and probably illegal on some level, certainly unethical. It was a bad move in the long run, not just from a business- point, but also in terms of the box covers and quality of the videos they were making. My money was the same per shoot, but the overall budgets got smaller, and checks would bounce now and then, and the short cuts they were taking just reflected in the end product. It was just a fucking disastrous nightmare, now that it's all coming back to me. I was above it, and should have said so at the time. The pressure was almost entirely on me as well as the company's biggest star to carry their product sales, and that wasn't fair at all to me. All of the other girls Charlie and John recruited were newcomers, and most didn't last more than a few movies. As the company's flagship star, I felt I deserved more money, and used it as the perfect opportunity to force Charlie to lower his percentage to 25% from 35%, which he reluctantly agreed to. He was acting real prick, looking back in hindsight.

Heading into the summer of 1997, I had my second nose-job, and the plastic surgeon was a complete asshole. I remember I stayed in this really nice aftercare facility in Los Angeles after the operation was over, in a little Bungalow with its own little bathroom and whatnot. It was a smart move, because at one point I blacked out like the first night after the surgery while I was in the shower and there was someone there to find me. They had nurses that checked on you, and had I been home, I would have been alone and helpless. I was down for two weeks after the nose job, so that hurt financially a little bit, but I was back out on the road featuring by the end of June. Things were still tough financially, in spite of all the money I was making between the dancing and movies. I had to give Charlie 25% right off the top, which was still a lot of money. Pay rent, my car payment, plus I was still paying down the debt Dick had run up in my name, and that was in the thousands of dollars, so it was a trying time in spite of my finally attaining stardom. That just allowed more opportunities for me to go out and make money that someone else took out of my pocket almost as soon as it came in. I guess that is life, but it still didn't sit right with me. Keith and I were also starting to have real problems around this point, because like every other fucking guy who lied about claiming he could 'handle my profession,' he was starting to pressure me to get out of porn. Well, naturally, that was the last fucking thing I wanted to hear, so it gave me refuge to steal off and be with Ralph, the Scorpions' bassist, which obviously didn't help Keith and I out either. Keith just couldn't deal with what I was doing, where Ralph never brought it up one way or the other, so that was convenient also.

In truth, I was starting to tire of the whole business myself, but I knew if I'd walked away from it then, I would have been forgotten about overnight. I had worked hard to build a reputation, and while I was now famous within porn, I hadn't yet made all the connections I would need to transition out of the business on my own terms. I was definitely starting to get burnt out though, but couldn't really tell Keith that because he'd just use it to his advantage rather than mine. I couldn't tell Charlie or John either, because now they were both my bosses, and had too much invested personally in the company to lose their biggest star while Crème was still a start-up company. Anyway, I really stayed home most of June because of the operation and from being fried in general, but I had to get back to work in July just to keep my head above water financially and to stay visible. That month, John also shot the second (and thank GOD final) fan-fuck movie, and like the first one, it was just fucking awful. It was called *Planet Jasmin: A Bang at the Park*, and it was just ridiculous. It was a fucking nightmare gone bad. It was basically identical to the first one, and was obvious to everyone at the shoot's conclusion that it needed to end. At that point, I was also weaning off of Ralph, at that point because I didn't want him fucking around all over town. I didn't like the fact that when I was with him and wanted to spend some time with him he would prefer to have these parties all the time with all these porn stars, who I had to see enough of at work as it was. It just got really annoying really quick.

Meanwhile, on the Keith front, it had gotten so bad that he would do shit like take me out to nice places to eat dinner, sit across from me telling me how great I was, and then in front of me drool over all these other women. Or he would go on and on about his ex-girlfriends, as if that was something any woman would ever want to hear about from her man? Then he started starting fights with me all the time over my 'porn friends' hanging out, then the fucking hypocrite went to his own porn shoots and fucked the girls he was modeling with, but he claimed it wasn't cheating because it was work. You fuck in movies, not on the sets of photo shoots — did he forget I was a fucking model too? I was too far into it now to quit, and his betrayals gave me no further motivation to consider it. If anything, this made me angrier because he more than anyone else should have understood the dynamics of it. You see I was too far into the game to turn back. I had everything; fame, interviews, publicity. It's all that represented independence to me at that point in my life. I was suffocated enough anyway by the fact that I was Charlie and John's main star at the new company, and so the last thing I needed was to feel controlled at ALL by my boyfriend. Well, the same day of this one particularly nasty fight we'd had where I'd thrown him out of my apartment, I was I was on the phone with my travel agent Elizabeth, going over an airline ticket itinerary for a feature I had coming up. Anyway, while talking with her in my kitchen, I suddenly get this instinct to turn around, and standing in my fucking living room is Keith. He'd climbed up two stories onto the balcony in broad daylight like a fucking burglar, and was now beginning to walk toward me in a manner I found extremely threatening. So from my kitchen I started screaming and throwing knives at him, whatever metal objects I could get my hands on that I thought would hurt him. While all this was going on, I still had Elizabeth on the phone, who called the police for me on her cell while she kept me on the phone. Keith is yelling at me, 'What the fuck are you doing?!' and people outside the apartment could hear him, all around Marina Del Rey. Anyway, I managed to keep him at bay till the cops arrived a few minutes later. Of course, they immediately got the picture, and once I made clear I did NOT want Keith there, and he refused even then to leave in front of the L.A.P.D., insisting he wanted to 'talk.' I was turned on by this and it made for great, hot sex later. Neither of us pressed charges. Ultimately, I ended up forgiving him and taking him back, but I knew things were doomed to end at some point. I just needed someone in that moment, and probably fooled myself like all women do on some level in thinking I could make things better between us.

As the summer came toward a close, things weren't much better at Crème. I was bored, John had me doing the hard core, boy/girl anal scenes, which was my bread and butter as a porn star, but he wanted me to develop an even bitchier attitude as part of my larger public persona as Jasmin. I thought I was already hard core enough, but I suppose I felt motivated to continue to stand out on some level because all around me, Charlie and John were bringing in all these clone chicks who were riding my coattails on the way to the top. The problem was they weren't stars, and therein only cluttered my movies but made me stand out that much more in another way, so it worked in reverse of what both John and Charlie had been hoping. I think over all, I was just really over the whole thing, and had no enthusiasm for it anymore. I mean how could I? How could I top the gang bang movie? Whenever I bitched about these hack bitches like Kendra Jade sharing my screen time, John would say I was jealous, but I was right: how could he or Charlie focus on me with all these other girls as clients? Moreover, it was an inherent conflict of interest that Charlie was acting both as my manager and employer as part owner of the company because he had no incentive to push for me to get other projects and opportunities outside of the confines of Crème. This meant he couldn't shop me to Vivid or any competitors because they were *HIS* competitors and that put me at a great disadvantage looking back.

Charlie Fry: I don't know if I agree with her depiction of the Jasmin clones. At her peak, Jasmin definitely had imitators. In fact, we had to send a cease-and-desist letter to one club feature dancer who was using Jade St. Claire with a very similar look to Jasmin. It was obvious she was trying to ride off Jasmin's name — there are a lot out there that were based off of Jasmin's name and look. My opinion is that once I did go onto the next girl, Jasmin got jealous because she'd lost the attention and positive male feedback that she craved. Because of her negative self image, which came in her case NOT from the dominant male figure in her life, but the dominant FEMALE figure, being her mother. I think by playing the role I did in making her a star as quickly as I did, she came to rely on that positive male feedback from me, and in general. So part of our fall-out came when I started looking to create the next star, like Kendra Jade, which is how I kept commissions coming in, but she perceived it as something where I lost interest in her and creating situations which kept her at the pinnacle of the porn world. In my defense, she had started getting more heavily involved in wrestling, which was not my forte, and as a result, I think we grew even further apart as her interest in adult film waned. I think its remarkable she kept her brand name alive in other commercial realms, be it wrestling or the music industry, but there wasn't much more I could do for her after she lost her passion for porn.

Jasmin: Charlie was just taking complete advantage of me wherever he could at that point — he even tried to get me to do a club date for free that I'd blown off a few months back. It was laughable, but showed how little value he actually put on me. I had July off from shooting any movies, which was a nice break. I'd actually made a couple girlfriends, as I like to joke, one — my friend Dawn, was a co-star, and the other-this gay make-up guy named Sean — was very sweet, he's so much fun to dress up with and go out. Like he'd come over to my place. He'd come dress me up and do my hair and makeup. And we'd go over to his place, he'd put something on and we'd sneak out and go dancing. It was so much fun. We go to department stores, and it was always a funny experience because we'd go to the makeup counters and fuck with the make-up people working there. He'd like borrow their eye-shadow right there and he'd do my makeup right there. He's a natural. I was very fortunate to have him — personally and professionally — because he knew hair and makeup. He made some people who really needed it — like Kendra Jade — look great. We went to another dumb convention in Vegas whose name I honestly don't remember. The most memorable event from that weekend was my breaking my own rule by hooking up for a one-night stand with this hot piece of ass porn star named John Doe, which was not typical of me. He'd come up to me that day during a booth signing and asked me out that night for drinks and I thought he was cute — big, tall guy, really kind of cute. So we went out for drinks, and he was a complete gentleman for a change.

I don't know if he was just so good that I was on cloud nine, or if the experience just really cleared my head. Once I was back in L.A., one thing I had taken full charge of in my life was getting Keith out of it entirely, only to replace him with a full-fledged male porn star named Earl Slate. I'd met him during the shoot for my August movie *Ridden Hard and Put Away Wet,* which was a one-off I did for Metro. Earl wasn't a star on that film, but was visiting the Metro set, and we just hit it off immediately. His real name was Anthony Stern. He seemed nice, was in shape, was *COLLEGE-EDUCATED* — a definite exception to the norm — and seemed like he had it together, too. He was doing another business on the side, some dental thing, and I found it attractive that he had something else going on outside of porn. That was how I thought — to the future — so it was refreshing to find someone else in the same mindset. He was also in some kind of AA-type substance abuse recovery program, which spelled out responsibility to me, so that was a plus too. We started dating in August, and had actually had our first sexual encounter together on a movie, which was tricky, because it's such a gray area once you begin making it personal. At first, we had that agreement that when it's off camera it is play, when it on camera it's work. It's really hard, because I look back at it and you can't really. It's hard to share those emotions with other people. It's a really fucked up thing to do. I knew it wasn't it right. Deep down, I fucking knew it wasn't right. But it was the only one I thought I could deal with by doing that. He was the same way; he didn't care. Eventually, as I started to fall for him, it would bother me that he was leaving my bed to fuck other women, but I didn't ever say much about it, but it did bother me. You know, at the time he was the only person I could really go out with, because of what I doing, too. At first, I didn't feel one way or another about it, and I had gotten busy again — I went back on Springer's show in September — and between my signings, features, movie shoots, and just living life with him in between all those commitments, there wasn't time to think about it. I know what I was hoping it would become in time, I was hoping he would grow to care enough about me that it would occur to him on his own to quit. That's obviously the hope anyone on a human level has about someone they share their life with.

That September, I went to New York to do another appearance on *Howard Stern*, in the process blowing off some high-profile features gig in Spain, which of course, made Charlie livid at me. I was already feeling ill, and he had me booked on a flight with 6 layovers, so I didn't feel too bad about it ultimately. Charlie really couldn't say shit to me anyway at that point because he needed me so badly at Crème. I was the company's only high-profile star, which allowed me to take advantage of loosening the leash with Charlie a little — especially on shit like that. He could yell at me till he was red in the face — like the Satan he was- over the loss of a commission, but he stood to lose a lot more money if I left his movie company, so I had him by the balls on that front. He kept working on my behalf ultimately because he couldn't afford not to, and that fall, actually did his job for a change and got me something new: a deal with Erostar, a company that did molds of celebrity busts. It was a $10,000 payday for me, so I was excited as ever — until I found out Charlie got $2500 of that money right off the top, prick. When all was said and done I walked away with $5000 after taxes, and for the time it took, that was bullshit money. First, they put this mask of mold solution all over your face and skin — it's like a free beauty treatment, but it covers my whole face, and I had to sit with it on for hours. They put a tube in my mouth to breathe, and my hair was pulled back in a cap, and my whole body was covered in this shit, my breasts, my vagina, my ass — everything they were molding. The toughest part was my face because you feel like your blacked out, your eyes are closed, but I was so freaked out after a few minutes that I got up and started walking around. One girl had to come and grab me and lead me back to sit down, or I'd have had to do the whole process over again. Anyway, after a while, they cut the mold — which is now a cast formed from an impression off my face — and they do it with this exacto-knife, a little at a time almost surgically. By the time they'd repeated that process in the more private areas of my body I spoke of above, I was embarrassed, and ready to leave. That might sound odd coming from me, but it was really involved — more like a doctor's appointment than a porn shoot, where the focus isn't entirely on you. Anyway, when the whole thing was said and done, it was really cool looking but weird, because it felt like real human flesh. That month, Earl and I also made the decision to tell John about our affair which we have been hiding from everyone. He took it okay, and really couldn't say much at that point. Besides, he was much more focused on shooting the latest addition to my distinguished film library — *Butt Sex*. I had a dancing feature up in Oregon that month and Earl came up to see me, and I could tell he'd been drinking, which I guess looking back I should have seen the beginning of the end, but I was in love with him and wanted it to work. I was tiring of the movies at that point — or their titles at least. Things had just been more stylish and distinguished at Metro — from the titles to the box covers to the film sets to my co-stars. I was just ready for a change I knew wasn't coming anytime soon.

As October began, Earl and I were spending a lot of time with each other. He felt like the perfect guy. He had no problem with my career and what I was doing. He helped me out with my stuff. He fit the profile of everything I was looking for in a guy. My movie that month was titled *Blow it Out Your Ass* and as over the top as ever in terms of the hard core. I was even bored enough that I suggested this wild idea to John where we could insert this party-popper type thing into my ass. Right into the top of the butt and a cord went around to the front where you would have someone in the back, pumping fluid into it, and a streamer would come out! That's how out of my mind with boredom I was at that point with the whole thing. I had a bunch of video store signings scheduled that month as well, in Houston, Dallas, and in each of those cities where I did signings I was getting huge draws. I had one in Northern California that was so big someone called the Fire Marshall, so I made a shit-pot of money that month. It was just easy, easy money — I would sign the box for the video, or an 8x10, and the store would pay me a $2000.00-a-day rate, before Charlie's cut of course, but it was still good money. One of my signings that month was with Kendra, who Crème was trying to promote on my coattails. She was nice enough; I just thought she was too much of a clone of me.

Charlie Fry: Jasmin perceived Jenna as competition — rightfully so — and there was a real genuine tension there, sort of a 'Don't Rain on my Parade' attitude. For instance, in Vegas when Jenna came to Jasmin's show at the Sahara Hotel, Jasmin basically said, 'I want her out of here.' Exercising her power for me to do it, and here I am having an audience of hundreds of people and I'm dependant on her to entertain them, so I said 'Fine,' and had her escorted out. Jenna and Jasmin were pretty much equals at the time in terms of their notoriety, and if anything, Jasmin had more — she'd appeared more times on Howard Stern, had more press and brand name recognition. They were definitely not friends behind the scenes.

At the time, this was a show I produced at the Sahara Hotel. Jenna was down the street at another, smaller hotel, and Jasmin's showroom held around 900 people, and was PACKED, billed as 'Starring Jasmin St. Claire, Hosted by Ron Jeremy,' and Jasmin was the main headliner for sure. Jenna's showroom by contrast held around 300 people and wasn't full. Ours on the other hand was filled to capacity.

Jasmin: It's very true that by this point in my 2 year-old career, Jenna Jameson and I were really locking horns in the porn press — by her instigation at all times. I had climbed from a no-name to the front-page of our industry in so short a time that it was bound to catch eyes, only in Jenna's case it was more like a jealous stare. Want an example, just look at the Vegas *All Nude Review* show at the Sahara Hotel back in November 1997. I was a star in it, along with Angel Hart & Gina La Marca, who was Penthouse Pet of the Year in 1996, and Ron Jeremy was hosting the with me. I had a billboard with my face on it on the Vegas Strip, and all of this happened to coincide with Howard Stern announcing on air that I had been his highest-rated guest, over and above Jenna or any other adult film star. So she had gotten pissed, showed up drunk, unannounced and uninvited to my revue, and started running her mouth. I hadn't said a thing to her and my manager quickly shut her up by having her thrown out, but it was still embarrassing, and the adult film press had been there to record the whole event. So later that night I was out at another club, and she must have been stalking me, because she showed up there and began trying to start shit again. When the owner went to throw her out, she even blurted out to him, 'What, do you think Jasmin has more power than I do?' Then when he ignored her and again asked her to leave, she said, 'What, you wouldn't fuck me?' To which he retorted 'Lady, I wouldn't fuck you with a dildo.'

Charlie Fry: I would book her and Ron Jeremy at clubs together, so you had in essence the biggest male and female porn stars of the porn industry, so we'd just pack places with that combo. They worked well together in that regard, and packaging them together was a really big thing at that time.

Ron Jeremy: I loved going to Vegas with Jasmin, I remember there being a GIANT billboard outside of the Sahara Hotel and Casino that said 'Ron Jeremy and Jasmin St. Claire: The Ultimate Review.' There were two marquees: a big one that was right in front of the Sahara and one that actually attached to the Sahara on a wall, both saying the same thing.

For a while there in the later 1990s, Jasmin and Jenna Jameson were neck-and-neck in popularity, and there was definitely a competitive rivalry.

I remember when we were doing the *Ultimate Review* at the Sahara Hotel, we were sold out and they were doing at the Riviera, and in fairness to them, they were close to sold out too. I thought we had a better Review because we were doing it with comedy, personality, and dancing, where there's was more just dancing. Ours was each girl dancing on her own working with a choreographer and making it the best possible dance. We had a Penthouse Pet named Leslie Glass, who later died of cancer, and later started her own organization called 'Pets for Pets.' Anyway, so Jenna came by one night to check out the show, watch the rehearsal and the attitudes were flaring up a little bit. Jasmin was going, 'I hate that girl,' and Jenna was saying, 'I hate that girl.' And they both had done a lot of Stern, and it was a rivalry.

Felicia, Jenna's friend, was really getting mad at Charlie, Jasmin's manager, for things he was saying about her (Jenna) in the porn press, and so that night, she came in with Jenna, and started a scene, screaming at Charlie and Jasmin, more than Jenna was. Jenna was just in the background, letting them fight it out, and Jenna wanted an apology from Charlie because he'd embarrassed her in the media. He'd said something to the Las Vegas Journal about our show having Jasmin St. Claire, and Jenna's show having 'that other girl,' and Jenna thought that was a cheap-shot. So once Jenna and Charlie had yelled at each other, Felicia just started screaming!

I remember very clearly, after the girls left, that I was trying to cheer Jasmin up because Felicia had started screaming at her. I sat her down, and she was saying 'I can't go on tonight, I'm all upset, I'm all upset. I'm pissed off.' And I said 'Jasmin, Jasmin, Jasmin, Jasmin! Relax.' Once she calmed down enough to listen, and continued, explaining to her that 'it's all good. Relax. Rivalries are good for press; it's a lot of fun. This is great press. I'll put it on a lighter scale: Schwarzenegger and Stallone never had a problem with their rivalry, it only helped. Andrew Dice Clay and Sam Kinison used to have a severe feud and a war, which made headlines, and they loved it. They had insulting comments in the press to each other, and it was great, because it gave them both more publicity. What do you care about war, war is wonderful, and maybe a few months from now, or a year from now, you end this war with a nice sexy girl-girl scene.' She didn't exactly go for that, but got my broader point of trying to tell her, 'Relax, it's not a bad thing. This war is fun, and is making more headlines and making the shows in Vegas even more popular.' She seemed to come around to that way of thinking a little.

Jasmin: Near the end of the month, I was in Connecticut to do some features, and appeared on the *Howard Stern Show* (again, ☺) to promote something or another. It was becoming part of my job description by that point to go on Howard Stern and Jerry Springer, and one of the only parts I didn't mind. It was my birthday that month — I turned 23, which was much nicer than my 22nd, mainly because I had Earl in my life. We went to Argyle for my birthday, and my gay make-up artist friend Sean came over and did my hair and make-up, and Earl gave me a diamond necklace as my present, it was just a beautiful day. By that point, we were staying over at each other's places a lot, acting like a regular couple. November went by quietly that year, until my mom came out for Thanksgiving. She was meeting Earl for the first time, which was hilarious because he told her he repaired boats for a living. It was just an inside joke that kept he and I laughing to ourselves the whole time she was out, because she really was a prosecutor about it with him, I mean grilling him up and down on boat maintenance and repair. Thankfully, he chose that occupation because Earl actually owned a boat and was quite versed as an owner with its ins and outs (pardon the pun in context of our real profession.)

I spent a large amount of December on the road, which was convenient because things had started to go a little sour between Earl and I, which led me in search of a variety of distractions — including Keith. I knew it was a mistake, but he'd been calling me again — A LOT — and I figured with my travel schedule it wouldn't get too heavy. I literally spent the first 3 weeks of the month on the road. To give you an idea of what my life on the road was like in months like that, my signing and features itinerary read something like this: Sugar and Spice Adult Video Store, December 8; December 8-13 Pete's Lounge, West Palm Beach, Florida. On the morning of December 13, I had to drive up to Fairville Mega Plex Video in Cape Canaveral, Florida for a signing. I was then home for two days, and then on December 17-20, had to fly back out for a feature at the Cat Walk in New Haven, Connecticut. Earl stayed back in L.A. filming this whole time, and I'd begun speaking to Keith more than I even was to Earl — officially my boyfriend at that point. I guess what started it was I stopped trusting Earl because he'd started drinking again, which he actually attempted to blame me for. That led me to be lonely on the road, which in turn led to my finally returning one of Keith's many calls.

When I was home, Earl was working every day, and he never made any time for me. When he wasn't working, he was drunk flirting with crack whores openly on his set, at strip bars, or off tooling with his boat. He had stopped spending time with me, and the fucking hypocrite had become more and more hostile toward my profession, even though he did the same thing! He even got so possessive at one point he asked me to marry him! It was laughable given the state he and our relationship were in. Anyway, I decided to try and give things one last shot with him, so we agreed to go meet his parents and spend Christmas up in Montana. That trip definitely let me know where his alcoholism came from. Anyway, prior to leaving on that trip, I'd called Keith while Earl was out getting drunk and screwing around. I wasn't necessarily trying to reconcile with Keith, but he did fuck my brains out, so that was a nice release from the vices Earl was trying to put on me. Shortly after that, Earl and I left for Montana to go spend the holidays with his family. He was raised by his father and grandmother. Both of who were sweethearts and very welcoming. He told them I was model, but he actually told his own father he was an adult film star!

By that point, he'd started telling anyone who would listen, and that made me like him less. He didn't stop to think for a minute how it would reflect on me either, as his girlfriend, but he never thought, so I guess I shouldn't have been very surprised at all. Anyway, we went skiing at Red Lodge Resort in Montana while we were up there, and I'd been many times skiing before with Joe, but I had a horrid time on this trip because Earl was drunk the whole time. I don't know how many of you have skied before, but it's a challenging enough sport that being drunk doesn't enhance performance at all — on the ski slope or in bed for that matter where Earl was concerned. Half the time we were on vacation, he couldn't get it up at all, which just made me long for Keith on a physical level that much more. He was as cold to me as the weather that year; he even called me a 'weak bitch' at one point when I complained about the temperature. At this point, Earl was doing blow again too. We'd had a huge episode earlier in the month where he'd gone off somewhere and got drunk, then dragged me off to some chili dog place where he was saying awful things like 'You are too skinny, why don't you fucking eat, you anorexic whore?' Just mean shit that, so much so that I was really getting scared because I'd never seen that side of him. He apologized the next day when he sobered up, which I accepted out of weakness, although I knew I never should have. It just let him feel okay about being abusive to me.

When we got back from Montana, I was hoping New Years would be better, and it was at the very least my most interesting New Year's

Eve ever up to that point, because I spent it with none other than O.J. Simpson! Earl and I went to St. Marks — this beach spot near Venice, and I had somehow or another befriended O.J.'s new Nicole-look-a-like girlfriend. They were looking for some blow, which of course, got Earl involved, and we ended up joining their party of 5 for the evening. I have to say, O.J. was the nicest guy. I know some people will hate me for saying so, but he was a complete gentleman, and people around us were giving looks. Some were mean, and others were gawkers more than anything else, but he was chill and knew how to handle it, which made all of us around him relax as well. I'd been recognized in public by that point, but I had no sense of a real 'celebrity' until I hung around O.J. I mean, he was almost notorious more than just famous. That would be the proper way to frame it, I thought he was very nice though, very charming.

He was a very classy person. I think it is possible he didn't do it, but we didn't talk about the murder at all. His girlfriend, however, told me in the bathroom that she thought it was his son who had done it, and that O.J. had taken the rap for him, which explained the D.N.A. similarities. She said he just wouldn't talk about it. That was their rule, so we respected that. He knew who I was, which was kind of cool. Anyway, as the night rolled on, Earl got drunker and more coked up, and eventually O.J. invited us to come back on to his boat for kind of an after party, which of course, I was extremely psyched for. Earl quickly ruined that possibility by being so publicly intoxicated we couldn't go anywhere but home. What sucked most about how I rang in the New Year was figuring out how I was going to get home with this guy all fucked up on drugs. It wasn't like I could ask O.J. to give me a boat ride back to fucking Marina Del Rey. Believe it or not, I ended up WALKING the 20 minutes back home to my apartment by myself because Earl — like all men when they become drunken assholes — wouldn't give me the keys to drive us both home. He was too macho, and kicked me out of his car before we even left the nightspot because I wouldn't A) let him drive, and B) wouldn't take him to the hood to buy more crack or whatever the fuck he was on. It was just a side I'd never seen before of him until that winter, and I made it my New Year's resolution that I wouldn't let the relationship continue in its present state, which was easier said than done. We were already so deep into things that I found it harder to break away from him than I'd thought it would be initially.

I tried everything, from going to AA meetings with him, getting to know his sponsors so I could be in touch when he was falling off the wagon, stopping drinking around him, everything. It was sad how far I went in context of how far gone he already was, because he couldn't see any of it. Maybe he just didn't care at that point, but I still did, and had to find a way to emotionally separate myself from him once and for all. I certainly wasn't doing myself a service by staying with him, so I made the decision heading into the New Year to work toward ending the relationship. It would take me another six months, but I knew it was the right thing to be focused on as a goal. What sucked was outside of that relationship, everything else in my life was going well — I was happy financially and in my career, and there were a million other girls who would have killed to be in my shoes professionally going into 1998.

PART XII

Time to Move On...

As low as some people were sinking in their jealousy of my steadying rise in international popularity, as the New Year began, and my prospects looked even brighter still, I took the high road, preferring to focus on everything good that was happening for me at that point. Unfortunately, other people close to me had taken note of that as well, and were taking every advantage they could of our good fortune. My long-time director, John T. Bowen had signed a deal with Crème Productions, and he had also expanded his star roster to include a couple new comers — Zoe and Kendra Jade. This was motivated in part out of some financial troubles his company was experiencing, which I had stood by him through. That's just something that's in my blood, and if you look at my life, I've always been loyal to people around me, and for John, that meant tolerating his inability to produce the bigger-end movies that I wanted. So I was patient with him, and to be fair, he was getting me better male talent. So I was working with guys like Brandon Iron, who was really hot and had a big dick. There was no movie in January, but I had many bookings. I was also still dating my alcoholic loser boyfriend Earl, and even though I wasn't very happy, I was so caught up in being Jasmin that I wasn't thinking about what was the healthiest thing for Rhea. I was expected to be Jasmin 24 hours a day, and even though I knew there were normal guys who would not want to date me because of my profession, so my attitude had become: if you can't beat them, join them. And Earl was in the business as well, so it was just easier.

That sense of internal surrender had really bothered me too, because for as big as my public persona had become, I had always viewed my adult film career as a stepping — stone to somewhere better. The sacrifices hadn't just been professional so far though, they'd also taken a personal toll that drove my sense of self low enough to date a douche bag like Earl.

His alcoholism was at a high point, and I didn't know what the fuck to do. I wanted someone in my life to be my partner, and I definitely didn't have that with him. I knew he was cheating on me, and cheating in porn means that when you have sex with someone else off-camera when you're not working. It was also hard during that time of year to be having the problems we were, because I'm very old-fashioned about love no matter what, and Valentines Day was no exception. At that same time, I had also grown sick and tired of my manager Charlie taking 25% of my money. I had figured out by that point that he was a scumbag, after anyone shook his hand they felt like they'd been talking to a used car salesman. You feel like you have to wash your hands afterward, but because of my contract, I couldn't leave him yet.

February put me back before the camera, working with Hershel Savage on '*Smell My Fingers*,' another classy title. Hershel was an older guy, but really good looking and really nice, and was from New York, a commonality in our background I picked up on and used in our conversations before shooting the scene to make him feel more comfortable with me. It was the same routine with a lot of the male stars I worked with, where I had begun making it a point to speak to them because it made everyone feel a little more comfortable. I never saw myself — and I still don't see myself — as an intimidating woman to any man, but I tried to work with them because when a male star can't get his dick up because he's so intimidated, when that shit happens, what am I supposed to fucking do? Sit there all day? It's like being a photographer, you show up with your shit, and you're ready to shoot, but some of these guys weren't showing up with a hard-on like they were supposed to. But in the end, we always seemed to get the problem straightened out. I took a trip in March of 1998 for GVA, who distributed my videos, to do a signing in Cleveland, Ohio, and the strangest part of that trip was Jenna Jameson coming up to my booth and talking to me as though we were long-time friends.

Dominic Accara: When she'd show up for a shoot, she was all business, and that intimidated a lot of people. We did a shoot with porn star Mark Wood, and it was one of his first scenes ever, and Jasmin was again all business, 'Get your dick hard and fuck me — NOW,' and this dude crawled out of that room. That was Jasmin in general.

Jasmin: I was also doing a lot of feature dancing, and the time on the road gave me some distance to realize just how fed up I was with John T.

Bone's whole operation. He'd brought Kendra and Zoe in without consulting me, and John was also starting to fuck around with Kendra, which is just not good business. If John had had his eye on the ball instead of on her ass, he wouldn't have made the colossal mistake of letting the Jerry Springer scandal that followed later that spring happen. The whole thing was unhealthy for our business in general, and it was a dirty way to think, which I know sounds ironic given we worked in a business where actors and actresses are paid to have sex on-screen. But there was a big distinction — at least to most of the actors — between being an adult film star and a prostitute, so when John suggested my next film should be another fan gang bang, which was beneath me at that point. But then again, that's how low things at Crème Productions had begun to sink by that point in general. Still, I did my best to stick with all of them — John, Charlie, Earl — all of them, because one of my biggest faults is I like to see the good in everyone, and wish and hope for the best. I grew up with a lot of negativity in my life from my mom, and I would always scream it out and wouldn't listen to it. I think, looking back, I was doing the same thing here. At that point, I really didn't know what to do, but personally I was becoming more and more desperate to get away from it all.

That desperation finally boiled over on one particularly ugly night in March following a fight with Earl, wherein he'd drunkenly thrown my cat Chloe against the wall. She ran out of the front door and off into the night, and I quickly booted Earl in the same direction. I was in pieces, first because I thought my cat was gone forever and also because I'd begun thinking, 'What's up with my life?' I felt totally abandoned. I sunk into a deep depression that caused me to take every single pill I could find in my apartment, trying to escape it. Thankfully, I'd forgotten that I had a girlfriend coming over that evening, and it's a good thing, because if she hadn't, I'd have been dead.

When she found me, she later told me that she and her neighbor had raced me to Marina Del Rey Hospital. I had flat-lined. All I remember was feeling really warm and seeing white, which I know you always hear everyone say, but I also saw my dad's face, and I was ready to go. At that point it was okay with me, it didn't make a difference, and it certainly didn't make a difference to anyone around me, it felt like no one really cared if Rhea was gone, in spite of how popular Jasmin had become. I wasn't speaking to my mom, and I felt like no one really would have cared. It's a good thing I was wrong and my friend found me, because she saved my life. I owe my life to her, and sadly, she's dead now, but I'll never forget her and will always be grateful to her.

Thankfully, once I had been revived, they moved me quickly to a private room because one of the hospital staff working in the emergency room recognized me. They also told me they were going to keep this quiet, and I remember a doctor saying to me 'We're going to act like this never happened, you're alive now, but you should be calling a therapist after you're discharged.' Anyway, once I'd gotten out and back to my apartment, I had the best home-coming present I could have asked for: my cat Chloe was waiting for me on the doorstep. The whole event had been a big wake-up call for me, and it forced me to ask myself: 'Who in their right mind wants to kill themselves like this?' So I decided from that day on, the only two ways I would die would be of natural causes, or by someone choking the HELL out of me while they're fucking me. Anyway, I knew suicide wasn't the way I wanted to go out, because what would I have died as: a *PORN STAR* and I didn't want that. That strengthened my resolve to keep my eye toward the goal of graduating out of that business as soon as possible. I didn't tell Charlie or John, or even Earl about the overdose, and the next day decided to take my first step toward a fresh start by going to the pound and adopting a second kitten. I found a cute black cat, and he ran up to me, and when I came back the next day, he ran up to me again, so I named him Trent and took him home with me.

Going back to life as usual — albeit with a new sense of resolve to get out of this business sooner than later — I shot another of John's tastelessly-titled movies later in that month, *This Little Piggy Went to Porno*. I finally started to get a better picture of what John and Charlie were trying to do with piggy backing Kendra and Zoe off my popularity, which wasn't cool. For instance, for any type of live gig, Charlie would say to the club owner or promoter 'Well, if you want Jasmin, you have to take Kendra or Zoe the next month.' I didn't see a percentage of any of their earnings, in spite of those monies coming in partially off my professional name. At that point as well in the mid-spring, my passion for wrestling was starting to grow stronger for that time, and I became an active fan and student. I watched as many matches as I could on T.V. — I was also making more of an effort to have my own life outside of porn — going to concerts, mixing with metal personalities, flying to New York now and again to see my mother when I could, and developing friendships with regular people outside of the adult film industry. I tried more and more to treat my work in adult film as a profession that Jasmin pursued, but personally, Rhea was a different person, so I also wanted that reflected in my associations.

Earl was still in the picture, but cheating on me, and so I ended the month by getting a little revenge via my first scene with Brandon Iron for *This Little Piggy Went to the Whore House.* He was a Canadian guy who was hung like a horse so he reminded me of a nice guy with a big dick. We were just friends really, but he was huge, and it was a nice little break from Earl's bullshit, which heading into April, was at an all-time worst and we weren't really seeing each other as much. I'd used the opportunity to break away from him and bring another guy into the picture — Keith — and we started having an affair behind Earl's back. We were going to the beach, and it was a lot like having a normal boyfriend for a change. He wasn't in the business, he seemed to care, he was handsome and built, and I wasn't thinking about Earl as well. I didn't have a film to shoot that month and things were relatively peaceful for a change until one day my beeper went off, and a hell of a different sort started to break loose. Basically, behind everyone's back, John T. Bowen and Kendra Jade had orchestrated a sex tape with tabloid talk show host Jerry Springer, and now the rumor had officially leaked. Well, of course, as with every leak, the pipes quickly began bursting all over L.A. and it didn't take long before it spilled over and flooded into my world.

According to Wikipedia, 'in May 1998, a photo story about Springer having sex with porn star Kendra Jade in Chicago's Executive Plaza Hotel appeared in the tabloids *News of the World* and *The Globe.* Kendra's stepmother Kelly Jade was also present in the hotel room, and Kendra, Kelly, and porn director John Bowen appeared on Springer's show the next day, discussing a 350 person gang bang.'

Kendra's comments on the Springer show also included the following specific references to Jasmin St. Claire in July, 1998: *'I also had seen Jasmin St. Claire's* World's Biggest Gang Bang *tape and thought to myself, 'I can do this!'...I wanted to beat Jasmin's gang bang record...I talked with Jasmin (St. Claire) the other night. She told me, 'when you reach my status, you'll understand why I had to move on.' I only hope that I can reach such status.'*

Once John told me he was going to do the next gang bang video with Kendra, I told her if she wanted to have that title she could, I was past all that shit. With Kendra, it's not that I ever had anything against her personally, but I made it a point also not to get to know her that way. So when you have private investigators and tabloids like *Star* and the *National Enquirer* calling asking you all these questions about who has the sex tape, telling me they'll pay me X amount of money to find out, it made me livid. I called John and told him what was happening, and his reply was: 'Don't do anything, don't say a word. I can't tell you any more about it.' I was shocked he would admit its existence so easily, and even more shocked I'd been left out of the loop on something that was already affecting my privacy. I shot back by telling him 'I've been here longer than any of these other people, when you were writing bad checks I stayed loyal to you, and you can't even tell me who has the tape.' At this point, I also figured out he was fucking Kendra, and he had lost all sight of his better judgment. That he couldn't recognize how out of line it was that my privacy was being compromised by people looking for drama, the straw that broke the camel's back with John and I was when Private Investigators hired by these fucking tabloids started stalking me outside my residence in early May. I had come back from breakfast one morning to find a pair of assholes standing outside my apartment door, looking like cops — I quickly realized it was bullshit when one of them asked me, 'Are you Jasmin St. Claire? We're looking for the Jerry Springer/Kendra Jade sex tape, and we want to know if you know who has it? We'll pay you a huge amount of money.' I told him, 'I don't know what the hell you're talking about, I was told by John T. Bowen not to tell anyone, so I'm pretty sure he has the tape, why don't you go bother him and leave me alone.' Then the guy actually took another step toward me, and I said, 'If either of the two of you step one more foot toward me, I'm going to kill you, stay the fuck away from me.' So they want back to their car, and I called John and told him what happened, and he didn't even care. In adult film, the anonymity of a star's private life is even more important than mainstream movie stars because of the nutty perverts and stalkers who can do real harm to you if they find out where you live. So the fact that John had not cared made really take a step back and open my eyes wide, thinking 'Wow, what a scumbag!' I had given a lot to that company, but it was clear they didn't value me the way I deserved based on my investment in them.

Charlie Fry: John and I eventually became partners in our own film production company, Crème, which was a mistake on my part, because John had a really, really bad reputation out there as a businessman, he had been notorious for not paying people and all this kind of stuff. My perspective was, being 3000 miles away in Florida, as long as I was getting what I needed for my girls, it wasn't my problem, which was naive. Because by getting involved with him, and unfortunately letting him control the money, things eventually started to fall apart in our relationship. The betrayal came with another star of mine, Kendra Jade, who was a newcomer to the porn business, a literal nobody from Connecticut. I'd gone to Jerry Springer's people, and successfully pitched them on a show covering a movie we'd done with Kendra for the entire hour. To get that kind of exposure for an adult film that introduced Kendra Jade was something you could have afforded to buy, certainly not a prime-time hour of T.V.

Well, John T. Bone decided behind my back and without my consultation or my approval, to convince Kendra it would be a good idea to seduce Jerry Springer — who was kind of a horn dog. John had sold the story ahead of time to the British tabloids, who had secretly set up cameras in the hotel room to catch him and Kendra in the act. So they essentially set up Jerry Springer, and that had several adverse impacts, for one, Jerry didn't know I wasn't involved because I was in business with John, so it put me on the outs with his camp. Moreover, it ended my relationship with John because I was furious and absolutely let him have it, and a further fall-out from that relationship ending was Jasmin was still making movies with John's company. So now you've got this opportunity for a rift to develop, where Jasmin is out in L.A. working with John every day, where they already have that director-actress relationship for him to play on, telling her every distrusting thing he can think of to put in her ear. And that ultimately led to her sticking with John, who ultimately proved to be what he is to her as well, and eventually we got back together, but it caused a lot of damage to our relationship. I think after she saw how he handled the whole Kendra-Springer debacle, she wanted out of their working relationship as badly and quickly, as I did mine with John.

Jasmin: Coincidently, the next day I had a photo shoot with another porn star, Tom Byron, who happened to co-own with another director named Rob Black a really hot film company called Extreme Associates. Also, amid the voicemails I had been getting from these fucking parasite P.I.s, there had been a few others on my machine hipping me to the fact that Rob Black was interested in working with me. Rob had even gone as far as having Gene Ross from *AVN Magazine* place a call, trying to make an introduction. That kind of courting was exactly what I needed at that time in my career, because its attention I definitely was NOT getting back at Crème, between John's obsession with Kendra, and her and Zoe's jealousy of my stardom. At the level of fame I'd attained by that point within the business, I truly and legitimately, I think, felt I needed to be in business with a company that placed my interests first, because I had worked my ass off to get to # 1. Kendra and Zoe were trying to jump the line, off my back, and I wasn't going to allow it. So at the shoot, I went ahead, did what I needed to do, and reached out to Tom to ask if he knew Rob. Once he explained they were business partners and he put me in touch with Rob. We began a dialogue over the phone about what I had in mind for my future, its extension beyond adult film, and he was very receptive, which gave me hope for the first time in a long time.

As May rolled on, the furor over the Kendra sex tape had also finally started to calm down a bit, and I was still seeing Keith. Earl was at this point living on a boat, and starting to shoot amateur porn, and in one of our only sane conversations that entire spring over a rare Sunday breakfast, I asked him what his long-term plans were, and he stated he'd intended to do porn for good. From that conversation, I realized Earl and I had very different ideals, and up to that point, I had held out this silly, false hope that he might change, but it was finally sinking into my head and heart that he never would. In any other circumstance, looking back in hindsight, I might have argued the intersection of my realizations about leaving John T. Bowen and Earl were coincidental, but I firmly believe more was at work here. It felt like a brighter sign of things to come, and since my faith in John, Earl and my manager Charlie had collectively dimmed by that point I felt I had little to lose.

With that in mind, near the end of May, my clandestine phone chats with Rob Black finally transitioned into our first face-to-face meeting at his company's offices to discuss my possible future with Extreme Associates. I was so nervous about the step I was taking that when walking into the courtyard of his office building, I thought I saw John T. Bowen sitting there waiting for me! I wasn't delusional, they just so looked frighteningly alike that I ran into another office and hid by a receptionist's desk until one of Rob's employees — some former Military Police Van Damage came and escorted me to Extreme's offices. It turned out the ghost of John was in fact some factory worker on his lunch break, but the incident is a reflection of how internally nervous with excitement I was at the prospect of getting away from Crème. Rob and his father were both at the meeting. They took me out to lunch, and proposed an offer that I almost couldn't afford to refuse: $8000 a month for one movie, which was twice what John had been paying me at my peak with Crème, plus a signing bonus of several thousand dollars. The deal clincher for me though was when Rob mentioned that he had a professional tie-in with NYC-based ECW Wrestling, which was the business I secretly was aiming to transition into as a way out of porn down the line. He'd even agreed to bring my hair and make-up artist Sean along, and said he'd put it in my contract! I also loved their company logo: Respect, We Don't Earn It, We Take It.

I left the meeting floating on air, Rob had been the best salesman I'd ever dealt with professionally, and he'd given me every assurance I needed to hear that things would be strikingly different if I defected to Extreme. Even though I technically had 6 months left on my contract with John T. Bowen and Crème, because he'd bounced a check, he was technically in breach, which allowed me to leave him early, so that became my plan. I kept all of this to myself, and Rob and everyone at Extreme made sure no details of our first meeting slipped out, which is a lot more than I can say for Crème. Everything there had become so unorganized and dysfunctional by that point with the Kendra/Springer sex scandal, that truthfully, no one would have picked up on anything anyway where I was concerned. The final straw that had broken the camel's back between John and I had already come though with the day that P.I. had shown up at my residence...that was my fucking home, and you just can't do that. I know some adult film actresses who live that way 24/7, to where they go to the grocery store or the gym looking like porn stars, and want the attention. And maybe their acting like that would allow them to bring stalking upon themselves, but I was very much the opposite way off-screen. So by that point it was obvious to me — between John's mishandling of the Kendra debacle, bouncing my checks or not having them at all, and a whole host of other incidents — that his respect for me had dwindled to almost zero. Most importantly, John had lost sight of the fact that it was my ass and my pussy that was paying for that fucking place, NOT Kendra or Zoe's. They were going to have to start pulling their weight soon enough, because heading into the summer, I was on my way out of Crème.

I did my last movie for Crème in June with Dave Hardman, and my affair with Keith was starting to taper off, and stupidly (I know, readers)

I decided to give Earl one more chance. He was in support of my leaving Crème for Extreme, who had even given me contracts to sign by that point, and wanted me to attend the VSDA show in July to announce my debut as their new top star. I had done some other shopping around as well- meeting with Evil Angel, another big adult film outfit, and with a few others, but ended up deciding on Extreme because of the wrestling tie-in and the monetary stability. I hadn't yet told Charlie about my move to Rob's fold, even upon signing the papers, because his interests were so co-mingled with John's that John would have found out immediately and tried to stop it. Charlie needed me to advance Kendra and Zoe's careers, where for instance he'd use my bookings to muscle the door open for them, and hadn't shared any of his commissions from their feature dance tours with me. That was probably the last straw for me with him, so in early July, for the first time in my career, I also started taking bookings from competing promoters — The Lee Network, and another from Continental bookings. Both of these firms were getting me just as well paid as Charlie had, and I never once had to worry about collecting my earnings. So I offered Charlie the option of staying on as my manager for a reduced commission base of 15%, and he naturally declined. As a result, I formally and finally (so I thought) fired him that same month, and upon signing with Rob Black, was scheduled for my first shoot with Extreme in August.

Even prior to that though, I attended the VSDA show in Vegas with Extreme's camp, it was my public debut signing at their booth, and everyone's reaction was one of 'HOLY SHIT!' My line at Extreme's booth was HUGE, a thousand people at least, and John T. Bowen's company Crème DIDN'T EVEN HAVE a booth of their own that year! They didn't even attend, and were getting smaller and smaller. The fact that they didn't even pay for a booth — which would have been a MUST had I still been in their camp and attended — showed me how much smaller now they had already shrunk since my departure. Once news got out to the public and adult film press at the VSDA show, it made even a bigger impact! I was told afterward that when John got word of my defection to Extreme, he acted like a family member died, and then Kendra and Zoe tried to spin things in their media reactions as though they'd conspired to force me out, which was laughable.

Consider Kendra's comments to one reporter following my departure in November, 1998, claiming I had been spreading rumors about her having STDs — which, for the record, is a FUCKING LIE — to which she replied in the press at the time:

'If you have the guts to back up your lies, I will rent a gym and fight you in the ring to shut your stupid lying mouth once and for all. I would like nothing better than to smash your stupid plastic nose out the back of your stupid plastic head. Your choice, gloves, bare knuckles, or baseball bats, either way you are going down. Put up or shut up, skank!... What was that white shit coming out of her (Jasmin's) pussy in Blow It Out Your Ass? *I would be more than willing to make my medical records public. I'd like her to do the same. I've never gotten any STD. I hate her. She's a cunt. I challenge her to a fight... I can't wait until the day I see her. She will meet up with me and we'll see how much she runs her mouth then... If she's so happy with Rob Black, why doesn't she just leave our company alone?'*

For the record, I wanted nothing more than to leave that cesspool, but they kept trying to keep the feud alive in the press, still trying to coattail my success as always. Anyway, Kendra was right about one thing, Rob and Extreme were running a very professional show, they flew me and Earl there first-class, and Rob had even put Earl on his payroll so he could be more than just my suitcase pimp. That definitely made things better for Earl and me personally, and he also went on the road with me for my dance gigs that month, so we traveled through upstate New York, then New York City, and everything went extremely well. Many of my fans who showed up for signings during my dance tour told me how happy they all were to hear I'd parted company with Crème and John T. Bone, which made me feel reassured in my decision. Also, a lot of my peers were pretty supportive of what I did. Adult film media like Hustler Magazine and others were supportive as well. It was very important to me that my friends supported my move, and my fans most importantly supported what I was doing. A lot of people thought it was a smart move.

When I got back to L.A., I took a few days off, and I felt stable in my life for the first time in months. Rob at that time was a good boss to me, and to no surprise, Charlie suddenly popped back up in August, wanting to mend fences and work together again. I had been featuring a lot without him, and he also had seen the steady downfall of John's company following my departure, so he knew to follow the talent and get out of there while he still could. I took advantage of that as well, and told him he had to cut my commission down to 15% from 25%, which I told him it had been at for way too long, which of course he went along with.

I shot my first film for Rob, called *The Pornographer*, and when we shot the box cover, he gave me my first $2000, and I had hit it off with one of the other Extreme senior stars, Ashlyn Gere, who I looked up to because she was beautiful and classy. It was much better to be around other stars, as opposed to up and comers trying to climb over me to the top. Also, the male talent was much better, and my first scene for *The Pornographer* was a double-penetration scene, with Luciano and Earl. Earl worked with me in a lot of my movies at Extreme, and believe it or not, we worked really well together, and got along better because of it. Then I had a few dialogue scenes to shoot with Rob, and then the box cover with Scott Preston, who did amazing photos. He didn't DO this Gonzo bullshit John had been doing with stupid fucking titles and crap box covers, and it was time to graduate out of that. While things were good for a bit between Earl and me, I remember some of the more fun times in our relationship at that point were the Sunday rides he took me on his Harley up and down Pacific Coast Highway.

When the fall began and September rolled around, Rob was getting me more and more press, and in interviews, more and more journalists were telling me how smart it was to leave John T. Bowen. Then I received the best news I had gotten in a long time: Rob introduced me to Bubba Ray Dudley from ECW Wrestling, who flew out to L.A. to meet with us and have a discussion about ECW doing something collaboratively with me. Paul Heyman, the owner of ECW had even talked to Rob directly about the Pay-Per-View special they had in mind in November for me to make my debut in. At the dinner, it even got as far as Paul talking about flying me out in later September to New York to shoot some promo video spots for the *November to Remember* PPV. It was like a serious wet dream come true!

The only downside was Earl had begun to drink again, mainly stemming from his depression over the amount of press I was getting comparative to his, that was really irking him. There was nothing I could do, I'd go to his AA meetings with him, but if I got recognized, it just made him more irritated. I'd even been supportive of his shooting his amateur porn films on his stupid boat. He'd actually gotten some kind of indie deal to shoot x number of films, largely based off his work with me, and as a favor to him I even shot a scene with him for his first film to help him get started. We shot the scene on his boat and it was fucking horrible. Deep down, I didn't want to have a pornographer boyfriend, but he looked good on my arm and that was that. He didn't seem to give a fuck what happened to me, but Charlie did, as he was back in my camp 100% and had cut all ties to John T. Bowen. I was happy we were friends again, and he put me right back to work, sending me up to Canada for a club tour at the end of September. My friend Sean came with me, because Earl and I were at a low point and I had asked him not to come. I had a blast in Montreal, they threw a big party for me, and I hooked up with a little fling named Kaleb — this local from Montreal. We started hanging out a lot in between my press and dancing gigs, and finally after a couple of days I was in bed with him having the best sex I'd had the whole year.

Its funny, because saying that probably makes you imagine me in one of my on-screen sex scenes, but to be honest people often ask me: do you have better sex on or off camera, and the honest answer is I don't remember much about the scenes on camera. All the great sex I've had in my life has been off camera, because it's more personal and I don't have some director telling me what to do. I'm smiling now thinking back about how amazing it was, and I've always wondered what happened to him because he was so handsome, and we had so much in common, and to top it all off, he was definitely the best sex I ever had. It was really therapeutic, because I just really needed someone at that point who treated me as me, and wasn't going to judge me or treat me like a 'stupid whore,' as Earl used to do. When I got back, I was floating on air, and throughout the rest of October, I did some photo shoots for Rob, and though I didn't have a scene that month, was paid my full $8000 just to hang out with the company. We were a tight-knit family, where at Crème I'd felt like a red-headed stepchild.

As November rolled around, I was preparing for my first wrestling pay-per-view with ECW, and even prior to that, I'd been asked to host my first 'New Jersey Metal Fest.' So back-to-back, I had two dreams come true for me in that professionally I was working in two of my favorite worlds: wrestling and metal. The metal fest gig had come about at the VSDA show that year, when the promoter Jack Koshick approach me and asked me to host. For me, it was a natural fit, and even though I know at first people just saw me as a porn star hosting a metal festival, but in truth, I grew up listening to Carcass, Cannibal Corpse, all the New York death metal. There were thousands of fans at the festival, and their reaction to me was great, which led to my getting a good deal of mainstream rock press, from *Spin Magazine*, *Revolver*, *Metal Maniacs*, etc. It was a fucking blast, I was partying with all the bands at the hotel, and everyone was puking out the windows all night, it was so fucking awesome! The highlight for me was introducing my favorite band of all time: SEPULTURA.

Right on the heels of that, following a scene I shot with Rick Majors for *House of Whores Pt. II*, I left for New York to prepare for the *November to Remember* ECW Pay-Per-View. I flew out for a few days early with the whole Extreme crew: Rob Black, Tom Byron, myself, and a couple others. We took a red-eye flight out, and when I arrived at L.A.X. to leave, I actually ran into Johnny Cochran, who was really nice, and then when I got on the plane, Macaulay Culkin was sitting in first class with us. I thought it would be really funny of one of the Extreme crew went over and gave him a business card, and Tom Byron actually went up to him and did so! Once we got into New York, we actually had dinner at Sparks Steak House, where A Mob Boss Paul Castellano had been gunned down in the mid-80s. After dinner, we went and visited all the porn shops in Times Square asking which of my films they had in stock, and every shop was sold out of all of my titles — every single one. So I really felt on top of the world, even ahead of the Pay-Per-View. We attended a pre-PPV party that ECW sponsored the night before the match, and I met the Dudley boys, who were ECW's tag-team members, as well Chris Chetti and Danny Doring, among a bunch of other wrestling-related personalities, and I felt like I instantly fit in.

When I woke up the next morning on the day of the match, I was so anxious with excitement I actually got a little scared. I sucked it up and headed up to the event, which took place on November 7th at the Asbury Park Convention Center in New Jersey. Upon arriving with Rob, Tom and everyone at the venue, I was escorted backstage to start prepping, and one of the first stars I was I met Spike Dudley, Tommy Dreamer and his girlfriend Francine, who was known in ECW's circle as the 'Queen of Extreme.' She taught me how to take my small bumps in the ring, and it was planned that I would take what was called a 'Stone Cold Stunner' from her once we were live in the ring. Basically, it was choreographed that she would put her hand around my neck, pull me down, and I had to do the movement of going down on my knees and falling back, and Spike and Bubba Dudley were helping me practice.

One funny thing I took note of right away about the wrestling culture that differed from that of adult film was the etiquette, such that when you come into a dressing room, you have to say hi to everyone and then excuse yourself. There wasn't as much socializing, and when you're through with your match, you thank your opponent back-stage and that's it. It's not as personal 'on-set,' but much more loyal and normal off-set, unlike porn, where so many of the actors and actresses live that way 24-7. For me personally, I enjoyed and appreciated that different right off the bat, and knew this was definitely the next profession I wanted to seriously pursue.

Once the event actually started, you could hear the crowd thundering with applause from backstage, and when it was my turn to go out to the ring, I got this huge adrenaline rush as soon as I hit the floor. When I stepped into the ring, the plan was for me to announce to the crowd that I was the new 'Queen of Extreme.' Essentially challenging Francine for her title, so I gave my rap to the crowd: 'My name is Jasmin St. Claire and I'm the new Queen of Extreme,' and everyone was cheering and cheering. Then all of a sudden, Francine appeared out of nowhere and gave me the stunner, and then I was carried out of the ring. I'd been told to act like I was injured, which I did, and everything went off without a hitch. I really enjoyed the adrenaline rush that I had as I entered the ring and just the whole atmosphere of the crowd, and enthusiasm and warm welcome I got. I knew that this was for me, and that I wanted OUT of porn altogether.

Dominic Accara: After Jasmin left John T. Bone and signed on with Rob Black at Extreme Associates, those two fast developed what was very much a love/hate relationship. Jasmin, whether Rob wanted to admit it or not, was the biggest draw in his company — yes, Lizzy Borden was his wife, and did good scenes — but Jasmin was it.

Jasmin: After the match, I was escorted backstage, and Bubba took down my information, gave me some commemorative T-shirts, and told me they wanted me to come in on a more regular basis. I gave them my contact information privately, because I wasn't sure what Rob would and wouldn't have been supportive of at that point. That uncertainty on my part grew in part out of the fact that, as odd as some of the characters were at the PPV that night, the two most suspicious had Rob Black and Tom Byron. After we'd left the match, both of them kept asking me all sorts of strange detail-oriented questions about how things ran backstage, who did what, basically a whole run-down on Paul Heyman/ECW's operation. I got a bad vibe from the whole thing, but was in the same time appreciative and grateful for their getting my foot in the door to begin with. I tried to be cool about it and said I had been watching the PPV and not paying too much attention. Anyway, when we arrived back to L.A., my suspicions were further confirmed that they were up to something when Rob asked me to come into the Extreme offices to sit down and talk in more detail about how things ran backstage at ECW.

I went in to meet with Rob on a Monday, and the first thing he did to set off flares in my head was to pay me at the top of the week, instead of on Friday, our usual routine. So next he asked me, 'How did they run things backstage at the PPV?' And from then on, every suspicion I had that he was up to no good was confirmed. Here I thought Rob had flown me to New York with my interests in mind, when he'd really had his own agenda the whole time. They asked me so many questions too: who was where? What did they do? What was the order of command: who was running what? And again, I told him the same thing about being focused on the PPV and not paying too much attention, and kept my mouth shut. On top of that, when I saw Earl after arriving home, he told me he hadn't even watched the match because he'd been off shooting his amateur porn videos on his stupid boat. I knew he was never going anywhere in his life, and finally found myself standing outside looking in and shaking my head at the situation, and knowing the end was coming with Earl.

As 1998 came to a close, we'd received word from the Brazilian distributor that they wanted me to fly to Brazil for a high-profile appearance. Also, although I didn't have a movie to shoot that month, I was busy getting ready for the annual CES show in January, but amid all that, I'd had ECW following up with Rob about my doing more work for ECW, and there had been no progress. In the same time, when I overheard Rob at the office one day talking about starting HIS OWN wrestling company, I finally was validated in my suspicions of his actions following the *November to Remember* PPV. He never had had any intention of my wrestling with ECW past that one-off spy trip he'd used me to go on. The whole time, he and Tom had been studying Paul Heyman's business model with every intention of cloning it in the form of their own outfit, and their big star to get the whole thing launched: yep, you guessed it, yours truly! Once again, those managing my affairs were using my name to make themselves money outside of and in addition to what I'd signed up to be involved with business-wise. It wasn't right, and it was the very reason I'd fired Charlie and left John T. Bowen and Crème the summer prior, and here it looked like the plan was to do it to me again.

I left the office and immediately called Bubba over at ECW. I told him I was very interested in continuing to work with them, and he replied by telling me A) the feeling was mutual. They even had a regular routine in mind for me and Francine, the 'Queen of Extreme,' to carry on our mock rivalry in the ring and B) they had been in touch with Rob to that end with no reply. It looked as though Rob had trapped me contractually into a corner with this 'Related Projects' clause in our agreement. When I called my manager Charlie to tell him about it, I found out he was in cahoots on the whole thing. When he replied, 'We're making more money off the Rob Black stuff; I don't think we should make a big deal about it, especially if Rob's going to have his own wrestling outfit.' When I hung up the phone that night, I felt like I suddenly got an attack of claustrophobia, the same way I had when I'd been at the end with John T. Bowen and knew I needed to leave, but didn't yet know how. I couldn't count on Rob or Tom, or my manager Charlie, and to top it off, Earl kicked off the holidays by leaving me out in the cold in the barrio while he was off scoring crystal meth in the ghetto. He made it up to me by taking me up to Montana for the holidays to meet his family, which gave me some sense of temporary faith in our relationship.

I met his father and his grandmother, and they were both really nice people, and Earl was on his best behavior. He didn't get fucked up, and was a gentleman, so that was a pleasant change for us. It was almost like he was someone else though, not Earl. We went to the Red Mountain Lodge, which was cool, and then I went to New York by myself for Christmas to see my mom. I think by that point, she had begun to have suspicions about what I was doing because my cousins were telling her they'd seen me on TV and heard me on the radio. That pissed me off because I've never — to date — really exposed my mother to that aspect of my life, there's no need to. It was crazy that I couldn't tell my mom anything about what was going on in my life, and at that point, she was the only person I had left. In my own sick way I think I was hoping that Earl would be another part of my life at some point — outside of adult film — but as each day went on, I realized it never was going to happen. Our best days were usually Sundays, where we'd go to breakfast together, then attend his AA meeting, and then take a bike ride up and down the PCH, and those good times were fading as time went on.

Looking to the new year, wrestling was my life's passion now, it was something I really wanted to do, but I knew it wasn't going to come easily to me, and especially not because of Rob Black. It was my turn to get out there to do something for myself. I made it my resolution for 1999 to get out of the business, get rid of Rob, Charlie, and move on from Earl — who left me to walk home from St. Marks at 2:30 in the morning because Earl was too drunk to drive us home. I was astonished by his behavior, but like an idiot, I stayed with him, even as I resolved to progress with my plans to leave porn behind me in the New Year. On another level entirely, I couldn't live anymore with my mom possibly knowing all this shit was going on, but I knew we could both live with wrestling, and I knew most importantly within that year that it all had to be accomplished.

PART XIII

The End of an Error

I started off January preparing for the forthcoming CES show, my first with Extreme since I'd left Crème, and I guess that first cycle of my life in adult film had come full circle, because I ran into none other than John T. Bowen and his wife at Extreme's booth. It was the first time we'd seen each other since I'd left the previous summer, and not surprisingly, he was very cold to me, and wouldn't say anything. Then John's wife stormed up to Lizzie, Rob Black's girlfriend and an Extreme executive, and yelled 'You people stole Jasmin from us, you stole Jasmin!' She threw a bottle of water at Rob, it was a nasty scene, and in my defense, I kept my mouth shut when I could have told John's wife, 'Yeah, well your husband was fucking around on you with Kendra!' I should have though; I probably would have been doing her a favor. I was happy to find out years later that she'd since left John, got a real estate license, and was doing really well, and have no hard feelings toward her now. At the show though, John's wife's anger was really a reflection of how big a star I had become since leaving Crème. Especially after the Pay-Per-View, because in addition to how busy my booth was the whole show, at the awards ceremony, we won 'Funniest Movie of the Year' for *The Pornographer*.

Everyone in the press at the show hammered me with questions trying to confirm I had future wrestling plans, and Rob told everyone generically that there definitely would be. Obviously he kept it generic so he wouldn't let word slip about the wrestling company he and Tom were quietly planning to debut later in the year, with guess who as their main attraction. There was some humorous tension that week among the Extreme camp because I was getting invited to bigger and bigger places and parties that Rob and Tom weren't. So my friend Sean and I went, along — of course — with Earl, who had to tag along everywhere I went. Earl was getting more and more work from Rob Black, and it was done as a favor to me, because he was my boyfriend, and he knew by being on my arm, the adult film press would give him substantially more coverage. Looking back on it now, Earl — in the porn world — was at that time a lot like K-FED was to Britney, because I was essentially a pop porn star by that point. It was a designation that only Jenna and I really held, and Earl knew how to ride my coattails. The only party everyone was invited to was the one Extreme threw for me at a ritzy Vegas club, and it was PACKED. It was my second year in a row, and my Billboard was even bigger that year. Professionally, I was just riding a wave that I hoped would eventually carry me to the next level of fame as a wrestler and retired porn star.

On Super Bowl Sunday weekend, I had a competing booking in Miami, which was a $7000 payday, and Rob had inadvertently scheduled me that same weekend for a trip to Brazil to promote for my distributor down there, which I couldn't afford to make. I had also pre-booked a vacation after the Miami gig to go to Acapulco and I had pre-paid a $1000 airline ticket for. So Rob and Charlie had replaced me with some low-end porn girl for the Brazil trip. The night before she was supposed to leave, I got a call from Rob at 3 in the morning telling me she had conveniently lost her passport and couldn't get a Brazilian visa. I thought it was bullshit, and that the Brazilian distributor had raised enough of a ruckus about my not coming, they finally caved and promised I'd be there. That is just my hunch, but by that point, everything with Rob was suspect. So sure enough, the next morning I get a knock on my door from one of Rob's assistants telling me we had to rush over to the Brazilian embassy to get my visa. Anyway, Charlie convinced me that the Brazilian trip was important enough to Rob's broader distribution structure down in South America that I agreed to bail him out and go. Little did they know I had (and still do have) a Brazilian passport as well, and could have just used that. I really needed a vacation away from everything and some ME time.

Charlie re-scheduled my Miami booking and the girl they got to go in my place made $1000, which was a considerable price cut, which was a huge relief for me. Anyway, everything was rushed getting ready for the flight, from the visa to my packing, and I just made the first flight to Houston, only to find out upon arrival there that my flight to San Paulo had been cancelled due to a pilots' strike. That news came as no surprise since the entire whole trip had been a debacle from the start. I lucked out with a really sweet airline employee who upgraded me to First Class for the remainder of my flights, rescheduled me out of Dallas to Miami, then to San Paulo. My therapy to deal with the huge mess this entire trip had been thus far to get completely shit-faced on the flight down. I arrived in Brazil on the day of the big promotional party I was the star of, had no prep time to get ready upon touching down, so I actually did my hair and make-up myself in the airplane restroom. I jumped off the plane into the waiting limo, and headed straight to the gig.

When we got to the gig, there was a HUGE line of cheering people waiting outside the club to see me. When I actually got inside, forget about it. The place was packed. I guess Rob had pre-booked Earl to be down there for another part of the company promotional plans, so I just ignored and walked right past him without saying a word. Anyway, I was already drunk and continuing on with that party throughout the night, to the point where I guess they told me later that a bouncer had to take me into a shower in the back of the club to wake me up. Then Earl left with me slung over his shoulder to head back to the hotel. I woke up with a horrible hangover and had a shoot to do for Hustler, which I got through solely based on my professionalism. The rest of my trip consisted of a bunch of similar promotional events, plus a couple of scenes they wanted me to shoot in Brazil, only I refused to work with any of the local male talent, due to the horrible health regulations, etc. Thankfully, Tom Byron was down there, so I agreed to do the shoot with him in Rio, which I left for after a few days in San Paulo. Before we'd left, I'd also done an appearance on the *Jo Suarez Show* AGAIN.

Rio was a big improvement, first because the hotel they booked me into was right on the beach, the Marisol Hotel, and it was beautiful. I went to the beach, and to punish Rob a little for dragging me away from my vacation, I bought a mini-wardrobe on his dime. It was fun too because I was a pretty recognizable star by that point in Brazil, and was treated accordingly by the locals. Every guy I ran into down there was pretty hot, and my scenes with Tom Byron went well, so the only real torpedo that could have slammed into- and ruined- my good time at that point was Earl, and of course, that's exactly what happened. On one of the last nights we were in Rio, he'd been out drinking and partying at the local whorehouses and showed up drunk at my hotel room door in the middle of the night. He had started throwing shit at me in a drunken rage when I'd rightfully given him trouble for his behavior. I was so scared that I ended up calling Rob's room in the middle of the night, and he had me stay in the extra bed in Tom's room.

When we got back to the states, in later February, I shot another movie for Extreme called *Sluts, Butts and Housewives,* which I shot with Earl and Luciano. The most memorable part of making that movie was the continual embarrassment Earl was causing — based this time on the news that had gotten around to everyone — including me — that he was injecting his cock with a liquid form of Viagra to keep it erect during his sex scenes. After his behavior in Brazil, coupled with this revelation, I had a strong feeling that he was going to fuck things up for me professionally if this went on much longer, and so I made a definitive decision that I would end the relationship in the near future.

Throughout the rest of the spring, Extreme released a compilation called *Extremely Yours, Jasmin,* and I took a vacation to Mexico, and then headed to New York for some feature dance gigs. In the course of that trip, I spoke to ECW Wrestling again, and found out they had been trying to contact me about coming back to do another PPV, but that Rob Black had been blocking access to me. I didn't raise too much ruckus about it at that point because things were still going relatively well with Extreme, and I didn't want to fuck that up. In April, I shot another new movie called *Acid Sex*, which featured me in 2 scenes with Tom Byron and Earl, who Rob had decided to give a last chance to at my request. I also followed up with Charlie about ECW, and he shot it down with the typical Extreme party line, 'We've got something better planned for you.' I also had another trip to New York that week, and ran into my old friend 'Sickie,' who I'd lost touch with years earlier when I'd first moved to L.A. I had brought Earl with me — for the last time — on a road gig, and of course, he let me down and acted like a total alcoholic loser the whole time, and our relationship was really in its waning days by that point.

Later in May, I shot another movie for Extreme called *Inheritance* that co-starred Ashlyn Gere where I played her younger sister. The plot involved two sisters who conned guys, killed them and then took their money. That was one of a bunch of my movies that got edited down and sold to Playboy and Hustler's T.V. channels, which had come from my deal with Extreme. One of the many things I hadn't had with John T. Bone, so I was trying not to rock the boat yet with Rob. Still, by this point he had started becoming more vocal within the company about his plans to start his own wrestling company, starring his porn actresses along with former ECW wrestlers he planned to hire. His basic plan, confirming my suspicion following the ECW PPV the previous year, was to clone ECW's model of operation and become the west coast equivalent.

At the beginning of June, I had a routine dance gig to do in Connecticut and attended Ozzfest while I was back East, which took an unexpected turn when I met the drummer from Slayer, Paul Bostaph. Things with Earl were finally on their last leg, so I had no problem exchanging numbers with Paul, and he even came to hang out with me at my last dance gig on that week of bookings. I was quite happy about that, and really looking forward to getting to know him better as time went on. As the summer rolled along, I traveled to Brazil in July for the big Sex Expo and they had a booth there I was going to be signing at with Ashlyn Gere. Rob brought his waste-of-space girlfriend Lizzie, along with Tom Byron, Earl, and a couple others, but I my mind was elsewhere the whole flight in, thinking about the scene I was going to shoot with this HOT Brazilian guy Christian I had met briefly on the last trip. I had thought he was really hot, and once I got wind of the fact that Earl was trying to hide his dick injections in another of our party, Tom Conneley's, hotel fridge, that was my last straw. Apparently it was as well for others at Extreme who had tolerated Earl up to that point, including Tom Byron, who gave him shit for being a drunken embarrassment when we all went out to dinner the first night, as well as Rob and others at our table.

Earl's answer was to storm out loudly and unapologetically off to a whorehouse near the hotel pissing everyone off and embarrassing everyone at the table. I can safely say — looking back on it now — that my feelings for him at that point had disintegrated entirely into hatred, so I took the moment as an opening to pack his shit, leave it at the front desk, and get my room key switched. I next called Rob and I wanted Earl out of my life entirely, which meant asking Extreme not to give him any more work — especially with me! Rob explained he had no problem with that given I was the SOLE reason they'd hired the douche bag to begin with. Since Rob had given him all of his scenes as a favor to me to begin with, it was an easy excuse for Extreme to dump him now that I had. On top of all that, to really rub his face in shit, the next day I shot that scene with Christian Wave, and it was amazing. I let him fuck Earl entirely out of my mind, body, spirit and soul, and it was exactly what I needed. I enjoyed myself so much that I decided to continue the party and invited him to stay in my room that night, and it was exactly what I needed, and Earl and I weren't talking at all at this point. They ended up sending Earl home early.

Waking up refreshed the next day, which was also the start of the convention, my ego was really boosted by the number of fans who turned out at my booth signing. I was there for 3 days, and there were several thousand people there to see me, and so I wound up enjoying this Brazil trip A LOT more than the first one, most notably because of Earl's absence for the balance of the Expo. Having that contrast was the equivalent of an epiphany for me that my love life — and life in general — would be much healthier without Earl. Even though I was working, the trip felt more like a vacation — all on Rob's dime: I shopped, went clubbing at night, and even started using my Portuguese, my 2nd language. Christian and I had a long goodbye before I left back for the States, and I even told him he could stay with me if he ever decided to visit L.A. I was just so relieved to have gotten rid of Earl, and knew in my heart that our break was a permanent one this time.

That August, I took everyone from Extreme with me to Ozzfest. We all hung out backstage, and it was a lot of fun with the exception of Rob Black's ego, which was inflating out of control by the day because he'd finally publicly announced his first XPW Wrestling show for later in that month. He had gone so far in copying ECW's blueprint that he actually hired ex-ECW wrestlers to work for XPW, it was shameless. He would even have these guys imitate ECW characters, and was even trying to hire wrestlers still actively under contract to Paul Heyman at ECW away. It was totally unethical, and at first, I wanted nothing whatsoever to do with it. Thankfully, I was already booked to host the Milwaukee Metal Fest that year, so I had an excuse not to be at the debut show. They has me shoot promos before I left for the next show, and clearly Rob planned for me to be one of his main stars, as with the films, so I knew there was no way around participating in his wrestling venture, even though my heart was with ECW.

I had become friends with an ECW wrestler named Big Dick Dudley, who had been hired for the show, and he even stayed with me while he was in town working — on the couch, I might add, to clear up the rumor going around that we were fucking. He was more like a big brother to me; we had the same mischievous nature, and would pull pranks together on people at the gym all the time. Rob's ego kept growing further out of control as the fall went on. I was also becoming better friends with Paul Heyman, and keeping him in the loop on this — among others — because the one thing I definitely didn't want was to have even a remote impression on Paul's part that I was in co-hoots with Rob. I loved ECW, they had given me my start, and still wanted to work with me, and in hindsight it was a smart move on my part to show where my loyalties lied, because within the year, I would be working for Paul as one of ECW's wrestlers.

Personally, with Earl out of my life completely, things were getting more and more serious with Slayer drummer Paul Bostaph, and it was nice to be with someone who wasn't an abusive, dependant, alcoholic loser for a change. I was also focusing on my time off on wrestling training — which I paid for out of my own pocket because I felt Rob Black's 'school' wasn't good enough. I studied with Sue Sexton, who had worked in Pro Wrestling for years, been a champion, and was truly the best of the best. I was so committed that — even though she lived 2 hours from me — I still made the trip 3 times a week. Later in that month, my training was put to the test when I joined Rob's second XPW wrestling show at the Reseda Country Club, which seats about 1000 people. The crowd was at capacity, but only because of the XPW trade ticket of *papering* all of their shows, which involved giving away hundreds of free tickets just to make sure that they had a 'sold out' crowd.

The plan was to make it a big surprise when I entered the ring for the first time, so they sawed a hole in the ring floor, and had me pop up out of the floor. It was a huge adrenaline rush, and the crowd reaction was awesome, people recognized me both from adult film, but also from the ECW debut, which made me feel really validated professionally since it was the direction I was planning to head in. It all went over really well with the crowd, and I was a hit — competitively with Nicole Bass and Missy Hyatt, among other more established wrestlers there that night. I was really happy to be wrestling, but not that deep down below the surface of my elation, I was frustrated that I was making my transition into the profession with XPW and not ECW. Now that I had finally worked so hard to get to the point where I was at, I knew — much as I had near the end with Earl — that I wasn't going to have the future I dreamed of staying with Rob and Extreme. That night was pivotal because it truly marked the beginning of the end for my adult film career and association with XPW. I knew I wanted out, and set my mind to figuring out how quickly I could escape.

The next show of Rob's I appeared in was even worse than the first one. It was held in San Bernardino, and it was pathetic — there were maybe 50 paying customers in the whole audience, it was nothing. I was one of the main female stars in that show, but didn't feel I was getting the respect I would have at ECW because people saw Extreme as a 'porn-wrestling' company, and they should have for the most part because all of Rob's female stars were porn actresses. The only people who gave me any credibility were the ECW wrestlers Rob had working there, and his plagiarism of Paul Heyman's model was getting even more ridiculous and blatant. For instance, Rob had tag time called the 'West Side N@ggers,' which was horrible, and a clone of Paul's 'Original Gangsters.' It was just getting more and more tasteless.

After the first show, my manager Charlie had begun renegotiating my contract with Rob, which had really been the beginning of the end, because Rob had begun deducting $500 a week from what were supposed to be my $2000 paychecks, supposedly to recoup expenses from the Brazil trip. I felt he had no right to do so, as I had been on business for him, and in every single other case in my professional career, when I traveled to a dance booking or a signing or a festival hosting appearance, my travel expenses had always been paid. It was an industry norm, and the fact that Rob wasn't holding up his end of our agreement was another sign to me that things were going downhill with Extreme. The last straw was a day in October when I went to the office to pick up my check and though Rob's car was in the parking lot, he lied and had his secretary say he wasn't there. I'd earned more respect and given his company more profile than to be treated that way, and when I stormed out to the parking lot to leave, THERE HE WAS in his Mercedes trying to flee the scene. When I tried to confront him, he rolled up his windows and acted like he hadn't seen me!

Throughout this entire debacle, I had become better friends with Missy Hyatt who was known throughout the industry as the 'First Lady of Wrestling.' she worked for Rob Black as well, but had been the original diva of wrestling. I had been having a great time with Paul, but knew it wouldn't last because of my work, and I understood that, I totally understood that. We had a great time together, but in the end he just wasn't for me, but I wished him the best. He's one of the most talented drummers out there. Anyway, Missy set me up with a wrestler from the WCW named Billy Kidman, and I needed the good time. We went out for sushi, got shit-faced together, had a blast back at his hotel, and it was a nice booty call, but I wasn't really interested in seeing him again. Then Damien Steel started making moves on me, and I went for it. He'd told me he was leaving his wife, and so we began spending more time together, until he had me over to his house while his wife was out of town. I thought that was really sleazy on both our parts, and he had a really small dick anyway, so I didn't have any faith in that relationship lasting past the fling-phase. After just coming off of Earl and then Paul, I wasn't really looking to start any new long-term relationships at that point — unless it was with ECW.

In late October, I had another wrestling event for XPW at the Reseda Country Club, and didn't want to go, but was trying to be a team player while I figured out my next move, and most importantly, I attended because of my love for the sport. Rob Black must have picked up on the fact that this was a last chance of sorts for him because he gave me a lot more in-the-ring interaction with the wrestlers than he had in past shows. He also had hired more legitimate wrestling personalities, rather than just stocking the ring with his porn actresses. I hadn't done a movie for Rob since the last Brazil trip, so I was beginning to consider myself retired, regardless of what anyone else thought. Anyway, the show went off really well, and I worked a lot with Nicole Bass, but again, the story lines for Rob's show were almost carbon copies of Paul Heyman's at ECW. Also, Rob's ego was getting bigger and bigger, along with his stomach, as each day passed, and to not think anyone would notice his ripping off of Paul's ideas was just foolish.

As November began, I had some dance engagements in New York, and hired Big Dick Dudley to roadie for me, as we were becoming closer friends by that point. During that trip, I confided in him about my unhappiness with XPW and even he — who still worked for Rob Black — told me I was better off without Extreme and XPW and that I belonged in a bigger and better arena — not Rob's silly little country club. Rob's promises had become almost entirely hollow to me by this point as well, 'We're going to do this movie and that movie,' it was all bullshit. Even Ashlyn Gere had begun growing tired of Rob's empty promises. I shot what would be my last movie for Rob in November, *LA 399*, with Evan Stone, who was hot and had a big dick. Luciano, Herschel Savage and

Tom Byron were all in it as well, and though I hate to give Rob any credit, it was definitely one of my favorite movies I did for Extreme. It had a lot of comedy, and was hysterical, but not nearly as funny as Rob's next suggestion for my career trajectory: that I do a sophomore gang bang *IN THE WRESTLING RING!*

Not only was I offended on a personal level, but that he was that disrespectful of my desire to keep the two worlds separate — something I had voiced out loud to him MANY times over — let me know for certain that my time with Extreme was up. We'd had a good run, but it was time to move on, and I took a deep breath inside knowing I would start the new millennium free of porn and Rob Black forever. Professionally, I didn't want to make any more movies, I was tired of the business, and personally, I wanted to have a real relationship with someone and settle down. I could make enough money from my feature dance gigs and signings, and pursue a wrestling career without having to live with the stigma of being an adult film actress always cock-blocking my heart's happiness.

Dominic Accara: As she began exiting out of porn, in hindsight, I don't know if she regretted it or whether she just had had enough of all the bullshit that came along with being a porn star of her popularity. When she was done with it and reached that point, it began to hit her exactly what she'd done over the past 3 or 4 years. I don't know whether she regretted the fact that she didn't fully understand the full impact that doing as much of the type of porn that she did would have on her life. When you become a porn star it's exaggerated because she was more popular with a bigger name. The only thing people ever associate with you is fucking and you couple that with her having the background of being a little crazy and she could never really get away from that image. Even after she went onto wrestling and metal — especially because of the extreme nature of things like the gang bang. She'll still always be a sex symbol first and foremost, for better or worse.

Jasmin: In the course of my exit from adult film, I was looking to reconnect with some childhood boyfriends of mine, including Tommy and another ex of mine Damien, who to this day is one of the only men — aside from my father — who showed me how I should be treated by a man. I missed his friendship, and with Tommy I'd always wondered what would have happened had I stayed with him instead of Dick. I might not have ever gotten into adult film, and my life might have been totally different. But it wasn't meant to be, it wasn't the time, but looking back, I have fond memories of my time with both of them.

I spent Christmas of that year with my mom, who actually flew out to L.A., we had fun, did the tourist thing, and although people would recognize me when we were out, she still had no idea I was a just-retired porn star. She knew I was getting into the wrestling, and it was a huge relief to me that I didn't have to hide my celebrity from her anymore, because it was a success I wanted to be able to share in with her. That month, even though I was through with the film side of his business, I agreed to be a team player and do a couple final wrestling engagements with Rob's company. I got 3 sprained ribs because of Nicole Bass choke-slamming me and not letting me take my own bumps because she didn't know what the fuck she was doing. She told me much later on that Rob had paid her extra money to do that to me, my severance package from Extreme I suppose. He also paired me up against a former ECW wrestler named Chastity, but was giving his girlfriend Lizzy in all the story lines with real wrestlers, and putting me off to the side. He was alienating other wrestlers as well, putting BIG DICK DUDLEY up in a fucking Motel 6 for that December show, which in L.A. is often the equivalent of a crack-whore motel! I thought that was bullshit, came and got him, and let him stay at my place. That was just pathetic, and another example of why I was relieved to be on the way out — Rob could try to muscle me to the side at his little bullshit show, and he never realized how far ahead of him I already was.

I was fairly confident ECW would take me on in the new year because I had quietly been plotting that move for a couple months at this point. I even found out from Ashlyn Gere, Van Damage, IROC, and Tiffany Mynx that month that they're quitting Rob's company, which made me feel even more validated in my decision. Amid all of this, Charlie was still trying to get me to stay working in the business, suggesting I switch companies from Extreme to Metro, another big adult company. Even in those end-of-year conversations about my future, I kept emphasizing my desire to switch primarily to Wrestling, which Charlie replied to me by making the point that 'This needs to be money for me too.' I think that's what I needed to hear from him as well realize he was no more my ally than Rob had been. If I was going to make a truly clean break from this business and turn a new leaf in my life, it had to mean getting rid of all the garbage in my life — including Charlie.

I spent New Year's Eve at the Rainbow Bar and Grill with my friend Gina, and we wounded up partying with one of my favorite bands of all time, Lizzy Borden, in the upstairs lounge of the bar. We were doing blow, drinking our asses off, and it was awesome! I had an unapologetic blast, and woke up January 1st of 2000 with a new sense of freedom I hadn't felt in years.

PART XIIII

Reborn

As January — and the process of breaking away from Rob Black and Extreme — began, I had to get ready for the annual AVN Show in Las Vegas, which I still attended under the Extreme banner because of how much money the booth signing brought in for me- independent of Rob. I figure for all the money he had taken from me throughout the fall, I was due one final payday on his dime. Nicole Bass was at the booth signing alongside me, and in spite of the crowds we were drawing, Rob still had the gall to stick both Nicole and I, along with the rest of his flock, in some off-the-strip fleabag hotel. Thankfully, Charlie found one of our sponsors to put me up at the Luxor Hotel on the strip, and I hardly said two words to Rob at the show, hanging out instead with Edsel from the band Dope, and Ashlyn and her husband. Rob's brother was even so embarrassed by his actions that he chauffeured me from the hotel to the convention center and back each day. On his own dime!

For all of the disharmony among his ranks, it was obvious by that point to anyone looking, that Extreme's porn business had suffered financially from dumping so much money into the XPW, which was reflected in Rob's cheapening on everyone's accommodations that week. So the disenchantment among his employees was louder than ever at that year's show. It was clear I had made the right decision in leaving Rob, and the sooner it was known publicly the better. I had left that task to Charlie, who thankfully got a first-hand taste of Rob's Vince McMahon-sized ego at the show when Rob showed up dressed like a Rock Star/PIMP, in Gene Simmons leather rocker boots, an orange fur coat, and his requisite bad-ass sunglasses. He looked FUCKING ridiculous, and thankfully, Charlie was there to see what I'd been talking about first-hand. Moreover, Charlie — along with everyone else who worked for Rob — got to witness a huge fight between Ashlyn Gere and Rob Black that day which resulted in HER quitting as well! The fact that Rob had been outted so publicly as a deadbeat made it easy for me to leave after that without creating a further scene, and besides, he was taking care of that just fine on his own. After the fight, he went into a casino and threw away hundreds of dollars he could have been paying me, or Ashlyn, or Big Dick Dudley, or any of the other disgruntled employees he allegedly also owed money to at that point. It was an unforgivable slap in everyone's face as far as I was concerned.

The night of the AVN Awards show, Charlie had attended with me, and he was even so visibly disgusted with Rob's behavior by that point that at one point, he leaned over to me and said, 'Let's go do something better with you, you don't need to be here.' I still sat at the Extreme table that night to avoid making an unnecessary scene, but it was a relief to finally have Charlie 100% on my side about leaving Rob. I announced some stupid award for 'Best Boy/Girl Scene,' and the whole thing was a big fucking joke to me by that point anyway. When we got back to L.A., Charlie immediately — as in that very Monday — began speaking to Metro Video about my switching companies, which went against my wishes to leave porn entirely. I figured since he and I were going through the final motions of our own split anyway at that point, so I let it play out. The deal he wound up coming up with for me with Metro involved a scene they wanted me to shoot with a bunch of guys BUKAKKE (i.e. all cumming at once) all over my face, and I put a screeching halt to the deal, and said NO WAY. In addition to having 50 guys jerk off on my face — yummy, yummy, yummy — I would also get to be one of the hosts of Houston's gangbang, which was an insult. That Charlie couldn't seem to respect the fact that I didn't want that in my life anymore, let alone all over my face, to me was the same as him spitting in it himself. I told him more firmly and finally than I ever had prior to that moment that I was 100% through with porn, and by the end of March, he and I were also finished.

In February, Rob and I had our final kiss-off when at his next stupid XPW wrestling show he tried once again to persuade me to do a live gang bang in the ring! I thought he'd gotten the message when I'd said no the first time, but that he had the audacity to ask again was even more infuriating and offensive. I agreed to wrestle in the show only, and that's all he got. Looking back in hindsight at all the men I had to stand up to in my personal life, I take almost as silver lining the hell they put me through in terms of the spine it built up inside me by the time I departed from Rob and Charlie. The steel I had to flex in my resolve — both in and outside of the ring — in the course of showing people I was to be taken seriously about my career change from porn to wrestling was put to the absolute test with my exit. In part, I suppose the resistance from Rob and Charlie had to do with how big a star I still was in that business and the money they stood to lose by my exit. Rob wouldn't even pay me the money he owed me, telling me after the show and my refusal to do his stupid gang bang that he wouldn't pay me a dime till I shot more scenes for Extreme.

Being free of Rob Black once and for all was one of the best feelings I've ever had in my life, it was better than the best sex I had ever had — on or off screen — and gave me the first complete sense of self I'd had in my life. I was beholden to no one at that point, and what I was choosing to do took balls, because I was the first in the business to leave at the top of my game professionally. I could have opted to stay in front of the camera. Or I could have whored myself out to Rob entirely by going along with his fucking spit-in-the-face ring-gang-bang idea. I thought better of myself, and knew that if I was going to have any shot at making it in mainstream wrestling I needed to be 100% devoted to that pursuit. Rob's attempt to mix the two in the ring ran contrary to that goal on my part, and it felt good to know I had left Rob Black — and the business — on my own terms. Immediately thereafter, my first act as a free agent was to pick up the phone and make a call I'd been dreaming of making for more than a year, to Paul Heyman, owner of ECW Wrestling. Thankfully when I told him of my decision to leave porn and the desire to come work for ECW full time, he took me in with open arms. He'd say, 'We'd love to have you here, but need to figure out where we're going to fit you into the television program, but in the meantime, keep going to wrestling school.'

It made me feel so good that he encouraged me to keep training because I read it to mean he took me seriously as a wrestler. My working with ECW wouldn't be just a gimmick — it couldn't be — because the caliber of talent that Paul Heyman employed was a lot more established and regarded than any one Rob could attract. You couldn't walk into a ring at an ECW show and not know what you were doing. It was the total opposite of Rob's operation, and I welcomed the challenge. Throughout the spring, I continued my training 3 times a week with Sue Sexton, and did feature gigs on the weekends to sustain myself financially. I was also watching the WWF shows a lot more, and noticed that many of the women who were featured in the ring didn't know a thing about the sport of wrestling — athletically speaking — they had no training and couldn't be taken seriously. To reinforce my theory, I attended a WWF show held in L.A. in March where with the Dudley Boys, who I'd stayed in touch with after they'd gone to work there after leaving ECW. They arranged for me to meet backstage at the show with the talent coordinators, and the only spot they would offer me was to being a Ho for a character called The Godfather, where I'd walk him out to the ring with 5 or 6 other girls. Naturally, I turned that down flat, and its not that I expected them to stick me right in a live match, but I wanted to be a character in the story lines — for instance, a manager who walks the wrestler into the ring.

Anyway, attending the match proved to be a good networking opportunity for me, and I met some big wrestling stars, like Mick Foley and Chris Jericho. After the show, I went with a lot of the stars back to the Marriott Hotel bar to unwind, and I saw Damien Steel, who worked for Rob, sitting in a corner of the bar with a hooded sweatshirt on, spying on me! He had no business whatsoever, from a professional standpoint, being there, and lived locally, so that was the only explanation that made sense. Once I pointed him out to the WWF wrestlers, they all started looking at him like he was a stalker, and he got the hint and quietly left. Not long after the WWF event, Paul suggested I start working in the Memphis Championship Wrestling, a subsidiary of the WWE, which was like the minor leagues of professional wrestling where future stars go to train even more intensely than I could have locally in L.A. It was a prelude to my making a professional debut with ECW, and I knew Paul wouldn't have sent me there if he wasn't serious about taking me on as a full-time wrestler with ECW. I was training there a few days a week for free, and would work their shows in exchange for the free lessons, and Jerry Lawler ran the federation, so it was also an opportunity to build a rapport with him.

I also attended the March Metal Meltdown in New Jersey that month, which I'd been hired to host, and I wound up meeting the Blue Meanie there for the first real time, and we became fast friends, staying in close touch afterward. I was so stoked to see one of my favorite black metal bands too: DIMMU BORGIR. Amazingly, while I had been off doing my training and dance engagements, Rob had apparently not gotten the message that I was no longer working for him. I found out that in spite of my quitting his outfit completely two months earlier, he had gone ahead and booked that disgusting gang-bang scene in a wrestling ring, and told 8 of the male actors that I still intended to star in the film! This was even after word had gotten out within the industry that I had retired. I was livid and decided to get my final revenge on Robby no-showing him on the day of the shoot and I did it with class. I called each of the 8 male stars the night before the shoot, including some heavy hitters like Brandon Iron. I said, 'Look, it was really nice working with you in the past, and I hope I'm not costing you work, but I'm not going to be doing that gang-bang scene, please don't tell Rob anything.' So I apologized to everyone and did the right thing, and they were all really supportive, 'Good luck with everything,' and so forth. I guess a couple of the voicemails I'd left didn't get to a couple of the male actors in time, and when one showed up and saw the nasty skank they'd hired to replace me with, he got his shit and walked off the set. Rob was pissed, and of course tried to tell everyone he'd fired me, and of course stiffed me on the money he still owed me.

By early April, I was back down in Memphis with the Blue Meanie. The WWE had sent there to lose more weight, and I had been in contact with Continental and the other agency that booked my dance gigs to tell them I was 100% on my own, which felt really good. I did a big wrestling show that Jerry Lawler ran and right away, he put me in a story line with the Blue Meanie. Our teaming went over really well with the audience, and I guess word got back up the chain to Paul, because 3 weeks later, in early May, he brought me up to the pro ranks and made me a formal member of the ECW camp. He didn't give me any breaks either, because my first match for them was against an African-American female wrestler named Jazz who could wrestle like a guy. Francine, the 'Queen of Extreme,' you could tell right off, didn't like the fact that I was there. As I'd got to know the Blue Meanie and other ECW wrestlers better throughout the spring, I'd also learned that she was fucking one of the talent bookers at ECW, Tommy Dreamer, and was extremely jealous of new female talent. You could tell why too because she looked horrible up close, like the donkey from *Shrek*, and when my debut went over huge with the crowd, that couldn't have helped. It didn't matter after that though because the demand was there, and she couldn't argue with that. For instance, on ECW's website, they had a section called 'Perv Pics,' which wasn't nude photos or anything, just little bikini teaser pictures. Anyway, it got back to me that A) I was the site's most popularly downloaded pictures, and that B) that fact REALLY bothered Francine, who'd been Queen B before I arrived.

Anyway, the ECW Arena was packed with 2500 people that night, but I swear it sounded like there were 3000, and part of why was the audience hadn't expected me to come in the ring as a real wrestler, which I think I proved I was that night. I gave Jazz a clothesline in the ring, and then she got up and answered that with a bulldog, which involved her putting me in a headlock and dropping to her knees while I was slammed forward and POWERSLAMMED! Then with the second move, after I'd gotten back to my feet, she picked me up over her shoulders, dropped down on her butt and I went down on my back. It's funny to me, looking back now, when I hear people say 'Wrestling is all fake,' because while yes, the moves are choreographed, when you hit the mat, you hit it HARD! People, I suppose, have a right to be misled because a big part of being a wrestler is selling, making it seem like you got hurt really bad. You always have to get carried off stage, because that's part of the storyline, to make it look real in how it comes across to the crowd. There was a lot of wrestling press covering the show, and the Blue Meanie and I as a team went over really well. At the end of the night, we did some interviews, and then shot some promotional segments for the next week's television show.

I was happy to have the press, but it was important to me that I'd earned it, rather than being one of these divas from the WWE who just wants to be in front of the camera, and never gets physical in the ring. I was a manager of a wrestler, but I also participated as a wrestler in live matches. The night was a massive success, and I was particularly happy with the exposure it gave me coming right off my retirement from adult film, because ECW was not only a weekly national cable TV show, but also pay-per-view. My profile couldn't help but go up based on that fact alone, and naturally, I drew fans from my former profession, but also was delighted that I was making so many new ones via the ECW crowd, who really embraced me as a member of their camp. It was heartwarming to say the least, and I hadn't felt that way professionally in a long time.

After the show was over, Brian and I returned to Memphis, but only for a brief period because his Grandmother had taken ill back in Philadelphia, his home town, so he returned home to care for her. I was still based in L.A., but between my dance and signing engagements, training, and starring in the weekend ECW televised wrestling shows, I was very busy as well, and it worked perfectly for me to schedule my other bookings around ECW's television or Pay-Per-View engagements. It was like living an entirely different life overnight from what mine had been 6 months ago, and I tried to savor every minute of it, because I'd fought so long and hard to arrive, and things were really good. I was also making a little money from Paul Heyman, but a lot more was starting to come in from eBay selling my adult film memorabilia. Brian also had wrestling fans of his own, so he and I would team up for signings; we had a huge one in L.A. in May, and thereafter started doing A LOT of signings together at different conventions. We made a great team.

Whenever we weren't working on an ECW T.V. show, we also took a lot of indie bookings together, almost every weekend. Those weren't televised, but were still packed with fans. We'd get paid for those appearances, then on top of that, combine them with signings where I'd sell photos and clean up big time. As the spring turned to summer, I continued training during the weeks with a new trainer, Mando Gurrero, in L.A., and on the weekends, found myself taking A LOT more signings and a lot LESS dance engagements, which was a nice change of pace for me. I finally felt like I was starting to live a normal life, still with celebrity, and being able to pay my bills from signings, and not having to dance nude before a bunch of strange men.

It was still work: we traveled all over the place for our autograph engagements — Philadelphia, Michigan, Wisconsin, Florida, New York, New Jersey, Texas — everywhere. We were typically flown in, and though we had to cover our own hotel, I didn't have to pay anyone a commission off of the signings, and just in every way, things were looking better and better for me. It was also fun for me to be able to have my mom see me on T.V. each week with the wrestling show, and then some aunt of mine in Europe saw me on the cover of a wrestling magazine in a supermarket in London. I was grateful, devoted to my work, and appreciative of the fact that the fans were always there to support me — whether at the matches or my signings.

As June rolled around, and we had quite a few wrestling shows that month. Even though Francine was constantly trying to cut down my on-air time out of jealousy, fan demand kept me in the regular ECW rotation for the television and PPV shows. That same month, the Blue Meanie and I were booked to appear at the Milwaukee Metal Fest in Wisconsin, and what was unique about that festival was the promoter incorporated both Metal and Wrestling. We were booked for the wrestling show for 2 days straight. I had my big tag match ever, working with the Blue Meanie against Doink the Clown and Sheri Martel. She was amazing and I loved working with her. I'd always seen her on T.V. growing up, and I thought she was so cool and really admired and looked up to her, so it was quite an honor to work with her. The first time I met her after we'd arrived in Milwaukee, I really wasn't sure what to expect, but to my relief, when I walked into the dressing room, she was sitting there smoking a joint. Once she'd offered me a hit off her joint, I relaxed, and again, she was cool as fuck to me. She knew I was new to the business, and really went out of her way to make sure I felt comfortable. I loved being a part of this community, because it really was like one big family.

Brian, a.k.a. the Blue Meanie, and I were also getting closer at this point. He was flying out to L.A. a lot. We were kind of a couple at this point, where we were dating but it wasn't anything too serious. We were briefly involved romantically, but were really more like best friends who tried to have a relationship. I'm almost happier that it didn't work too because it allowed us to be that much closer as friends, and Brian was always with me. He's one of the nicest people I'd ever met, and he had drive and ambition, and we worked well together on a lot of important levels professionally and personally that allowed us to accomplish everything we eventually would together. That July, Brian and I had a big, mainstream signing to do in New Jersey for K&S Promotions, and maybe by fluke or fate — I believe the latter — I was reunited with my long-lost friend Sickie! I couldn't believe it when I ran into him, and he was hanging out with the Iron Sheik of all people. We became best friends again after being reunited, and it was like no time had passed.

In addition to my reunion with Sickie, I felt that particular signing was noteworthy because it marked a shift in the kinds of signings I was being offered, mainly because I was no longer associated with the dirty porn. That was slowly but surely moving into my past in the perceptions of others, and that was underscored by my last appearance on the Howard Stern Show. He'd asked me to fly in and appear on-air with Houston and Spontaneous Ecstasy to speak about gangbangs. I missed my flight due to some cancellation, but still did a call-in interview, and throughout the interview, I laid low and mostly let them argue amongst themselves, because I felt the whole thing was really stupid. I'll always be eternally grateful to Howard Stern for playing a big role in launching me into stardom, and being supportive of me throughout my career by having me on his show so many times, so my feelings were — and aren't to date — any reflection on him. It was more that I was just over it, and I was tempted right then and there to blow the whistle on the whole gang bang myth, but I didn't. I just kept thinking throughout the entire interview: why am I sitting here talking about this with these idiots, one of which was Houston. Once it was over, I knew I wouldn't do an interview like that again — no matter who offered it to me — because had I, it would have given off the wrong impression about my being finished with porn. Thankfully, wrestling gave me enough profile to not have to worry about it anymore.

As the summer steamed on, everything was going great: I was getting more and more indie bookings and mainstream signings in-between ECW events, and was becoming friends with more and more of the wrestlers. And even though I didn't have a thing to do with Rob Black's joke XPW league, I did keep in touch with Big Dick Dudley, who still wrestled for Rob, and he kept me in the loop on their camp. I was happy when he quit working for Rob in later that year in September. That August, ECW had a Pay-Per-View in L.A. called the *Heat Wave*, they had me shoot a promo for it on the beach with Sinister and Mikey Whipwreck, which opened the PPV. I also met for the first time a WCW wrestler working on the show named Gorgeous George, and boy was she gorgeous! She was very, very pretty, tall and beautiful, and you could right away tell that Francine did not like her. She was very nice, the opposite of Francine, I loved her. Francine ended up getting her fired in September out of jealousy, and I thought it was a real loss for the company.

The only downside of the ECW PPV was the presence of Rob Black's goon squad. It is not a cute little wrestling nickname for his team of scum fucks, most notably including Krysti Myst, who was sitting in the front row of the PPV and at one point, stood up and started flashing her tits to the audience. All I could think was, is he that desperate? It was rude, and our wrestlers responded to his squad by jumping them in a brawl that led out to the street, and Rob's whole crew — even Krysti — got their asses kicked! We beat the shit out of them, it even united me and Francine, who wanted to beat the shit out of her.

According to a recounting of the incident at Wikipedia.com, 'owner Rob Black purchased six front row tickets for the show. The tickets were given to a cadre of XPW talent, and their mission was to make it clear that

ECW was on enemy turf. This was not a storyline. At the beginning of the main event, the XPW contingent donned shirts emblazoned with the XPW logo, gaining the attention of security and ECW wrestler Tommy Dreamer. Security ejected the XPW group from the building and later, a brawl broke out in the parking lot between members of the XPW ring crew and the ECW locker room. The XPW wrestlers were not involved in the fracas, during which the ECW wrestlers brutalized the XPW ring crew with several of the ring crew members left in pools of their own blood. Initial reports claimed that XPW valet Kristi Myst had somehow touched ECW valet Francine Fournier and that this is what prompted the incident. Fournier herself has since gone on record as saying that she was never grabbed or in any way touched by any of the XPW crew, and other eye witnesses support the story that Fournier never had a hand laid on her. XPW were never mentioned by ECW announcer Joey Styles during the pay per view telecast. The XPW contingent who had sat a ringside consisted of wrestlers The Messiah, Kid Kaos, Supreme, Kristi Myst, Homeless Jimmy and XPW announcer Kris Kloss.'

Jasmin: There was no working relationship between XPW and ECW, they were rival companies, and the fact that Rob was that jealous was just pathetic. It was even sadder that Rob wasn't man enough to show up himself, and instead dispatched these minions to do his dirty work. Paul Heyman showed a lot of class I thought by not showing the disruption Rob had caused during the show, because even though it would have held great entertainment value, it would have also given Rob exactly the attention he'd been seeking when he sent them in to begin with. It was talked about for about a month afterward in the wrestling, and as the summer ended, things really couldn't have looked more up for me.

At the first big ECW show that September at the Hammerstein Ballroom in New York City, I ran into another ECW wrestler, Elektra, who was a manager at a strip club, a 'House Mom' as they called it, when she wasn't wrestling. We were friends, and she also consulted on casting for The Sopranos at their strip club, The Ba'Da Bing. She was really cool and I loved working with her. Anyway, she told me that the casting directors for the Sopranos had a role they were looking to cast that ended up being the stripper that Ralph gets pregnant and then beats to death in Season 3. I turned it down because she didn't tell me any of those specifics, and if I'd gotten it, I would have been on the show for five episodes! All she'd told me was that it was a generic stripper at the Bing. The Pay-Per-View at the Hammerstein was great, and the day before that we had a televised show that went over really well.

I continued with my usual routine of attending indie shows/signings in between my ECW matches, and though rumors had begun to swirl about financial troubles within the company — largely due to TNN's decision to cancel 'ECW on TNN' that month. Even still, everyone was so loyal and morale was still so high that the whole family kept momentum flowing into October. For instance, without naming any names, many of ECW's wrestlers were continuing to work the shows even though their pay had been cut, including myself. I had never been more committed to anything in my professional life. Still, being a businesswoman, I did decide to take a light look around and in talking to WCW, found out they were also having financial difficulties.

Anyway, I stayed working with Paul because he was the first to give me my chance — NOT ROB BLACK, or anyone else — PAUL HEYMAN and ECW were the ones who had put me on that map, and brought me back after I'd left Rob's shitty little joke of an operation. Rob wasn't anywhere near Paul's level either, because rumor had it that Vince McMahon, the kingpin of professional wrestling, was one of Paul's backers. Rob Black could never have commanded an audience with Vince, let alone a monetary investment. Vince's position was what it was, he was a living legend by that time, but the fact that he had enough respect for Paul's share of the wrestling marketplace to recognize it as legitimate is something he NEVER would have done with XPW. It was just two different levels. A lot of ECW wrestlers went up to Vince's major leagues. Others from WWF went to work for Paul — Vince and Paul always had a respectful working relationship, Rob Black never could have gotten in the same room as Vince, unless maybe he sent a spy in like he had at ECW. We did a Pay-Per-View that month in Minnesota at the Mall of America, which was a lot of fun.

Things briefly took a darker turn later in the month when the Blue Meanie and I got into a fistfight. He sent me to the hospital with 18 stitches. It was a week before a signing at the Allentown Convention Center, and we'd had an argument that was the culmination of his bitching continually 24-hours-a-day, 7-days-a week about his family taking money from him more so than he could afford. Anyway, he ended up head-butting me and pushing me down on the ground, with his mother watching, who of course did nothing. It was ugly, my forehead got cracked open, blood was shooting everywhere, which caused Brian to react by crying like a little bitch once he'd realized what he'd done. He didn't realize his own size, because he's like a big fucking monster, he looks like SHREK! I got up, gave him the finger, left and rushed off walking to the emergency room. Fortunately, when I arrived, the doctor who treated me recognized me as a wrestling fan from my work with ECW and stitched me up, and I was a wreck. I was crying, looked like Frankenstein, and had to go do my signing that weekend with everyone asking me what happened? Naturally, I made up a lie to cover his abuse — as I had with Dick in the past — and said I'd had an accident while Brian and I practiced some wrestling moves and hit my head. After that, things changed between us, we kept working together professionally, but personally he was a big, fat piece of shit to me. Eventually I forgave him for the sake of our professional partnership, but things weren't the same between us again personally in the aftermath.

I spent the holidays of that year with my mom in New York, and returned to L.A. in-between Thanksgiving and Christmas, and spent a lot of my time that month tending to my flourishing eBay business, where I sold everything from (photos to videos to worn outfits.) This meant I was able to do less dance engagements, and spend more time doing indie shows/signings, and training locally in L.A. when I wasn't in the ring. I was very appreciative for the fans that had come out to see me dance. Honestly, it was a tired routine. I'd go to these clubs where I'd spend all this time getting ready to hit the stage, and by the time I walked out of there at the end of the night, my clothes and hair smelled like smoke. The traveling was grueling; my sleep schedule would get fucked up from all the flying, so being able to tone down that part of my life was a nice change. I didn't necessarily have a problem with feature dancing, as I'd been doing it before porn even, and considered it an entirely different profession. I would still schedule a gig if we had a signing to attend, but I found myself more and more able to market to that fan base online without so much travel necessary, and loved the fact that the money was as good. I even made a New Year's resolution to stop feature dancing completely in 2001.

I was relieved to have the extra source of income with eBay, because the rumors about ECW's financial hardships had swirled into a whirlwind around the community of wrestlers and employees of the company. At that point, the cat was more or less out of the bag as their weekly TV show,

'ECW Hard Core TV,' would also aired its last episode on December 30th of that month. That was a great show, I stole most of Francine's thunder by taking a big fucking pile driver off the second rope from Rhino, which was pretty scary, but exhilarating at the same time. I knew I'd found my calling, and wasn't planning on going anywhere. Unfortunately, the same couldn't be said for ECW. Paul wasn't telling anyone too much, but we all knew the writing was on the wall, and while it was a sad time on one level, I was inspired on another out of my sheer love for the sport and desire to truly make my own mark on the business. I wanted to do something no one had ever achieved before in the male-dominated world of wrestling: Become its first legitimate female promoter. My official move in that direction wouldn't come until later in 2001, but the seed had been planted in my mind. I ended my year a long way from where I'd begun it, and knew that I was exactly where I wanted to be in my life, and I wasn't planning to leave anytime soon.

PART XV

Still Going Strong

In early January, I appeared on what we later found out would be ECW's final Pay-Per-View, 'Guilty As Charged,' which aired on January 7th, 2001 at the Hammerstein Ballroom in New York City. According to Wikipedia's accounts of the PPV's highlight matches; Bilvis Wesley defeated Mike Bell, Cyrus and Jerry Lynn defeated Christian York and Joey Matthews. Before the match, Da Baldies attacked Christian York and Joey Matthews; Danny Doring and Amish Road Kill defeated Hot Commodity (Julio Dinero and EZ Money) (w/Chris Hamrick, and Elektra) to retain the ECW Tag Team Championship. Nova defeated Chris Hamrick (w/Elektra); Tommy Dreamer defeated C.W. Anderson in an 'I Quit' match; The Unholy Alliance (Yoshihiro Tajiri and Mikey Whipwreck) (w/Sinister Minister) defeated Kid Kash and Super Crazy and The F.B.I. (Little Guido and Tony Mamaluke) (w/Sal E. Graziano) in a Three-Way Dance. Whipwreck and Tajiri pinned Guido with a Double Tiger Suplex to become #1 contenders to the ECW Tag Team Championship. Simon Diamond and Swinger (w/Dawn Marie, The Blue Boy, and Jasmin St. Claire) fought Balls Mahoney and Chilly Willy to a no-contest. The match ended after Rhino came out and attacked all four wrestlers. The Sandman defeated Steve Corino (w/Jack Victory) (c) and Justin Credible (w/Francine) in a Three-Way Tables, Ladders, Chairs and Canes match to win the ECW World Heavyweight Championship. Sandman grabbed the title to win the match. Rob Van Dam defeated Jerry Lynn (w/Cyrus); Van Dam pinned Lynn after a Van Terminator with Joel Gertner holding the steel chair; and Rhino defeated The Sandman to win the ECW World Heavyweight Championship.'

I knew the lights were going down on Broadway at that point because Francine had made a point of telling me at the final pay-per-view that there wasn't a need for me to come to any of ECW's house shows. She even went as far as to call me and Elektra up in January, trying to tell us not to come to the road show in Pinebrook, Arkansas, even though we'd been advertised for the show. Clearly, she knew attendance was going down and didn't want any other female star threatening what little spotlight she had left because she was a jealous bitch. Naturally, I showed up anyway. I had a big signing that weekend as well but I knew the writing was on the wall for my future with ECW. Thankfully, the Blue Meanie and I did among the wrestling community, and as a team, we continued our routine of independent wrestling shows and signings, which we built enough momentum from the previous year to continue without a hiccup. Brian had become a good friend to me at this point, even if we weren't romantically linked. We trusted each other, and shared the same love for wrestling, which was the most important thing in making our partnership work.

Regardless of whatever happened with ECW, Paul Heyman had created arguably the biggest independent wrestling company in the history of the sport, and Rob Black could NEVER even dream of coming close to hitting that mark. They were desperate to get any kind of affiliated press they could, even if it centered on pointing out the latter contrast between the levels the 2 camps were on. I know this because Rob Black's camp had continued to talk shit about ECW after we'd so publicly and completely humiliated them by kicking their asses out of the ECW Arena the previous fall. XPW's claims kept getting wilder and wilder than the craziest story line I could ever think up for one of my matches. I even heard that Rob's girlfriend Janet was talking shit about me, claiming she had to hold my hand when I did my in-the-ring scenes, and that I couldn't do anything for myself. I beg to differ, it was quite the opposite: I was probably one of the most independent women working in that business, and I didn't require anyone to help me with anything. She's just a dumb cunt trying to run her nasty lips, and what she didn't understand was: A) NO ONE in the wrestling or related media took Rob seriously, and B) All her shit talking did was gain me more press, which meant I was doing something right. The day they stop talking shit about me is the worst day ever. People have always loved to hate me, and that's good. I used it to my advantage in the ring because the fans LOVED it! They ate up the notoriety and the controversy, and Francine couldn't STAND it that I got so much love from that crowd, and Rob definitely had to HATE it! The bottom line was XPW had no street credibility. Just to underscore that point further, in February, Paul Heyman sold ECW to the WWF, something Rob could NEVER have pulled off, given how much smaller his little joke of a company was.

I was getting indie wrestling and dance bookings left and right, and amazingly, Francine and I kept working together at a lot of the signings, because promoters would book us together. I knew it was business, and went along with it, and I consistently outdrew her, which was an added bonus. She was really fucking snotty to fans at signings, and I told her she needed to stop or she wouldn't get the kind of signings we were, and I made sure that it didn't reflect on me by being as cool to fans as I'd always been. I had a lot more practice at that than Francine did, both because of the considerably larger size of my fan base due to my followings in both porn and wrestling, and she just never understood that fans are the reason she had any fame at all. I know that seems obvious, but not every celebrity sees it when they're living in their own little bubble, as Francine was. She didn't seem to realize that bubble was already leaking air and was about to burst.

At that same time, I was getting a lot of offers from other independent wrestling federations to come wrestle for them, but I felt guilty about talking to any of them seriously because none were interested in the Blue Meanie. One of those who'd called had been the XWF, which sounded like a legitimate operation and like something too good to pass up on. The event they wanted me to appear on wasn't until later in the summer, and I agreed to do it contingent on their also taking Brian along, which they agreed to. I felt like he and I were a team — both professionally in the ring, and personally in that we clicked so well as best friends, even though we weren't involved romantically, in spite of press reports at that time. It's how we spun it because it sounded better, and made Brian, a.k.a. the Blue Meanie and I appear more like a package deal to promoters, some of whom never would have been interested in booking Brian without me. The same extended to a lot of the signings we did and truthfully, many of our indie bookings as well. I was paid for each indie booking, plus I got to keep all the photo money I made from the wrestling fan signings, so I was absolutely the main bread winner in our dynamic. I felt bad for him as well because wrestling was all he knew, he had no experience earning money outside of that niche, so I did everything I could to help his profile stay afloat. In between gigs, I even paid him to roadie for me at dance gigs until the next indie booking came along. We'd get flown in for some shows, but for a lot of them, we'd get our hotel and gas money paid for. As happy as I was living my dream, Brian would get so depressed at times I felt like I had no choice. At times, when we were out on our endless road trips to and from gigs over the course of March and April, there were times when I would even wonder the inevitable question: did I do the right thing by giving up porn for wrestling? It's always 20/20 with hindsight, but I felt that I had done the right thing, so much so that another accomplishment for me that spring was shutting down my porn site completely, I didn't want a thing to do with it anymore. Unfortunately, the asshole who was hosting it for me didn't want to go along with it, so I had to battle this domain company to get it taken down offline. Eventually, they took the domain name away and gave it back to me since I'm the trademark owner of my professional name, Jasmin St. Claire.

I even tried out for the WWF that spring, but there were so many politics to that place, and because of my porn past, they were worried about how it would go over with mainstream wrestling fans. I thought that was bullshit, because I don't believe one's past should dictate their future, but apparently Vince McMahon did because I was passed up for a spot in their federation. Paul Heyman did everything he could to get me in the door. Everyone was really nice to me at my audition, all the female talent was really cool — a nice change of pace from Francine — even Vince was nice to my face, because he had to be. As nice as everyone was to me, as usual, Brian was treated like shit, they even kicked him out of the arena's backstage locker room, and I felt really bad for him, because the morale he had about his own self was lower than ever at that point. Thankfully, Jimmy Hart, who ran XWF — another wrestling league — had been in touch with me throughout the spring about coming to work for his company, whose first shows were scheduled for later that year. Brian and I continued our road shows throughout May, and my dance gigs and indie bookings carried us through the uncertainty wrestling was going through as a business as Vince McMahon continued to consolidate his chokehold on the industry. One thing I definitely took note of was the opening in the market for new indie blood in the way of Wrestling Federations, and quietly ideas were beginning to brew about starting my own company. Part of what first gave that idea was the fact that ex-ECW wrestlers who Vince hadn't picked up were even going over to Rob Black's company XPW to get work.

Heading into the summer of 2001, things between Brian and I were at a low personally because he'd thrown a public tantrum before an indie show in Indiana, which pissed me off. That's not how you behave, and I wasn't having it, even though the show itself went well. He was lucky that the wrestling community- especially on the indie circuit- is like one big extended family. For everyone to be like a family in porn would be incest, but in wrestling, because of the love I got, the promoters were willing to deal with Brian. It wasn't all his fault — the WWE was horrible to him, they'd made him lose all that weight, and then hadn't hired him back. I thought he was a talent, which is a large part of why I stuck with him, and without me, he absolutely would have been dead weight, professionally-speaking. Thankfully, things brightened that July when XWF sent me my contract to review, which was a big relief. I was eager to be hooked up again with a mainstay operation, and they had a television syndication deal in the works, so I happily signed on the dotted line. There was every reason in the world to feel confident too: they had a lot of money behind them, a wrestling legend in Jimmy Hart at the helm of the ship, and a great slogan: *'No more prima donnas, no more politics, in your face!'* The company was owned and operated by wrestlers, with partners including Brian Knob, Greg Valentine, Hulk Hogan, Rowdy Roddy Piper, Jerry Lawler, and a host of other wrestling legends I'd grown up on, so I was elated to be in their professional company.

I spent the balance of the summer training in prep for the XWF shows, and things were going well until September 11th, when the World Trade Center was attacked. I was in L.A. when it happened, and was freaking out all day as I tried to get in touch with my mother and friends, and luckily everyone was safe. Like everyone, I was in disbelief, but relieved my loved ones were okay. I shot a cover for a Cleopatra Records Limp Bizkit Tribute album the next day, and tried to go on, but as a New Yorker born and raised, it changed my sense of security. We returned to New York that October before the XWF shows, and you could still smell the smoke and burnt flesh in the air, it was horrible.

Even flying to Florida for my debut with the league in early November was eerie, but I was so excited about making my debut with XWF that I did my best to keep my mind on the positive. XWF paid for everything — airfare, hotel, and meals.

Preceding the show, XWF had something of a conference to introduce or in most cases re-introduce everyone to one another from all the different leagues Jimmy Hart had drawn his league's talent from. It felt good to be among the company I was in, because being in the presence of legends like Hulk Hogan and Rowdy Roddy Piper and Greg Valentine let me know I had created enough profile during my time with ECW to qualify as authentic with fans. That was the key, and it was part of my strategy throughout all the indie-circuit gigs I took as a team with the Blue Meanie. Building profile has always been one of my bedrock principles as a businesswoman, no matter whether I was in porn or wrestling or even now in metal. I always try to keep my finger to the pulse of what the next big thing could be, and this certainly felt like it had a shot at the time. They held the show and conference at Universal Studios in Orlando, Florida and paid everyone a lot of money to be there. They were well organized, and it was huge production. I spent down time hanging out with Gorgeous George and other girls formerly from the WCW, of course, there were plenty of haters. When Gorgeous George heard some jealous bitches making light of my porn past, she stood up for me and told them to shut the fuck up, that it was my past. I felt like I belonged, and the fact that my presence intimidated other female wrestlers let me know that George and I were the biggest female stars there.

We shot a bunch of promos at Universal Studios to promote the XWF debut and the first show was amazing! It was held at one of the Universal Studios' arenas, and the crowd turnout was huge, they even had pyrotechnics at the show! In the show, I was managing the South Philly Posse, who was a formerly known as the Public Enemy when he'd worked with ECW. The last day I was there, XWF had a big press conference, which was held in a wrestling ring, with the media set up around the ring. You could see that the hype was building, and as the final day of the trip concluded, I flew home with my spirits were raised as high. The plan had been to run shows every week, just like the WWF.

According to Wikipedia, 'The XWF taped more than ten hours of wrestling at Universal Studios, Orlando, Florida, of November 13 and 14, 2001. Primarily, these tapings were pilot episodes to show television executives in the hope of securing a major TV contract. The stage, lighting and overall production was considered to be of the highest quality, said to be like that of the World Wrestling Federation. While the XWF awaited finalization of a national television contract, the promotion also experimented with live arena shows, likely to enhance their pitch to television executives.'

When I landed back in L.A., while I was waiting on everything to follow-through with XWF, Brian was still staying with me, and I felt horrible that he hadn't been included in the XWF's debut. He was an extremely talented wrestler, but that was all he knew, which worried me even more for him because I could see he was depressed. The Blue Meanie was great at his profession, but he had no other options, and ironically, it was his having painted himself into that corner that first sparked the idea for that we could starting our own wrestling league. I hated seeing him so depressed about the state of his career. Even as mine continued to rise, we had a great reception whenever we teamed up together on the road, so I knew between that and my reception at XWF that the fan base was there to build upon foundationally. In addition, I had made a great number of contacts between the indie shows, ECW, and XWF, so I had a rolodex of talent to call upon in the case our idea ever moved past theory. At that point, I was still holding out hope that XWF would take off, but weeks passed with no word on when the next show would be.

As the year came to an end, the only shows XWF had since the big debut a month earlier had been several local shows in Florida with the older talent like the Nasty Boys and The Road Warriors as the stars. They hadn't invited me down to participate in any of them, even though we all knew it was the local shows that grew buzz for the bigger events, and gave the fans a chance to become familiar with new talent. Everyone already knew who the veterans were, and that couldn't carry the day alone, it never did. I'd seen it with ECW, on the indie circuit, where I would get just as much crowd response as any veteran I was in the ring with, and now I was seeing the same sad charade play out all over again here. The difference by this point rested in the fact that I'd learned enough about the business over the past couple years to know what NOT to do, which was overstock your talent roster with older faces. Wrestling fans have a short attention span as is, and not only weren't the older wrestlers physically capable of pulling off the same wild stunts they'd been famous for 10 years prior, but more importantly, the crowd could see that, and it put them to sleep every time. My eyes were wide open to this, and I saw it as a solution to Brian's depression, as well as perhaps a possibility to carve out some security for my future in the business. XPW, Rob Black's joke of a league, was also a sinking ship at this point, the greatest evidence of that being Vince McMahon's lack of interest in throwing them a lifeline. He'd bought out ECW when its sails started to sag, recognizing Paul Heyman as a talent that Rob Black would never be. He wasn't out of business yet, but there was definitely an opening in the market I spied that I knew would eventually open even wider as Rob's hopes continued to dim. I spent the holidays of 2001 with my mother in New York City, and brought in the New Year back in L.A. with the Atomic Punks, a popular Southern California Van Halen tribute band. My resolution for 2002 was to immediately dive headfirst into the planning stages for my own wrestling league. From my time in the sport, I knew how to take a hit, and felt I could withstand whatever chauvinistic pressures would be applied initially in an attempt to keep me out of the managerial level of the sport. Men had run the world of wrestling forever, and I knew it was time to change that paradigm permanently.

PART VXI

The Birth of 3PW Wrestling

By New Year's Day I was already selling the Blue Meanie on my idea for starting our own wrestling federation — which I wish to re-iterate again for the record was MY IDEA, from the outset. To Brian's credit, he did come up with the name, but it was my concept and my operation since I was planning to bankroll it entirely. I emphasize that because it pisses me off to this day because the sheer level of blood, sweat and money I put into getting 3PW off the ground has never been acknowledged. I'll never take any credit away from Brian in terms of his talent in the ring, and his coming up with the name, which I loved from the outset, but make no mistake — outside the ring and behind the curtain I was pulling the strings from day one. I was the brain behind the operation, and the wheels were churning in my head non-stop as I began plotting our future.

I had plenty of motivation due to the run-around XWF was continuing to give their contract wrestlers. By the start of 2002, the delays had become permanent, and what pissed me off most about it was the fact that they wouldn't be up front with us about the real reason why — Vince McMahon. He had seen the company as a threat, from what I heard and had been rumored to conspire behind XWF losing their T.V. syndication deal. As bad as I might have felt for them, they had they been straight up with everyone about it, I had no sympathy left by that point. If you can't get it together, just say so and be fucking honest, and let the talent look for a more stable home. It was tying the hands of wrestlers who'd been conned into thinking they had a future they clearly didn't, and while we were all potential competitors, XWF wasn't at that point so what did it matter anyway? This attempt to lead everyone on endlessly is what ultimately solidified my resolve to start my own wrestling league. I was ambitious, was a natural promoter, had a business degree, and for the first time, was being given an opportunity to combine all those assets into one investment. The most promising thing about my prospects for succeeding was my investing in myself and I knew that would keep me hungry.

I had nothing to lose at this point and new market share to gain if we played our cards right. While I had shut my porn site down, I continued with my dance feature gigs throughout the month, banking my considerable earnings from those shows toward our start-up costs for my new league, which by this point Brian — to his credit — had named 3PW (Pro-Pain-Pro Wrestling.) I also rounded up little investments from here and there, but the lion-share of our start-up capital came out of my pocket. For our first 3PW show, which was held at the old ECW Arena in South Philly on February 15th, 2002, I booked all the talent, coordinated the scheduling for hotels/airfare and even lined up the venue we held our debut at — the ECW Arena in Philadelphia, PA. I felt there was no better launching pad from which to announce that REAL indie wrestling had returned to the ring, and the venue owner must have liked my concept, because he gave me a great deal on the rent! We definitely were paying homage to the spirit of what ECW had stood for in its heyday, but wanted to make sure the world of wrestling knew we represented the start of a new era for wrestling: one where the sport's first female promoter was intent on making her mark!

I booked the first's show's talent based off who I thought would make us money, drawing from my years wrestling with many the likes of the Sandman, Steve Corino, Crowbar, CM Punk, and Colt Cabana among others. These wrestlers were all ex-expatriates of the big-name leagues that Vince McMahon had swallowed up: WCW, ECW, etc. Collectively, they made up what would be the start of many star-studded rosters to come over the next two years. I had a vision: to popularize our own championship matches, create new ring-rivalries that would be exclusively battled out in our ring, to make a TRUE indie powerhouse, for lack of a better term.

Of course, we got off to the same start as every other league had — we sold out about half of the house, even in spite of the fact that we flyered to death, and had tickets available at all the major ticket outlets — Ticketmaster, etc. We worked our asses off. While I was handling the booking of talent and venue, Brian was heading up the street-team and working on the website. Together, we were taking the credibility and experience we'd built up between us as a team at ECW and on the indie circuit, and pouring it all into the magic that became our first successful show was all the validation Brian and I needed to continue. We were also helped out by the reality that we were launching our company in the dead of winter in Philadelphia. Considering that we'd thrown the show together in just over three weeks, we both felt really good about how we began, in spite of what could have been better attendance numbers. We put on a stellar-show for those who did show up, and more than anything else, for me, the greatest high came from being in the ring again, on my own terms, calling my own shots. With only the fans to answer to, I knew things could only get better.

By the time of our next show, May of 2002, it was clear we were onto something. Buzz had spread to wrestling fans throughout the East, because our sophomore show was twice as packed as the debut had been. In the interim, my competitors on the indie circuit had already started talking shit about me, and the Blue Meanie and I were being given plenty of chances in the wrestling press to reply, clearly reflecting the media's interest in our new endeavor. It was intriguing, the idea of a female-run wrestling league, and my reputation for having steel balls must have preceded me, because in interviews, I never got anything but encouragement from the journalists chronicling 3PW's rise.

Consider Wikipedia's summary of my strategy for the company's talent roster starting out: 'Following the close of Extreme Championship Wrestling, many former ECW veterans, such as Raven, The Sandman, Al Snow and Sabu, made frequent appearances in the promotion…Independent wrestlers including Rockin' Rebel, Monsta Mack, Ruckus, Joey Matthews, AJ Styles and Lo Ki also competed in the promotion…In the beginning, 3PW brought in wrestling legends like Dusty Rhodes, Terry Funk, Abdullah The Butcher and Bam Bam Bigelow to compliment the roster of young and upcoming talent.'

As we planned our sophomore show, evidence of the aforementioned buzz came with former ECW booker Todd Gordon's phone call to us about joining the team. Brian and I were both elated at the idea, and brought him right aboard. He gave us a tremendous amount of street credibility, which is what we needed, and so rather than rush into another show the next month, we decided to take our time to plan our next show. We scheduled our next show for late May, and took the rest of the spring to set up our promotion properly. It had been so rushed with our debut show that we all wanted to take the time to do it right, which meant taking out ads in the paper, printing posters and flyers…I mean, we promoted the FUCK out of that show! The real draw though was the talent we booked for what became the first-ever 3-Way Body Bag match between New Jack, Sabu, and Sandman. We doubled our crowd at the second show, drawing around 900 people, and we even had a local league, Ring-Of-Honor Wrestling, try to run their own show head-to-head against me on the same night. We outdrew him as well, but it was more evidence to me of the fact that 3PW Wrestling was a fast-growing name.

When dealing with the inevitability of competitors trying constantly to steal our thunder, one thing I was a big bitch about was that I wouldn't let other people flyer for their events at my shows. That I guess is something they'd been used to getting away with before I came on the scene. I was also very strict about the locker/dressing room backstage; I didn't let anyone back who wasn't involved with the production. I didn't like my wrestlers' privacy being invaded because that's half of how all the drama at ECW had happened. It also prevented any spies in the vein of Rob Black's to infiltrate our operation and try to steal ideas from it. I was so good at what I did, and I don't care if people called me a bitch, or cunt, or whatever, I proved myself to be one of the best indie-promoters there ever was. Unlike a lot of the other operations out there, all of my wrestlers got paid on time, IN CASH, which no one else did, and Brian, Todd, everyone I had working for me did so on a salary. These people all worked for me as employees, and everything was negotiated through me. I was capable of playing as dirty or as nicely as my competitors wanted to, but one thing we made loud and clear with our second show's success was: 3PW wasn't going anywhere but UP!

Heading into the summer, there was another new company coming around called NWA TNA (Total Non-Stop Action) Wrestling, which was run by Jeff Jarrett, formerly of WCW, and they had some money behind them and were running pay-per-views at the time. Apparently they'd been keeping tabs on 3PW because they approached Brian and me that summer about appearing together on some of their PPVs. We didn't see it as a conflict with our own company, especially since they had a visibility level with television we were aiming to eventually graduate to with 3PW. It was also welcome because our June 3PW show was very slow; it's very difficult in the summer in that part of the country because you're competing with weekends at the Jersey Shore, which drew our attendance down. So we kept the budget relatively low on that show, knowing it would be a slow month. Still, the crowd went wild at that show when we rolled Bill Alfonso out of a body bag and into the ring for his match with the Sandman, and Sabu, and we called that show 'The War Renewed.' Our goal with that match was to pick up where ECW left off. That's how people described it when it was over. So even though the crowd was lighter than May's attendance had been our profile as a company continued to rise by the caliber of the matches we were putting together.

Then rumors started swirling that Rob Black's XPW was going to try and compete on our turf. To me, that was a fucking joke, and no more a real competitor than this little backyard wrestling federation that had started up locally around the same time. We decided to take July off and hold our next 3PW show after Labor Day, and spent the interim working on the side for TNA. Once I'd started wrestling for them, Francine was brought in to have a head-to-head match with me in the ring, and she looked so horrible I actually felt bad for her. The match began with she and I started to engage in a cat fight backstage, which they showed on the jumbo-tron once we got to the ring. I did all the microphone work, called her out to the stage, and we had an even bigger cat-fight in the ring — before Brian finished her off with a pile driver. It was funny to me because it pissed her off so much to be in that position, where she'd always cock-blocked my spotlight time in the past. This was the best payback I could have asked for, being in a new league, where we were both on the same level, and I was considered a bigger star than she was in how they scripted the match's outcome.

That August, we held a lower-key 3PW wrestling event, 'Babes, Belts and Blood,' which featured a title match for Dusty Rhodes vs. Bam Bam Bigelow vs. Kevin Sullivan. For that event, I also thought it would be a smart move to sponsor a promotional wet T-Shirt 'Miss 3PW' contest designed to promote the forthcoming September show. I remember inviting Ron Jeremy to come in and emcee the event, and it went off beautifully with the crowd.

Ron Jeremy: I was also impressed with the fact that Jasmin had retired from the porn business and was still popular. A lot of girls will often wait and keep performing past their prime. They go on the road and feature, and do a porn film once in a while to keep themselves current on that circuit, but Jasmin loved entertainment and being in the limelight, and knew how to keep herself there by expanding beyond porn and into wrestling. I think that was very smart, and others tried it after her and weren't nearly as successful.

Jasmin: As we went into planning our September 3PW show, I got word that Ring-of-Honor was planning to run a head-to-head show with us on the same night, so we took the gloves off. We hired who had just been released from the WWF — and I made sure he was off the market and booked for 3 shows after that. I utilized that strategy a lot when I was booking wrestlers for 3PW shows, wherein I would lock them in for 3 or 4 dates at a time, so they'd stay exclusively in our camp. Our September show, 'This One's For You,' which was held on the 21st at the ECW Arena, was fucking PACKED! Our main event was Sabu vs. Syxx pac (formerly known as X-pac of the WWE,) and I booked Missy Hyatt, the 'First Lady of Wrestling' to come down. She and I had an appearance together called the 'Three Way Strip Off,' where we stripped out of an evening gown into our bra and panties. It evolved into this huge catfight in the ring. It was amazing to be employing all these legends I had grew up watching — especially Missy Hyatt, who was one of my heroes in the sport. That feud between Missy and me in the ring was one of my highlights looking back at my wrestling career.

We passed fire code on the September show, and after that, the word was out, to the point where before the night was even over, we were getting requests for tickets to the next show, which we hadn't even planned yet! We were finally in demand, and we even turned a small profit on the September show. Most importantly though, everyone got paid, largely thanks to my knowing everything there is to know about budgeting while not looking cheap in the process: for instance, with the corporate rate deals I did with hotels I put our wrestlers up at. For the first couple shows, I'd had everyone at the Holiday Inn, but I found a better deal with the Ramada for the September show, and it was a nicer hotel at that. Anyway, once word got out that 3PW paid CASH, plus expenses, it became a chorus of 'That's the company to work for; they're fucking cool.' It's funny too because by this point 3PW had an 800 number, and we had every idiot in the industry calling up to get work with us, and many of them weren't humble about it either. Still, we put up with it because THEY were calling US, and my goal was to continue expanding our roster.

> '3PW is promoting an ECW style product. Unlike a lot of Indy shows 3PW brings in many name wrestlers such as legends Dusty Rhodes, Terry Funk and former ECW greats The Sandman and Raven. The promotion is owned by...Jasmine St. Claire'
>
> — *Wrestling101.com*, November, 2003

For as much of a high as we were all on from the success of the show, that exuberance was handicapped slightly by the death of one of my wrestlers, former XWF wrestler Fly Boy Rocco, who I managed as part of an in-ring tag-team. He died at the gym working out before the show, so that sadness hung over everything. Still, we all went out to the ring that night with his spirit pushing us all to the top of our game, and by drawing wrestling talent like Abby the Butcher vs. Kevin Sullivan, and Syxxpac vs. Sabu, the audience got swept up in 3PW fever as well! After that show, it was contagious, and we had solidified ourselves as one of the East Coast's most competitive wrestling leagues. It had taken 7 months, but considering how few shows we'd held in that time, we took the momentum as an opportunity to pay tribute to Fly Boy Rocco at our next show in October. We had a Ten-Bell Salute to him in the ring, and the show was dedicated to him. His old tag-team partner Johnny Durham was there, it was really nice. We had a ceremony in the ring, and then just put on a hell of a show in his memory. We had tag-team between the Blue Meanie and I, and Missy Hyatt and the Rockin' Rebels, and by now, we were drawing anywhere between 900-1200, which is considered a sell-out. I would go onto sell out that arena many times, but these first couple sell-out shows are still my favorites looking back.

I celebrated my birthday that year in New York with my mom, and was really happy, because we were gaining the momentum we deserved. The shit talking was already flying from rival promoters about how we were a flash in a pan, I even got word that Rob Black was trying to move in on our territory and was planning up-coming XPW shows in Philadelphia for later that fall. My attitude was — BRING IT ON, I was fearless, because of the old adage 'I had nothing to lose,' since I'd built this league from nothing, and Rob had been hanging around for years on the fringe, unable to rise to the level we had. They had even stooped so low as to sneak into our August show and try to give away tickets to OUR PAYING CUSTOMERS in the audience. If I hadn't been so strict about our parking lot's cars being flyered as well it would have been worse, but once I caught wind of Rob's latest desperate antic, I made sure NONE of his people got into the September and October shows. Still, I wasn't intimidated by the thought of the competition. He threw a show in November, trying to go head to head with us, and fell FLAT on his face. Rob's next move was even more laughable, and pretty under-handed at that, wherein he signed an exclusive lease with the ECW Arena owner Stein and Silverstein, which would force our move in the New Year to the Electric Factory — where we still outsold Rob 2-1!

I think Wikipedia could report the outcome of Rob's East Coast 'Takeover' best: 'Controversy arose when Xtreme Pro Wrestling (XPW) signed an exclusive lease with the venue in late 2002, preventing other promotions from using the building. XPW went out of business in 2003, and the lease was voided.'

Another insight as to why, perhaps, Rob's lease was voided: 'Ring of Controversy' January 9th, 2003, by R. Jonathan Tuleya, The South Philly Review. 'A new wrestling organization with a colorful past is drawing criticism...coming from residents...Viking Hall's (a.k.a. the former ECW Arena) new tenants have some residents in the area ready to tap out. XPW's (exclusive) lease on the arena began Jan. 1, 2003. Sources report the lease deal is for three years at $120,000 annually...For the last two years, an unidentified group or individual has been circulating a two-page flier, mainly via e-mail, warning people that 'pornography is coming to your neighborhood...' The missive makes allegations about XPW's connections to the hard core pornography industry, problems it has had with licenses for past promotions and even claims that the promotion's management had something to do with severing the thumb of one of its former wrestlers. Residents should be concerned, believes Bob Magee, the owner of an industry news Web site called Philadelphia Wrestling Between The Sheets (pwbts.com), where he writes a weekly column called 'As I See It.' Last week he reprinted a copy of the flier on the site...Magee said he is not affiliated with any of the local independent organizations — the major ones being Combat Zone Wrestling, Ring of Honor Wrestling and Pro Pain Pro Wrestling (also known as 3PW) — but he does promote them through his site, all except XPW. "I don't feel comfortable to promote people that blatantly don't seem to give a damn about following the same regulations everyone else does," Magee contended.'

We held our November show as planned, in spite of Rob's XPW 'competition,' and again packed in a sold-out capacity crowd. That must have been what spooked Rob Black into agreeing to pay the king's ransom he eventually did to steal the ECW Arena away from us. He couldn't do it on the merits of the crowds he drew, so he had to buy his way in, which in my opinion highlights the one thing Rob never got about promoting wrestling events. It's not about the quick buck, like porn is. It's about building a following the way ECW had, and now that 3PW had re-engaged that fan base and won them over through HARD WORK — something XPW had no concept of where wrestling was concerned — I knew Rob didn't have a chance.

Our November ring roster included Dusty Rhodes, Sabu, Kevin Sullivan, Syxxpac, Kid Kash, and I managed a wrestler named Jason Knight, and the show went off fantastically. I wish I could have said the same about the December 3PW show, our final at the ECW Arena before moving to the Electric Factory. To start with, Dusty Rhodes missed his flight and the match as a result, and another of my wrestlers, Ron Killings from the WWF, no-showed me. I later found out that Rob Black had paid him not to show up, which didn't surprise me in the slightest. In spite of the setbacks, the crowd was huge, and no one asked for their money back, which I saw as the ultimate fuck-you to Rob and XPW by the fans. Regardless of all the antics Rob had going on, I was satisfied in having a confirmation that I knew where Philadelphia wrestling fans' loyalties lay. We had earned their respect the hard way, and believe me, it was a trying time for 3PW.

Once we got confirmed word that Rob Black had signed the exclusive, lockout lease for the ECW Arena, our promoter Todd Gordon had already been out looking for a replacement. We'd accepted that it was a business decision on the owner's part, and decided to fight Rob on that level, rather than making it personal. We had a superior roster of talent, a superior reputation as showmen (and women ☺) and we outdrew them 2 and 3-1 once they started showing their faces on our turf. We had a show at the end of that December on the 28th, 'Year End Mayhem!' It was our final show at the ECW Arena, which was a little sad, but I was proud of what we'd accomplished there and ready to embrace the future of 3PW.

Over the holidays, I stayed in Los Angeles, having been back in the East for so much of the fall. It was a nice quite holiday at home. Brian and I spent New Year's Eve club-hopping, celebrating how far we'd come in such a short time. In *TWELVE MONTHS* we'd built the hottest wrestling league on the East Coast, with a popularity that was rising by the match. We were attracting all the top-shelf talent, and serving rabid wrestling fans the best matches in town. For Brian and me, it was an even more special celebration on a personal level because this had been our resolution a year ago to that night, and we'd achieved it. I was re-energized again about the life that lay ahead of me, and with my adult film past so far in my rear-view, I felt like I'd finally really started on the path to making something of myself professionally. I knew adult film had been an irreplaceable stepping stone, but wrestling was my love, and something I'd dreamt of doing since I was a child. People can chuckle at that if they want, but it really was — I was a metal-head wrestling fan who was now as a grown-up getting to live one of those dreams. Looking towards the New Year, my resolve to defeat Rob Black and drive him straight out of Philadelphia was my new resolution. It's one I don't mind giving the ending away to way ahead of time: I ACHIEVED IT, and in even less time than I thought it would take!

PART XVII

3PW Lives On!!!

By the New Year, we were busy moving our operations into our new home, the LEGENDARY Electric Factory, which held twice the capacity as ECW Arena! Todd Gordon had been friends with the booker who was a really big wrestling fan and specifically a 3PW fan. That allowed us to score a really good price on our lease (a third of what Rob was paying, which says something about the real cost to XPW of being our competitor at that time.) Taking a cue from Rob, I also made sure we'd secured exclusive wrestling show rights as part of the deal with the club. We were going to be bigger than ever: within that February, Rob Black would be kicked out of his lease in the ECW Arena, and out of Philadelphia altogether as a result of what went down — but I'm jumping ahead.

> 'The Electric Factory is a well-known venue for concerts in Philadelphia, Pennsylvania. The first 'Electric Factory' venue was actually a converted tire warehouse that was located at 22nd and Arch Streets. This first Electric Factory had opened in 1968, and it closed in 1973. The first performers at this venue were the Chambers brothers, on February 2, 1968. The 'Electric Factory' was resurrected around the latter 1994 or early 1995. It presently stands at 421 N. 7th Street between Willow and Spring Garden Streets. This place is more symbolic because it is an actual converted electric factory. The standing-room-only capacity in the Electric Factory is approximately 2500 to 3000 people. This includes the second-floor area. Since this portion of the area overlooks the stage from the left, people up here have a good view of the backstage. The Electric Factory is known to host major musical acts on a regular basis. These musical acts usually consist of heavy metal, rock and grunge genres. The Electric Factory has a rich history just like rock

and roll does...The Electric Factory is described as a legend in live music that has survived for more than 30 years.'

— *www.ticketnest.com*

'3PW was born out of the idea to see what running a show would be like. I had been in the business for 8 years and started to think of what to do for my post in ring career. Truthfully my body won't hold up to the punishment much longer so I figured I'd give promotion a try. Our first show was the blotter test to see if we wanted to go on. Things went smooth and we decided to go forward. So we enlisted the help of a good friend in Todd Gordon. Todd is very intelligent in the world of business and wrestling. So who better to come up with idea, Todd, Jasmin and I think of ideas for the shows. So far, so good. Our 2nd year anniversary show is coming up on February 21st at the ECW arena in south Philly.'

— Brian 'Blue Meanie' Heffron, *www.Wrestling101.com*

Our first scheduled head-to-head show with Rob in our new home in the Electric Factory outdrew him 2-1 from what his previous shows had been drawing. Held on February 15th, 2003, our one-year anniversary as a league, we went ALL OUT in celebrating it — beginning with a wet T-Shirt contest we held with Nicole Bass, of whom I was one of the judges. We had top shelf wrestling talent at that show. Prince Nana vs. Jeff Rocker, RAVEN vs. The Blue Meanie; Jason Knight w/ Jasmin St. Claire vs. Rockin Rebel; Kid Kash vs. Kid Kruel; Da Hit Squad (Mafia & Monsta Mack) vs. Balls Mahoney & Nosawa; a tag-team match between Josh Daniels & Damian Adams vs. Matt Striker & Rob Eckos. Low Ki vs. Homicide; RAVEN vs. Xavier vs. 'Pitbull' Gary Wolfe, and finally Terry Funk vs. Sabu in a title match.

Even with a snow storm, we packed the Electric Factory that night, and the kicker was Rob Black — once he found out what our draw was going to be — cancelled his own show! He'd lost his own game of chicken, and I felt validated that I was the BEST at what I did. It didn't stop with Rob either, every other male indie promoter in the region took a shot at us, and no one could rival our operation. I ran a tight ship for that very reason, and that's why it may have earned me the reputation of an all-business bitch over the years, it was worth every insult that kept my name in the press. In that same article, they had to write about why my league was getting so much attention — good and bad. Word was apparently spreading beyond Philadelphia that we were the league to beat because shortly after our February smack down, a major DVD distribution company — DGD Distribution — who wanted to offer us a contract, so I snapped that deal right up. On top of that, a company in England who syndicated a weekly wrestling show on the BBC's Wrestling Channel, wanted to run our taped shows.

For the first time in my life, I can honestly say I felt like I was exactly where I wanted to be, at the top of my game. I had wrestlers calling me for work — including guys who had no-showed me before to take what at the time were bigger gigs with Vince McMahon's league — and I told them no. I didn't do it to be spiteful, but to remind them they were dealing with a real wrestling league that didn't need them. That's not to sound arrogant either because those wrestlers who were loyal to us, we treated like royalty — they were ALWAYS paid on time, with full travel expenses covered since we had many wrestlers who flew in from all over the U.S. to work for 3PW. We were definitely becoming a force to reckon with. People were calling me for work and I didn't have to reach out. Even those little fucking skanks who'd talked shit about me over the past year to the porn and wrestling press were calling trying to get work from me, and it actually took me aback: the audacity of it. Naturally, I put my foot down and said: 'NO FUCKING WAY!' That autonomy extended to anyone — male or female — that I felt wouldn't bring us money in the form of butts in the seats. I knew from my dancing days that the bottom-line job of the talent is to bring in the customers, which sounds obvious, but in the wrestling business there were MANY times where I saw money thrown down the drain on 'talent' that were really just favors. In my league, if it didn't make dollars, it didn't make sense, and I ran my company accordingly. If Todd booked someone I didn't think made sense for the show, I had no problem dismissing them from the bill, it was always my call at the end of the day — and the talent can back that up.

Ron Jeremy: 'A few years later, when she was retired from porn and was working the wrestling circuit, running her company 3PW, she hired me to come out and emcee a match they were having. And I actually saw her in the ring wrestling, and remember being thinking it was great. Because when she first walked out to the ring, I remember initially thinking to myself, 'This is going to be cheesy and corny,' but she was authentic in the ring. She did a good job, and I remember thinking 'Wow, Jasmin actually learned some moves. She's got some moves.' I never really knew any other girl not to insult anyone else who tried to follow in her footsteps that succeeded the way she did. The crowds loved her, and she always went over very well with everybody because she had the looks, and the *moves*. It also helped her transitioning into promotion, because she really knew the business inside out. It was impressive.'

Jasmin: I had to fight twice as hard to be taken seriously because I was a woman running my own show, and that extended to every area of the business — from hiring and firing talent to physically kicking hangers-on out of the back-stage/locker-room area of the arena. I had my share of throwing people personally out of the arena, so as time went on; people who had second-guessed my authority in the past or press got to see it in action first-hand. I had put time and considerable resources into getting this business off the ground, and now that we finally had momentum, I wanted no dead weight slowing us down or holding us back. By this point, as my fortunes continued to rise, Rob Black's were fast dwindling, and for better or worse, it put a smile on my face when…well, maybe I should let the media do the talking:

> 'Rob Zicari and Janet Romano, better known within adult as Rob Black and Lizzie Borden of Extreme Associates, have been indicted on 10 charges by a federal grand jury for allegedly distributing obscene materials via the United States Postal Service and the Internet. Zicari, Romano, and Extreme Associates, Inc. were indicted for allegedly distributing three obscene videos to the Pittsburgh area through the mail and six video clips in various digital formats over the Internet to the Pittsburgh area. The tenth charge was one of conspiracy to commit the alleged crimes… According to U.S. Attorney Mary Beth Buchanan, prosecutor for the case, Zicari and Romano, if convicted both face a maximum penalty of 50 years in prison and a $2.5 million fine and probation. Extreme Associates Inc. faces a $5 million fine and could have to turn over their domain name. 'For over a year Extreme Associates, Inc. has been investigated by the LAPD Obscenities Squad,' the warrant reads, in the section entitled '*Summary of Case*: On February 7, 2002, PBS-Frontline interviewed Extreme Associates, Inc. during a movie shoot of American Porn. The PBS-Frontline cameraman and interviewer stopped shooting during the movie shoot. We believe they left because of the shock and disgust of the rape scene, which was subsequently released as *Forced Entry*. During

the PBS-Frontline interview, [Rob Black] (principal) and Extreme Associates issued a challenge to U.S. Attorney General Ashcroft [USAG]. They touted the USAG in regards to the content of their movies and that USAG could not do anything about it.'

— AVN Network

'Atty. Gen. John Ashcroft promised upon taking office that he would crack down on the distributors of adult entertainment material such as movies, magazines and Web sites. Much as his Reagan administration predecessor Edwin Meese III did in the 1980s.'Today's indictment marks an important step in the Department of Justice's strategy for attacking the proliferation of adult obscenity,' Ashcroft said. 'The department,' he said, will, 'continue to focus our efforts on targeted obscenity prosecutions that will deter others from producing and distributing obscene material.'

— *Los Angeles Times*, 'U.S. Indicts Porn Sellers, Vowing Extensive Attack,' By P J. Huffstutter, August 08, 2003

Jasmin: Now you see why I got out of the porn business as quickly as I did. And by the complaint being lodged from Pittsburg, it was clear this part of the country wasn't very welcoming of XPW's 'East Coast Invasion' after all. He wasn't very wanted back home in L.A. either, as I found out later he'd run for Mayor of Los Angeles in 2001, receiving only 789 votes. His ego was out of control, to where he'd even tried opening a wrestling school, which fell flat on its face:

'In April 2003, Rob Black and Lizzy Borden were indicted on obscenity charges due to pornographic material produced by XPW's parent company, Extreme Associates...The stress of the trial took a toll on the owners of the company, and XPW could no longer be subsidized financially.'

— *Wikipedia.com*

With Rob Black now out of the way, 3PW moved full-steam ahead into our second show at the Electric Factory, held on March 29th, and entitled 'Legends Collide' which featured as its Main Event a 3-way LEGENDS match between Terry Funk, Abdullah the Butcher & Dusty Rhodes 'The American Dream, as well as under card matches between Homicide vs. Xavier and Nosawa vs. Balls Mahoney, and of course, Jasmin St. Claire vs. Missy Hyatt — Panties & Pasties Match. We drew around 1000 people to that show and had a full show schedule for the remainder of the year. I was commuting back and forth from L.A. during the period in between matches, subsidizing income with dance gigs, and still running my wrestling league from the road. I'd liaise with Todd on booking decisions for upcoming shows, which was made a little easier by the fact I'd booked a lot of our name wrestlers into multi-match commitments, so we didn't have to go from show to show sweating out who our main-event talent would be. I was juggling a lot of balls at once, but loved the challenges I had before me now. For the first time in my life, I was 100% in charge of my own destiny, and living it to the fullest.

Our show that May, 'A Funkin Classic,' held on the 3rd, was as star-studded as ever, featuring a Title Match between Jerry Lawler and Terry Funk, we also had a hard core match between Ian Rotten and Balls Mahoney, and of course, a 'Miss 3PW' beauty pageant, which I hosted. We always made sure to feature girls for every type of guy, and our attendance was up from the March show to around 1500. Our other wrestlers included Trent Acid vs. Ric Blade, Rockin' Rebel & Jeff Rocker vs. Da Hit Squad, Homicide vs. Kid Kash, the Blue Meanie & Roadkill vs. Joey Matthews & Christian York, and Kevin Sullivan vs. 'Pitbull' Gary Wolfe. We kept the pace right up heading into June's show, and took full advantage of Rob Black's exit to welcome back in some of the ECW talent he'd tried to steal away from us a year earlier. Aptly titled 'A New Era,' and one which 3PW absolutely owned in that moment, the show featured a bevy of heavy hitters. It included a three-way match between Sandman vs. Terry Funk vs. ' Pitbull' Gary Wolfe, N.W.A. TNA's AJ Styles vs. Kid Kash, Da Hit Squad vs. the Blue Meanie and Roadkill, Damien Adams vs. Ricky Vega, and a tag-team match-up of Joey Matthews & Christian York vs. Matt Striker & Rob Eckos. As well as the 2nd round of the Miss 3PW Contest, hosted by yours truly. I'll happily admit, looking back, that it felt a lot nicer to be HOSTING a beauty pageant than to be starring in one.

Because it was June and we had our usual Jersey Shore competition, we drew around 1000 people, but we still covered our overhead and made a profit. Having just come off back-to-back shows, everyone wanted a little break, so we decided not to hold a July show and focus our resources on August's show, 'That's Incredible,' which we held in the middle of that month on the 16th. Our roster for that show included a title match between Justin Credible and Terry Funk, as well as match-ups between Sandman vs. 'The Pitbull' Gary Wolf, Ricky Vega vs. CJ ODoyle, the Sugar Shack with myself & George Frankenstein, 'Hot Stuff' Striker vs.

The Blue Meanie, and a tag-team match between Nick Berk & Damian Adams vs. Monsta Mack & Rockin Rebel among others. I had my own little brawl outside in the parking lot with some punk bitch who we'd caught papering our parking lot at the June show. I'd let him off with a warning, and then saw him again at our August show doing the same fucking thing, which made me livid! After my security caught him and alerted me to what was going on, I PERSONALLY beat the shit out of him in the parking lot. I was fucking pissed, and he started wining about the cops getting called, until we told him we had off-duty cops working as security on the show. After that, he put his tail between his legs and limped away to lick his wounds elsewhere. By that point, you could safely say word was out on the street that 3PW wasn't a league to be fucked with, we gave everyone their money's worth, but we also fiercely protected our turf, especially after what Rob Black had pulled over the last year. After going through all of that together, we had become a tight-knit gang.

By the end of the summer, we'd started running ads for our return to the ECW Arena, whose lease had now become available again with Rob Black's having been run out of town by all the powers that be. We had had a wonderful run at the Electric Factory, but the history of the ECW Arena dictated that we return with a show that took the fall to plan. I told Todd I really wanted to blow the roof off of the arena, and we promoted the HELL out of our return — between radio, local television and Newspaper ads, as well as a street-team that flyered all over town throughout September and October. Unlike Rob, we had earned the right to host our shows out of the ECW Arena, and if I had it my way, we weren't going to get kicked out of there again. Thankfully, the owner also wanted us back because he knew — again, unlike Rob — that we were reliable, and it made me feel good to know we'd earned our respect through sheer hard work, and our profile continued to rise as a result. Over in the U.K., we had our first year of shows in steady rotation on the Wrestling Channel. Residuals coming in from that allowed me to begin reimbursing myself for the TENS of thousands of dollars I'd laid out since the beginning to get my company to where it was at that point.

We titled the show 'Raven's Rules,' and in designing the dialogue and match-ups for the show, were really focusing on the character-driven story lines that had made ECW Wrestling classic to begin with. I truly considered ourselves the next generation of that legacy, so we decided our title match with Raven would also serve as a great surprise ending to fans when we unveiled his new title within our league as '3PW Commissioner.' I also gave a new female talent named Talia her first break, where she then went onto work at NWA TNA which to me, underscores why I felt 3PW was a great place to grow new talent, in addition to our routine rosters of wrestling legends.

> 'OPENING MATCH: C.J. O'Doyle defeats Ricky Vega; MATCH: Monsta Mack def Roadkill; MATCH: 'Hot Stuff' Matt Striker defeats Ruckus; IN THE RING: Bob Artese, Joey Matthews, Todd Gordon, Jack Victory + Raven...This was a drawn out segment leading to the announcement of Raven being named 3PW Commissioner...Raven's first act of duty was to stripe Justin Credible of the 3PW title...Raven said that he, Sabu and 'someone else' would fight in a 3-way dance for the 3PW title...Raven said that Joey Matthews' girlfriend (Alexis Laree) abandoned Raven's flock so he wasn't high on Joey...Raven set up a match between Joey Matthews & Low Ki...MATCH: Low Ki def Joey Matthews... MATCH: The Blue Meanie def Rob Eckos w/Matt Striker...Matt Striker came out dressed as Jimmy 'Superly' Snuka — his entire gimmick is of an 80s wrestler...Raven came out after the match, and said Matt Striker will face the real Jimmy 'Superfly' Snuka next month! TODD GORDON SUGAR SHACK: Todd Gordon, Jasmin St. Claire and Gary Wolfe...Jasmin said Todd Gordon had bought her lots of presents lately so she had one for him...Jasmin went to the back and brought out a hot blonde named Talia...Jasmin's said she is a piece of white trash and will be Todd Gordon's sex slave...Todd Gordon toyed with Talia, asking her to touch her toes etc...Todd Gordon then introduced Gary Wolfe and his ' mystery woman' to talk about his change of attitude...Todd Gordon said Damian Adams was trash talking Gary Wolfe, so he challenged him to a match...MATCH: Damian Adams def Gary Wolfe... SPECIAL ATTRACTION MATCH: Xavier def Homicide... 3PW TITLE MATCH: Raven defeats Sabu and The Sandman to win the 3PW title!'
>
> — Recount of the show's highlights from
> *Obsessed With Wrestling.com*

After the success of the November show, we were doing extremely well, and had reached a high point where I'd achieved something no other wrestling promoter had since Paul Heyman: which was to sell-out the ECW Arena. Rob Black certainly couldn't, and our profile continued to rise. I spent both Thanksgiving and Christmas in New York with my mother, while Brian stayed back in Philadelphia with his. We were on the outs a little personally from his pushing me earlier in the fall — but professionally we were known as a team and had an image to uphold. On top of that, we did work well together, he was a reliable employee of mine, and one of the only men in my life who I'd been close to that actually lifted a hand to really help me get one of my dreams off the ground. I can't ever take that from him, even though I was the mastermind behind what we eventually built.

I don't mean to sound like a broken record with that fact, but it became so misconstrued over the years in the media that this is my only opportunity to fully and completely correct that record — figuratively speaking.

At that point, we had a pretty harmonious thing going between everyone in the 3PW camp. We had no shortage of talent coming out of everywhere to work for us, and we wasted no time planning for our year-end show, which was one of my favorites because I booked a wrestling LEGEND, 'Superfly' Jimmy Snuka, as one of our headliners. We even named the show in his honor: 'Su-Su-Superfly' and it was a BLAST! Jimmy squared off in the ring against Matt Striker. We also had John Zandig and Wifebeater vs. 'Commissioner' Raven & Sandman, Sabu vs. Jerry Lynn, 'Pitbull' Gary Wolfe vs. Damien Adams, and of course, a Braw and Panties match between me and Gorgeous George who had changed her professional name to George Frankenstein for her appearances with 3PW. It was a lot of fun working with George. It was killer! I was in the company of greatness in the star roster and capacity-crowd we turned out for that show; it was a true triumph for us as a company, and for me as its owner/founder. We really were BOOMING as a business, and anything I've ever done in business I've done big, and with the goal in mind to be the best.

My resolution for 2004 was more of the same. To be bigger and better than we'd been, and part of my strategy for how to achieve that next level involved taking on investors, beginning with a wrestler of ours — 'Pitbull' Gary Wolf's — girlfriend, who had family money, and had expressed interest in investing in 3PW. At the time, we were looking for a domestic T.V. syndication deal for the 2 seasons of shows we'd taped and that had been such a hit over in England on the Wrestling Channel. Todd Gordon had first suggested the idea of taking Gary's girlfriend on as a partner, and I went along with it. I was inundated — between booking existing talent and the massive number of new demo tapes I was getting in from all around the country from up and coming wrestlers wanting to work for my league. On top of that, I had gotten involved in a new project with Cleopatra Records, which is owned by my longtime friend Brian Perera, one of the nicest and most loyal people in the business. He had a new DVD coming out called *Hollywood Rocks* and he offered me the job as host, which OF COURSE I jumped at. My very first interview was with Johnny tempesta from Helmet/Rob Zombie's band, then my second was with Joey Belladonna from Anthrax, and Brian thought I did a great job, and I think he was impressed with the depth of my knowledge of the genre. Metal has always been my other love — the heavier the better and I had always had a blast as hosting metal fests over the years. Anyway, my success with that first series of interviews gave me my other resolution for 2004: to expand my professional reach into the world of Metal!

Jasmin modeling Championship Wrestling Belt.

TOP: Wrestler Rhino Piledriving Jasmin in ring during ECW heyday.
BOTTOM: Jasmin getting started on indie wrestling circuit.

TOP: Jasmin and Blue Meanie, June 2002 on Wrestle the Radio.
BOTTOM: Jasmin celebrating 3PW 'One Year Anniversary' Show (featuring wrestling legends Terry Funk vs. Tabu for the Title), February 15, 2003.

TOP: Jasmin at the 3PW 'Raven's Rules' house show (starring Raven, Sabu and Sandman), November 27, 2003, Philadelphia, PA, Viking Hall.
BOTTOM: Jasmin at 3PW 'Not Enough Time' Title Match in Philadelphia, May 15, 2004.

Jasmin at the 3PW 'Su-Su-Superfly' Title Match (starring Raven and Sandman), December 27, 2003, Philadelphia, PA, Viking Hall.

Jasmin at 3PW 'Splintered' Title Match, June 19, 2004, Philadelphia, PA, Viking Hall.

Jasmin heating up a sold-out crowd at the 3PW 'Splintered' Title Match, June 19, 2004, Philadelphia, PA, Viking Hall.

The Blue Meanie defeated Roadkill wJasmine St Claire at 'Splintered' 3PW Title Match, June 19, 2004.

Jasmin in ring at 3PW 'Splintered' Title Match, June 19, 2004, Philadelphia, PA, Viking Hall.

Jasmin entering ring at 3PW 5 Star 4 Way, August 21, 2004, Philadelphia, PA, Viking Hall.

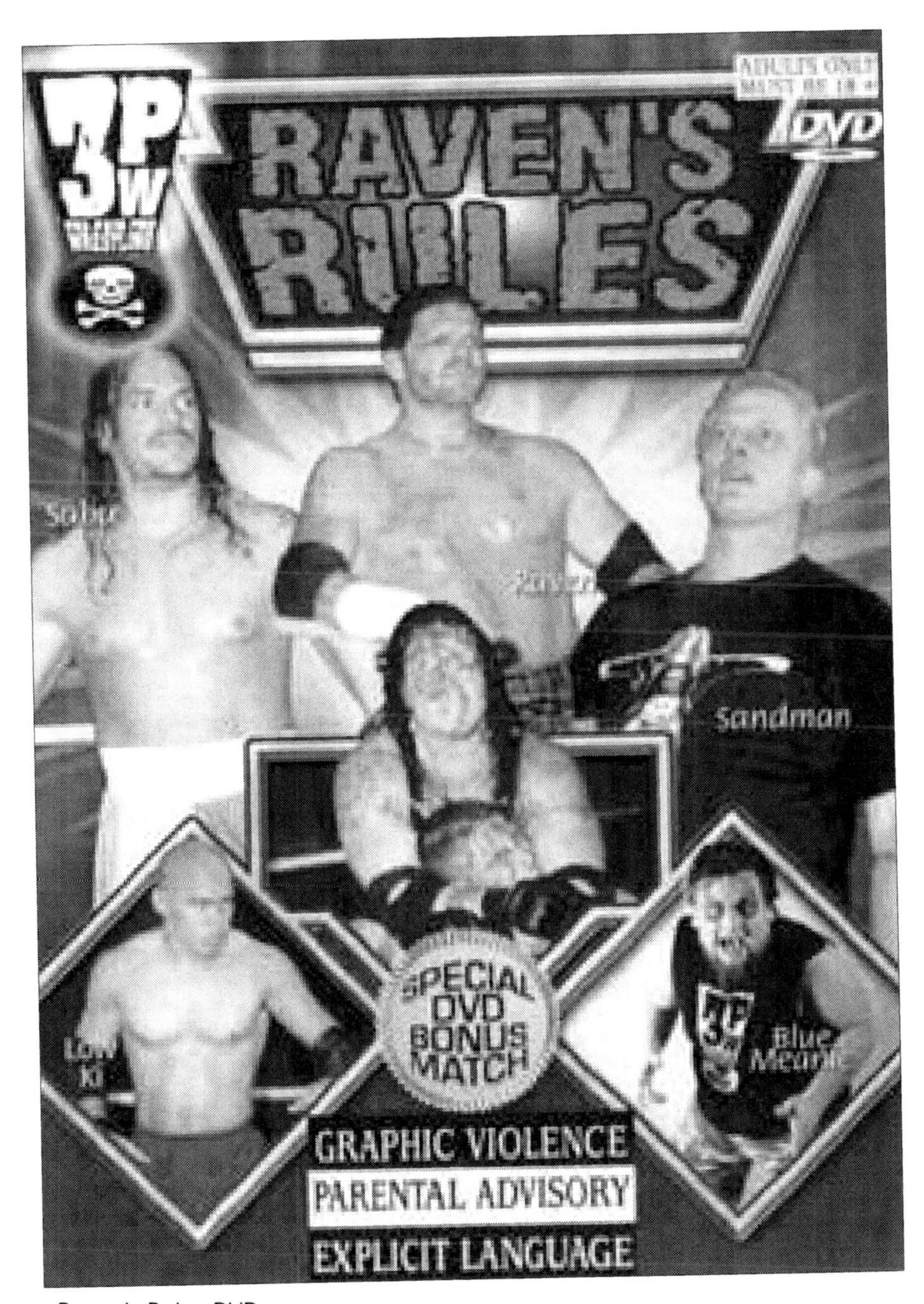

Raven's Rules DVD cover.

Jasmin entering the ring at 3PW 'Till We Meet Again' Title Match at October 16, 2004, Philadelphia, PA, Viking Hall.

Jasmin hosting 'For the Gold' Title Match, November 20, 2004, Philadelphia, PA, Viking Hall

Jasmin wrestling in the ring at 'For the Gold' Title Match, November 20, 2004, Philadelphia, PA, Viking Hall.

Wrestling Promo Poster.

PART XVIII

Metal, Metal & More Metal!!!

January marked the beginning of a new era for me professionally in which I had been bit by the metal bug and knew my ambition was hungry again for a new challenge, which I had to balance with 3PW's position in the business at that point. If we got the investments in for 3PW, great, if not, we'd keep rolling right along, and I figured I could have the best of both worlds with metal and wrestling in the same time. We had one of our best shows ever at the end of that month, with Al Snow, and the ECW Arena was beyond packed! I felt I'd finally made my mark as the most successful independent wrestling promoter — and a female at that.

That February, it was time to do our two-year anniversary show, which we held on the 21st and billed as '3PW: Second Anniversary.' It featured matches including: Derek Wylde defeating Rob Eckos; Slyk Wagner Brown w/April Hunter defeating Mike Kruel; the FLORIDA X-TITLE MATCH featuring Roderick Strong w/Ron Niemi defeating Mikey Batts to win a vacant title. Ruckus vs. Damian Adams; a TAG MATCH between Rockin Rebel & Jack Victory defeating C.J. O'Doyle & Blue Meanie; 'Macho Man' Matt Striker w/Miss Talia defeating Monsta Mack. The DOG COLLAR 3PW TITLE MATCH, which featured Raven defeating ' Pitbull' Gary Wolf to retain the title; and finally the TRIPLE THREAT match, which starred Joey Matthews defeating Sabu and Jerry Lynn.

We still did well with crowd capacity in spite of how crappy the weather was at that time of year, which made it really difficult traditionally to draw people in. We kept that show to a little bit of a lower budget by using some independent talent along with the headliners for the undercard matches. I felt it was nice to give up-and-comers an option to work somewhere

where they'd have a chance to wrestle before a large crowd, because the mainstream wrestling business at that point was getting tougher and tougher to break into with Vince McMahon's stranglehold over everything. Because of that, I had A LOT of wrestlers coming to me for work; I did my best to strike a balance between booking the headline talent that brought in the bulk of our crowd, but also introduce some new local talent via the opening matches. I knew 3PW fans had also become accustomed to seeing our shows. It was a potent combination, and one that I had masterminded from the beginning, and had watched it become our hallmark over the next two years.

Around this same time, I had been speaking with Cleopatra Records owner Brian Perera about starring in a DVD series called *Metal's Dark Side*, which would basically be a much larger scale, mainstay version of the documentary. He had me interviewing metal bands locally around L.A. up to that point. Perera had seen promise in it as something larger that could be distributed on a national level via DVD, and felt I was the right personality to host the series because of my talents as a host but, I believe he also recognized I was an authentic metal head.

In March, I headed back East for what was scheduled to be the next 3PW show, and ahead of the gig, which was scheduled for later that month. I shot a mainstream, independent film called *Communication Breakdown*. I worked for scale on the project because it was one of my first 'real' movies — as opposed to the type I had made in a previous life and I had jumped at the opportunity to break into that world. In any event, we shot on location in North Carolina, and of course, I underwrote our expenses (from meals to the Holiday Inn) because he had a bit part in the film and I still believed in him as a talent. We were a team in the eyes of a lot of industry people, so they felt I think in a way having us both in the film would play to our wrestling fan-base, in addition to my broader mainstream following. We shot on a soundstage where the set had been built to look like a radio station. Our director, Richard O'Sullivan, was really on his game with the movie, and eventually signed a deal with Comcast On-Demand to debut the movie, in addition to DVD distribution.

Once we'd wrapped shooting on *Communication Breakdown*, Brian and I drove back to Philadelphia to prepare for the next 3PW show, which was supposed to begin in early April. Prior to that, I had been cast to appear in another independent film, *Coalition*, which was shooting in New York, and starred Frank Vincent, who played mob boss Phil Leotardo on *The Sopranos*. My first day on set was the day following St. Patrick's Day, and because I had to be on location at 5 that morning, I'd taken it easy on my partying the night prior. In hindsight, I should have whooped it up because my being a good girl ended up making no difference when I shot up out of bed the next morning with a searing pain in my stomach. I felt like someone had stabbed me with a 12-inch blade, because it was a pain I'd never experienced before in my life, but I thought at first it was just food poisoning or something minor, and didn't want anything getting in the way of my movie shoot. I know that sounds retarded reading it now, but that's how much a professional I am, and how ambitious I was to break into mainstream film that I sucked up the pain, and worked through the day.

I had been cast as a Hispanic newscaster, and everyone on the set were all Italian guys who were also all big wrestling fans, which reflected where 3PW was at that time in terms of its street credibility. I'd like to think it's not the sole reason I got the job, but I knew it played a part, and that was fine. We'd shot all day in Williamsburg, and upon arriving back at my mother's house that night, the pain I'd been ignoring all day suddenly overtook me like a Tsunami wave, because all I remember is collapsing to the floor like a rock and passing out. When I woke up hours later I was in the hospital, and the doctors told me my appendix had burst. On top of the emergency surgery I underwent to have my appendix entirely removed, it also turned out I have a very rare blood type which they had to search the city over to find a match for. Thankfully, they eventually did, and when I woke up in recovery, my mother and some other family were all there with me. I felt lucky to be alive based on how close the doctors told me I'd come to death. While I was chomping at the bit to get out of the hospital so I could prepare for that weekend's 3PW show, they ensured me I would be putting my health at even greater risk if I discharged myself premature to a full recovery.

That essentially translated to mean that we were forced to cancel the entire show scheduled to be on March 20th — because of how involved I still was in running the day-to-day operations and the fact that I wrote all the checks. We simply couldn't have pulled it off. Everyone was understanding about it, for the most part anyway. Brian had gotten through making calls to everyone letting them know what had happened and it necessitated a cancellation of the main event. I was shocked to find out that one of our wrestlers — Matt Stryker, who I'd given his start to and eventually went onto wrestle for the WWF — had asked Brian if he could go to the hospital and get his money for him. Even though the event was cancelled, and we didn't have that kind of a clause in contracts with any of the talent, that he still had the balls to ask such a thing of me was a shock. I couldn't believe what a greedy, nasty son-of-a-bitch he was for saying suggesting something so horrible while I was lying in the hospital!

He was blackballed as far as 3PW was concerned after that. To add insult to my existing injuries, I additionally discovered that Raven — one of our main stars at the time — was trying to fly in on the ticket I'd booked for him in conjunction with the 3PW event to come in and wrestle for a competitor. Our show had been cancelled. On MY DIME — I don't think so honey. I was deeply offended by both of their actions, especially in the case of Matt Striker, who I had put into business in the first place, and had a lot to thank me for. I put him on T.V. and given him a profile he never had prior to coming to work for 3PW, but what Raven had done bothered me even more because he was seasoned enough to have known better. That he had the nerve to try and fly in on my dime to wrestle for a competing promoter was laughable and horrible in the same time. One of the few good things to come out of the entire experience was the chance I had to see the true colors of those I had surrounded myself with in the 3PW camp. Many showed their loyalty to me by not saying a word about the cancellation of the show. Others however, like Raven, cost themselves high-profile spots in my organization by the way they treated me during my health crisis.

I decided — while still lying in my hospital bed — to get my revenge by hiring Raven, who at the time was 3PW's reigning champion, for one final show in late April — without telling him ahead of time it would be his last. I set it up for him to square off against Joey Matthews, and had pre-determined that he would lose the match and ultimately be stripped of his belt. I was in recovery for over two weeks, and had to have follow-up laser surgery to remove the scar it left entirely. Everyone but Raven had sent me get-well cards in the hospital, and my VERY first day out, I called both Raven and Matt Striker and cussed both of them out, letting them know how low and out of line I thought their behavior had been. I had been a very good boss to everyone, and had deserved better, which was the bottom line.

The re-scheduled March show was held on April 17th, in an event billed as '3PW: The Future is Now,' which I thought perfectly captured the spirit of things as we prepared to exit Raven from our league. The show was packed at capacity, and our roster results included 'Pitbull' Gary Wolf defeated Ron Zombie; Slyk Wagner Brown w/April Hunter defeated Ricky Vega; CJ O'Doyle defeated 'The Amazing' N8 Matson. Matt 'Macho Man' Striker w/Talia vs. Rob Eckos went to a NO CONTEST. TAG MATCH: Jack Victory and Rockin Rebel defeated The Blue Meanie and Roadkill; Mike Kruel defeated Monsta Mack; Jerry Lynn defeated Sabu; and Ruckus defeated Damian Adams; all leading up to Raven's defeat in the title match by Joey Matthews. After the match was over, I felt redeemed, and decided that I was going to focus as much as possible on branching out beyond wrestling with my new *Metal's Dark Side* DVD series, which Brian and I had planned to officially launch that summer.

Making up for the lost time due to my appendix emergency in March, we held a 3PW show on May 15th, which we titled '3PW: Not Enough Time.' It featured a bunch of bad-ass match-ups including: Rob Eckos defeating Amazing N8 Mattson, a 3-way match wherein Ruckus defeated Mike Kruel and Damian Adams; a match where Jack Victory & Rockin' Rebel defeated Ron Zombie & Don E. Allen. CJ O'Doyle vs. 'Pitbull' Gary Wolf; a match with Roadkill and myself defeating The Blue Meanie and 3PW TITLE Matches between Jerry Lynn and Joey Matthews (Champ); Slyk Wagner Brown & April Hunter w/Todd Gordon defeated Matt Striker & Miss Talia; and the headlining match between Christopher Daniels vs. AJ Styles.

In June, I shot more interviews for the *Hollywood Rocks* documentary for Brian Perera out in Los Angeles, which I loved because I got to interview Helmet drummer John Tempesta (who also played in Exodus, Testament, White Zombie, The Cult, and Rob Zombie) and. We held another 3PW show, on June 19th, titled '3PW: Splintered,' which as usual featured a ton of exciting matches including 'Amazing' N8 Mattson defeating Ron Zombie; Damian Adams defeating Mike Kruel; Rockin' Rebel vs. Johnny Grunge (of Public Enemy fame); the Blue Meanie defeating Roadkill w/ME. CJ O'Doyle defeating 'Pitbull' Gary Wolf; a tag-team match between Slyk Wagner Brown & April Hunter vs. The Ultimate Striker & Rob Eckos. Sabu defeated Ruckus and the 3PW TITLE 'FALLS COUNT ANYWHERE 3-WAY' match wherein new

3PW Champion Joey Matthews defeated Jerry Lynn and AJ Styles to retain his new title.

With things going as well as they were with 3PW, I found I had A LOT of people hating on me at this point all over the internet. My rule of thumb with that is and has always been — that whenever people start bad-talking you, it means they're jealous and you're doing something right. Whenever the noise stops, the day when people stop saying anything bad about you: that you have to worry. I was proud to be hated, and always will be, because I'm one of those people everyone has always loved to hate on: from my adult film career through my time in wrestling, because I was a threat to what had been a male-dominated establishment. There had NEVER been — and hasn't since — been a female promoter who got as high up the latter as I did in that business, and people didn't know how to deal with that.

As well as we'd done with the May and June 3PW shows I decided to tighten the belt a little and stopped paying for our wrestler's hotel rooms. Everyone was making more money but the company, and we deserved to be turning more of a profit given how far we'd traveled to get to where we were at that time. Everyone in the organization supported it, and when I got shit from some of the other wrestlers, I told them, 'You guys wrestle on other shows together and share a hotel room.' The bottom line was: if our talent wasn't so picky about when their flights — which we continued to pay for — left, we'd have been able to possibly continue with the hotel perk. Even after that, I still retained a very loyal cast of wrestlers who regularly worked our shows, because they all got paid, and it was one of the biggest draws in town at that point. I treated everyone on the same level where compensation was concerned: my wrestlers were paid what they drew in crowd capacity, and by that point, we could tell who the crowds got most excited about.

Also, we gave raises to wrestlers as they got more popular working in our league, which is something NO other independent did. 3PW had built up all these independent wrestlers' profiles so well — including talent like Matt Striker, C.J. Styles, Rukus — and I'd always used headliners like Raven to loop fans in to see what else we had to offer, and by that point, it was paying off for us big-time. On July 17th, we held the '3PW: No Limits' show, which reflected where we felt we were as a league at that point. It featured matches including CJ O'Doyle vs. Monsta

Mack; Jerry Lynn defeating Low Ki; a tag-team match between Rockin Rebel & Jack Victory vs. Rob Eckos & Matt Stryker as Sandman); Ruckus defeating Damian Adams. Another tag-team match between The Pitbulls 2004 (Mike Kruel & Gary Wolf) defeating Roadkill & Blue Meanie; and 3PW TITLE Matches between Joey Matthews vs. Slyk Wagner Brown; and Christopher Daniels defeating A.J. Styles. The headlining match between Chris Daniels and A.J. Styles was really cool, because we had no time limit on the match for 45 minutes, which was unusual. We called it an 'Iron Man' match, with the intent being to determine who would be the contender new 3PW Championship belt. So we were setting the audience up for the August show, and it worked perfectly.

I continued shooting interviews for the *Hollywood Rocks* documentary that summer, including Tracy Michaels from the Peppermint Creeps, Pretty Boy Floyd, who was someone I always admired and thought it was really cool how hard he worked to promote his band. I also interviewed Chris Webber, who was the original lead guitarist in Hollywood Rose along with Axl Rose and Izzy Stradlin (who of course went on to found Guns N' Roses,) and spoke with Marc Ferrari and Ron Keel as well from the '80s band Keel. It was really fun for me to be hosting this documentary interviewing all my rock and metal heroes from childhood on up, and I was having A LOT more fun with it than I was with wrestling at that point. To the point where I'd started almost dreading going to my own shows, if you can believe that.

I had grown so tired of listening to all these steroid-pumped, grown-men prima donnas bitching about their airline tickets or their hotel bills. I felt a lot of these guys needed to be humbled the fuck out, and no matter how I'd tried to keep 3PW grounded — even as we had continued to grow in popularity — it was getting out of hand. I hung in there because it was my fault in a lot of ways that we'd become as big an indie league as we had, it was my ambition which had been a big part of driving us to the top. Now that 3PW was competing at the level it was, some of the talent were starting to get big-headed, and I wasn't having any of it. But it sucked having to be a hard-ass all the time to keep all these men in line, and I was one woman doing all of that side of it. Brian and Todd never had to be the bad guy, that role came with my title of BOSS, and I was finally starting to grow a little weary of it. In truth, it just wasn't fun for me anymore, but I did my best to keep my head in the game, even as

I started pursuing more and more opportunities in metal as the summer came toward a close.

Prior to the final 3PW show of the summer, I had another independent film to shoot called *Swamp Zombies*, which we shot in Pittsburgh. Everyone involved with the film was really in the game. They sent me a few weeks before the shoot to a Special Effects outfit in Burbank that made a plaster mold of my head for my decapitation scene. It was a hilarious process having a mold of my face made, because you can't see anything while they're doing it. The film was shot way out in the boonies of back wood Pennsylvania, and the director Len Kabasinski was really great to work with. The first day of shooting was in a hospital, and my character was a hospital manager who was in co-hoots with a surgeon played by Shannon Solo who was conducting illegal experiments on cadavers, trying to turn them into zombies. We actually shot the scene where I get decapitated on the second day, even though I didn't die till much later in the movie, which I thought was funny. I had the requisite topless shower scene, but still was happy because I'd had A LOT of dialogue scenes in the movie as well.

We left the shoot in Pittsburgh to head straight to Philadelphia the following weekend for our August 3PW show, which we had billed as the '5 Star 4 Way.' It was held on the 21st before a capacity crowd, and featured in the opening match, Ruckus defeating Slyk Wagner Brown w/ April Hunter. The ROYAL RUMBLE tag-team match, which featured Jack Victory & Rockin Rebel vs. Rob Eckos & Matt Striker, and Gary Wolf vs. Mike Kruel w/Me, and Slyk Wagner Brown vs. April Hunter; Monsta Mack vs. CJ O'Doyle; and Roadkill defeating Monsta Mack. All of these matches preceded the title match, which was delayed because of our headlining wrestler A.J. Styles' plane being delayed in Atlanta. We were freaking out backstage, but trying to keep the crowd cool while A.J. — after landing at the Philadelphia Int. Airport, was rushed straight to the ECW Arena! He ended up literally exiting the cab and entering the ring for what we'd set up as a 4-way title match between Chris Daniels, Joey Matthews and Chris Sabin. It was nerve-racking, but the crowd LOVED the climax of the show, and I was relieved we'd pulled off 3 successful shows that summer, when most of the East Coast is traditionally dead.

That September, I began working on what would become the first volume of the *Metal's Dark Side* DVD series, and my metal profile got an even bigger boost when I co-hosted the *Metal Sludge Extravaganza 9* with the Blue Meanie and Stevie Rachelle. I was excited about that because it gave me the opportunity to interact with Metal Sludge's online fan base as well, which was huge at that time. I also moved that month, which was a huge pain in the ass, but I was excited because I had a trip to Europe planned for October. Basically, by that point, our 3PW matches had become very popular on the Wrestling Channel over in the U.K., and we were on T.V. twice a week in England, Scotland, and Ireland. The owners of the Wrestling Channel had invited me to come over to the U.K. to host a big promotional party of some sort, and as it turned out, they also had a wrestling-oriented talk show that aired out of Ireland. They had invited me to be a guest on the show as well. I had also planned to celebrate my birthday in Amsterdam while I was over there, and was scheduled to depart for the trip right after the 3PW show that month.

We held our October 3PW show on the 16th, titling the event 'Till We Meet Again'. The show featured matches including the Blue Meanie defeating Rockin' Rebel and Rob Eckos defeating CJ O'Doyle. A triple threat match which featured A.J. Styles vs. 2 Cold Scorpio and Chris Sabin; Roadkill vs. the Rockin' Rebel and the title matches including Pitbulls 2000 (Gary Wolf & Mike Kruel) defeating Slyk Wagner Brown & April Hunter; Damian Adams defeating Matt Striker; and finally Chris Daniels defeating Joey Matthews to retain the 3PW Championship belt. Following the 3PW show, I flew back to L.A. almost immediately, and turned around to leave for Amsterdam, which I'd planned to visit before arriving in London to complete my wrestling promotional commitments. It was an amazing time of year in Holland, and I had a blast, and tried hash and pot for the first time in years. It was just a very free time for me, away from all the stress of 3PW back in the States, and I remember my last night staying at the Sheraton before I was to leave for the U.K., I ran randomly into Cleopatra Records owner Brian Perera! He was there promoting some dance CD, and I ended up partying with him until sun-up, and had so much fun I even slept through my flight — which I NEVER do. I had needed a break with the trip, and definitely got it while I was in Amsterdam!

I arrived in London on the 23rd of October, which is my birthday, and celebrated at my aunt's house with a lot of my European family. The next day, I flew from Heathrow into Dublin and was greeted like royalty by the people from the Wrestling Channel, which felt really cool. I was interviewed at a T.V. studio with an audience full of fans, and then they threw a big party for me after the show. I had a wonderful time, and as weary as I'd grown toward some of the grind of running 3PW back home, it was nice to see how much my — and our — hard work had paid off over in the U.K. It really made me feel like I'd accomplished everything I'd set out to in wrestling, and while I wasn't anywhere near ready to walk away, I felt clear-headed about putting more of a focus on metal once I returned to the States. To put a fine point on that, the day I arrived back in L.A. I drove straight from the airport to San Diego to see a death metal band called 3 Inches of Blood that I was a huge fan of. They were playing with Metal Church in this DIVE bar called Brick by Brick. I was without a doubt the band's biggest supporter at that show, and we all went out to eat at Denny's afterward, and it was clear to me I was most at home hanging out with these metal bands. I could relate to them as a fan, but also a friend, and it just made me feel that much more excited about the *Metal's Dark Side* DVD series I was starting production on in principle that November.

I spent Halloween at the Key Club rocking out to W.A.S.P., who I'd been a fan of since childhood, and started November interviewing George 'Corpsegrinder' Fisher, lead singer from Cannibal Corpse, as my first official interview for the 'Metal's Dark Side' DVD series. I'd been a fan of CC since childhood, and I was SO nervous because he was an idol to me. We were both big fans of the horror filmmaker Daria Argento, and we really hit it off on a personal level, which helped because I was shaking in my boots throughout the entire interview, but he was really cool with me, and we've stayed friends since.

George 'Corpsegrinder' Fisher: I met Jasmin in Philadelphia in 2003. We were playing at TROCADERO, and the day before we'd played in Pittsburg, and I didn't play the show because I had come down with a viral lung infection, so it feels like every time you take a breath, someone's putting a chokehold on your throat. It was the most painful thing to try to breathe, and went to the hospital, and I stayed in a good mood throughout because I knew the next day I was supposed to be interviewed by Jasmin. I was like 'Wow, this is awesome', and I couldn't believe it, 'Jasmin St. Claire!'

I remember when I was doing the interview, I was telling her 'Yeah, I might not be able to play tonight,' and my folks and brother were even at the show. I remember telling her all I could really handle was 3 songs, and she was like 'Awe man,' all bummed out I was singing more songs. And I was just shocked, and thought it was crazy she was a fan, and a real metal head, because you don't think any star is going to listen to this kind of music. No offense to our fans, because they're the best in the world, but I have a certain idea of metal heads, and just wouldn't ordinarily think that anybody that's had any kind of success in life is going to listen to this kind of crazy music. So I never knew before that interview that she was into metal, and was surprised she was a metal head — all the metal she was into, I was like 'Wow, get the fuck out of here!' She was a real metal chick, and I would never have assumed she listened to this kind of music.

At the time, I felt like, 'Wow, I'm just some schlep in a death metal band.' We have this magazine down here called *Rivot Rag*, and she did an interview for them but I was shocked beyond belief when they asked her who some of her favorite people to interview for Metal's Dark Side were, and she said she was nervous when she interviewed me! I was like, 'What? I was nervous when she was interviewing me.' And I didn't think she was nervous at all, and thought — even starting out — she was just as professional as anyone we'd ever done interviews with.

To me, she's not just a pretty face they hired to do interviews, which unfortunately seems like all they ever do, like when MTV had Headbanger's Ball, they had hosts who weren't really into metal, and SHE IS, and she was before she started doing this. She's into the scene, and she knows what she's talking about, she knows what's going on, and knows as much as I do about metal.

Jasmin: Later that month, we held the last 3PW show of the year on the 20th, the weekend before Thanksgiving, and titled it 'For the Gold' because of the multiple title matches at stake. Highlights from that show included Low Ki defeated Slyk Wagner Brown w/April Hunter; CJ O'Doyle defeating Rob Eckos; a Tag-team title match between Pitbulls 2004 (Mike Kruel & Gary Wolf) vs. Double Trouble (Monsta Mack & Damian Adams). As well as other title matches between Chris Sabin defeating Joey Matthews; Road Kill & Blue Meanie vs. Rockin' Rebel & Jack Victory; April Hunter vs. Don E. Allen; Simon Diamond vs. Matt Striker; and finally Christopher Daniels defeating AJ Styles during the Championship Belt title match. We also named Bill Apter, a big Wrestling journalist, the new Commissioner of 3PW during that match, which went over really well with the packed house of fans!

As successfully as that show had come off, I had reached a breaking point with everyone's greed and bad fucking attitudes. At that point, was seriously considering my accountant, Richard McDonald's offer to come in and take over the financing of the company, and having Brian take over as general manager. I was sick of everyone's mountain of bullshit, and was really starting to hate what I'd once loved so dearly, and had worked tirelessly to build. I can't give something 100% if my heart isn't in it, and at that point, my love for metal had overtaken any other professional ambitions I had driving me.

As November came to a close, I interviewed Damage Plan and Shadow's Fall, Bleeding Through, and Himsa for *Metal's Dark Side*, which marked the first time I met my future husband Matt 'The Mooch' Wicklund, who at the time was playing lead guitar for Himsa. I'll never forget, at the outset of my interview with his band, our eyes locked out of nowhere and I felt like I'd been hit by a thunderbolt. It was my first and only case of love at first sight, and I believe was the same for him. Even within our first conversation during the band's interview, I felt he was sexy, well spoken, and we had this chemistry that would NOT quit. The only damper on the moment came when he went to get us drinks and didn't have enough money to pay for them, so naturally I covered the tab — which should have been the first fucking sign.

We hung out all that night during an Arch Enemy concert, and even after I had to leave to drive home, I was getting text messages from him at 3 and 4 in the morning, telling me he didn't want our conversation to end. I have to admit, I didn't either. He invited me the very next night to come see his band play in Anaheim, and getting to see him play on stage added a whole other level of attraction to our mix. He had energy and talent, and I instantly believed and bought into the idea that he was on his way to somewhere big. His band still had a very long way to go at that point, but I felt sure they would get there, a fact that, when I shared it with him, brought us even closer together. We were both very ambitious and driven at that time, and though I was a lot more established than he was in the business, he didn't initially seem to care how I'd gotten to where I had, which was also a very big deal to me. I would be lying if I didn't say I started falling for him almost immediately, and the feeling was clearly mutual by his almost constant text-messaging in the first few days after we'd met while his band was on the road. He would tell me how much he missed me and how I made him melt, and as with any long-distance romance, our time apart just fueled the passion that was building up in his absence. He called me every day from his band's Canadian tour leg, and it felt right to feel what we were for one another — no matter how quickly it was happening.

Himsa's tour ended on December 19th in New York. I flew out to meet him, which also marked the first time all the passion we'd been banking over the past few weeks unleashed itself physically, so needless to say we didn't leave the hotel for the first couple days of our visit. When we were outside walking around the city together, it felt just like one of those romantic Woody Allen movies shot on location in New York, because we would just talk for hours and hours. While we were in New York, we attended the Roadrunner Records Holiday Party together, and the next day, were still so lovely dovey that neither one of us wanted the trip to end. I wound up inviting him to fly back to L.A. to me to see a Killswitch/ Slayer show at the Universal Amphitheatre I had tickets and backstage passes to, and by this point, we decided mutually we were a couple. I was crazy about him, and even though I didn't know where it was going, I couldn't have cared less because I was so happy. We were going to concerts together left and right, from Marilyn Manson to Strapping Young Lad at the Century Media Christmas party, and on the way home from that show, Matt told me he was in love with me. I told him the same, because it felt true, even though my head and heart were lost in a whirlwind as fast as everything had happened between us. He flew home briefly to Seattle for Christmas while I went home to New York to be with my Mom, but we quickly rendezvoused back to L.A. to head into the New Year together.

TOP: Jasmin and Judas Priest. BOTTOM: Jasmin signing at Tower.

TOP: Jasmin with Lemmy and Metal TV Show Co-Host Ron Estrada.
LEFT: Jasmin poses for the cameras the Expo Music Convention, 2008.
RIGHT: Metals Dark Side DVD advertisement.

TOP: Jasmin & Stay Heavy TV show co-host Vinicius, Brazil.
BOTTOM: Jasmin interviewing Yngwie Malmsteen for Metals Dark Side DVD Series.

TOP: Motorhead's Lemmy Kilmister & Jasmin.
BOTTOM: Jasmin and Chuck Billy (Testament).

TOP: Jasmin and Hank Shermann, Mercyful Fate guitarist.
BOTTOM: Jasmin and Johan Hegg (Amon Amarth).

Hard Rocker Magazine Cover Shoot.

TOP: Jasmin with Kiss's Bruce Kulick.
BOTTOM: Jasmin signing autographs at the Rock Brigade Magazine booth, Expo Music 2008.

TOP: Jasmin and Willie Adler (Lamb of God). BOTTOM: Jasmin at NAAM 2007.

TOP: Jasmin interviewing Ratt guitarist Warren DiMartini for Metals Dark Side DVD series.
BOTTOM: Jasmin & Frank (Suffocation vocalist).

TOP: Jasmin & Fred (Dragonforce) at Namm Convention.
BOTTOM: Jasmin with Almah.

TOP: Jasmin with Bill Hudson of Circle to Circle.
BOTTOM: Jasmin with the Metal Mayor of Kvarna, Bulgaria.

Jasmin with Paulo Xisto (SEPULTURA).

PART XVIIII

Booty Call Gone Wrong...

I started out 2005 in LOVE — with my new boyfriend Matt, with the metal scene I was becoming more and more professionally immersed in, and have to say that the New Year began, everything was going extremely well. Matt came with me to the NAAM convention in Anaheim, CA where I was signing at the B.C. Rich and Coffin Guitar Case booths, which marked my debut within that industry crowd because I'd been off wrestling for the past few years and off their radar. I guess metal heads are bigger fans of porn than of wrestling. Either way, it was an event, and I was thrilled by the response I got in the form of two of the longest booth signing lines of the entire convention. Everyone kept telling me how great I looked, and I could tell some of the other Coffin Case girls didn't like the attention I was getting very much, which I was used to.

I could tell the attention I was getting at NAMM bothered Matt on some level, which took me a little aback, but I was so in love at the time I couldn't have cared less. I thought the constant attention he was giving me was sweet, not able yet to see past my blinders to the fact that it should have been an early warning sign unhealthy possessiveness he was filled with. My past had never come up in our relationship to that point, other than he knew I had been an adult film star. I guess I can see in hindsight how it might have shocked him a little when so many of my fans came crawling out of the woodwork at the convention. My crowd ranged from suits to long-haired guitar techs, and even rock and metal star players, which I think really bothered him because he kept drinking more as the day went on.

It didn't really matter to me at the time because I was so happy we were together. He stayed in L.A. with me for a few more days before returning to Seattle to work on writing the new Himsa album, while I stayed back in L.A. continuing to shoot more interviews for the *Metal's Dark Side* DVD. We also decided to put our first 3PW show of the New Year off until later February, because of it being the dead of winter and traditionally a harder time to draw in fans, but also personally for me because I was fast losing interest in the company. We'd decided to bring in some outside investors who were going to be a little more involved in the day-to-day running of the company, and I wasn't happy with some of the direction they wanted to head in, so that gave me further incentive to stay away. I think my waning interest in wrestling had most to do with the stress of running a league, rather than out of some lost love for the sport itself — which is something I want to make clear for 3PW fans.

I wasn't seeking to step out of 3PW completely, just step back, and perhaps recoup some of my considerable personal investment in the company I'd bankrolled and built from scratch. More than anything, I was just SICK and TIRED of dealing with wrestlers bitching about their airline tickets, I was truly over it, and it just wasn't fun anymore. Besides, I just knew I was onto something new and wonderful with my Metal hosting and modeling gigs, and it's where my heart was — when it wasn't preoccupied with Matt that is. We talked and texted for hours every day until he came back to L.A. at the end of January to visit me again. I couldn't have been happier with life in general, at that point. I'd gotten a cover with *Femme Fatales Magazine*, and my publicist had gotten me hooked up with a part for the new National Lampoon movie: *Dorm Daze II*, which was awesome on top of everything else.

In February, I flew up to Seattle to visit Matt for his birthday. We stayed at the W Hotel, and had a wonderful time on my dime, but I noticed something while I was up there that should have been a warning sign to me of things to come. Basically he wasn't living anywhere steady — he was sleeping on the floor of his band's rehearsal studio or crashing on couches, which is common enough I suppose for musicians. But a trend had quietly developed where I was paying for *EVERYTHING*, from the hotel to drinks to meals, I was just too much in love at the time to care — about that or even 3PW. The latter came to a head on February 19th when the February 3PW show and Matt's birthday coincidentally happened to fall on the same day. I was so fed up with my role in 3PW at that point that I chose to blow off the show and spend the day with Matt in Seattle instead — which I know sounds bad. It felt right at the time to me, and I can tell you right now I had a MUCH more enjoyable time in Seattle with my boyfriend than I would have in Philadelphia dealing with prima donna wrestlers.

We spent the night at a Himsa concert he had to play and it was a very romantic day all in all, and I had no regrets about blowing off the 3PW show. Of course, the company felt differently, and the shit started to hit the fan in early March when the Blue Meanie went behind my back and signed away the rights to 3PW, which wasn't within his authority to do. I had a contract stating that I was to be repaid ALL the monies I'd invested in 3PW before any sale could go through, and the fact that he sneaked behind my back and trademarked 3PW in his own name was unethical and illegal. It wasn't his company to sell, and so I had no other choice than to begin litigation against 3PW that same month.

As the spring rolled on, Matt and I got into a routine where we'd travel back and forth to either Seattle or L.A. — depending on his Himsa and my *Metal's Dark Side* commitments — to visit each other. Of course all of it was on my dime, but again I didn't care because I had plenty coming in from my merchandise sales, signings and was expecting a big settlement at some point in the near future from my 3PW lawsuit. In the meantime, their show attendance numbers had started to drop WAY off once word got out that I was no longer involved with the league. That made me feel good to know I had some loyalty among the fans, but I was sad in another way that I was walking away from a movement I'd built from nothing. It was a mountain I was very proud to have climbed, but at this point, felt like I needed a new challenge in my life. Between juggling a long-distance relationship with Matt and my fledgling Metal hosting career in California, I didn't have time to keep up with all of 3PW's drama. I have never been about drama — unless it's centered around me of course, ;-) and I just felt my life was healthier without the negativity 3PW had come to represent at that point. Looking back on it now, it's a decision I still have no regrets over.

As well as the spring was going, when Matt came down to visit me in L.A. over Easter weekend, it marked the beginning of an ugly pattern that emerged thereafter of his starting to ask me more and more questions about my past. Since he'd visited me throughout the spring in L.A. and stayed at my apartment enough to see my merchandise (DVDs, signed posters, etc) which paid for ALL our bills, he'd begun to develop a complex about it. This ran entirely contrary to his claims from the beginning of our relationship that he didn't care about my past, and certainly he was biting the hand that fed and flew him from Seattle to L.A. and back on a regular basis, but it seemed like he couldn't help himself. He had developed this possessive, creepy, judgmental side to his personality very quickly in the course of that visit, and I didn't like or appreciate it one bit.

Already I'd given up a company I'd built from the ground up for him, and unfortunately, it marked the beginning of what was a lot more sacrifice on my part to come for that fucker. At the time, I was still drunk on love, and he was getting drunker and drunker by the day on alcohol, which really alarmed me, but I didn't know how to approach him about it. When he finally told me near the end of March that he'd decided to stop drinking for a while, I thought that would cure him of the possessive side of his personality — which seemed to rear its ugly head primarily when he was drinking. Sadly, I was wrong, because he kept getting worse and worse with his jealous judging of my past. On top of that, he had girls texting him all the time and wouldn't change his relationship status from single on his MySpace page, to which he retaliated by pointing out that fans of mine would leave comments on my website. He also had a sick talent for making me feel like his treating me that way was my fault, and of course I fell for it because of how madly in love I was at the time.

We ended up working it out, and just in time, because heading into April Matt had a falling out of his own with Himsa involving a disagreement over songwriting-credit related issues. That would result in his formally exiting the band later that summer, and I guess in a way I played a role in that exit, because ahead of his leaving he would constantly tell me how lonely he was without me in Seattle. I wanted him with me in L.A. so I didn't try to stop him, and I believed in his talent enough to support his decision without blinking once. His plan for the moment was to continue commuting as Himsa had gone head long into writing on their next album, and I supported Matt's career 100%.

As May began, things were full underway with my 3PW lawsuit, and as livid as they were making me trying to steal my company without compensating me properly, they had the nerve to try and get me to come back! Eventually, my lawsuit with 3PW was settled, and I was awarded all the footage we'd shot of the first two years worth of matches, which had been in syndication in the U.K. on the Wresting Channel and was among the most valuable of the companies assets. Brian was awarded rights to the 3PW name, which pissed me off, but I didn't blame him entirely — he had partners idiot partners in 'One Eye' Rich, my former accountant, and this power hungry limey named Mike who had no idea what he was doing. Neither had any idea what they were doing in trying to run a wrestling league, and paired with Brian, they were spending more than they were taking in at the shows, and the company was just heading downhill. I was just relieved I wasn't going along for the ride, and that I'd gotten out when I had. I had my eye to the future, and my first mainstream feature film with the *National Lampoon's Dorm Daze II* shoot, which began in principle that month.

While I was working on my movie, Matt was in Denmark with Himsa writing on the band's new album, and while the distance was hard, he would call me every day in between my scenes, and we'd talk for hours. I guess he wasn't getting very much in the way of a per diem from the band while he was there recording, so I sent him some money for phone cards and basic expenses. At the same time, he was still in the dark with Himsa over how much money he'd be getting paid from his publishing share on the album the band was recording. He was worried he wouldn't be getting his fare share of the writing credit reflected in royalties, so per his request, I got him hooked up with a lawyer through my dear friend Brian Perera at Cleopatra Records. It felt good to be supporting someone I loved, it came naturally to me, and gave me happiness, but as often as he called me to tell me how miserable he was without me. I missed him fiercely as well, and so we decided on my break in later May from the National Lampoon shoot, I would fly to Denmark to see him.

After the first half of my shoot was over, Matt was still in Denmark writing the new Himsa record, and I'd lined up some *Metal's Dark Side*-related business in Europe so I could fly over to visit him as we'd planned. From the moment I landed in Arhus, we had just the best time together. The northern lights were beautiful, and the whole vibe going on in that part of the world was just a welcome change from L.A. I put us both up at the Radisson Hotel so he didn't have to sleep in the shit hole the band was bunking up together in. When he'd get done with his sessions, we'd spend our nights together walking around Arhus, Denmark, and I felt for the first time in my life like I had a real partner. On the weekends, we were inseparable, and when it came time for me to fly back to the States to continue work on the Dorm Daze movie, he was nearing the end of his writing sessions. So I arranged for him to fly back as early as possible to join me in L.A.

I picked up shooting on *Dorm Daze* in early June, and I remember the first day I was back on the set, which was down by the Queen Mary in Long Beach. I had my own trailer, and was playing the wife of the ship's Captain, who was played by a really talented performer named Richard Riehle, who'd played Tom Smykowski in Office Space! As one of my — and America's — favorite cult film classics, that was a real honor, and he treated me as a total equal on the set, which was really cool. I was also acting with the Chris Owen, who'd played the Shermanator in the American Pie movies, and felt like I'd really arrived. I had my own trailer with an air conditioner and my name on it, and the catering on set was amazing, it was definitely a step up from the indie-sets of *Communication Breakdown* and *Swamp Zombies*. It was funny because when I walked on set for the first time, people were expecting me to be horrible, and I did what I do best on-screen: I winged it, and my scenes went over really well. I had one day of dialogue with this Frat kid named Oren Skoog, who was of the nicest people I worked with on that movie, which made me feel horrible when I had to torture and slap him in one of our scenes.

When I wasn't on-set, I spent my time in my trailer playing video games and talking to Matt, who was flying in from Denmark, I was into the second half of my Dorm Daze shoot. My dressing room was moved onto the actual ship the next day because I had scenes to shoot with Charles Shaughnessy, who played Fran Dresher's love interest on the Nanny, and I was again just so excited to be working with real actors for a change. I also got on really well with all the crew people, because there were a lot of female actresses on the set. Even though they were nobodies, would still play the whole L.A. prim Madonna part and not give anyone but the director in the film crew the time of day. I never treated anyone that way — dating back from my days on adult film sets, to signings when I watched Francine blow off her fans during my wrestling days, to where I was at by now with my film work in metal and mainstream movies. I always felt like the crew worked as hard — if not much harder — than any of the talent. They got up hours before we did, worked much longer hours and got a lot less sleep than we did, and it's just an etiquette I've always brought with me to the job.

Driving home with Matt that night after my shoot had ended, I got the happiest shock of my life when he told me about a dream he'd had while sleeping that day in my movie trailer: in the dream, we were living in Europe together and married. Then he shocked me literally to where I almost lost control of the steering wheel when he popped the question out of the blue and proposed marriage to me! I was stunned, and **IMMEDIATELY** said '*YES*,' almost as an emotional reflex — that's how natural it felt to me. He didn't have a ring, which I couldn't have given a shit less about — I was just so happy to be engaged. Naturally, our euphoria only extended as far as our own little world, because neither his parents nor my mother was very thrilled about the news upon hearing it. Though that made us a little sad, but everyone on the set was thrilled for us when I broke the news the next day, popping Champagne and celebrating in between takes. Our friends were also very excited for us, and I think I felt 100% content for the first time in my personal life because I had everything I wanted: a man who loved me for me, a burgeoning mainstream film and veejaying career, and no headache anymore with 3PW. In that moment, I was completely content with my life overall.

Matt had to head back to Seattle to deal with some Himsa business, and I flew back to New York to spend some time with my mother to calm her overprotective nerves about my wedding. While I was still in N.Y., I got a bit of a shock when Matt informed me that he had quit Himsa, which everyone of course blamed me for. The truth was Matt was unhappy with the musical direction the band was heading in, coupled with his dispute with fellow members over his publishing splits. And even though the lead singer had literally threatened to beat Matt's face in for leaving and blamed me for his exit, I'd been the loudest critic of his decision when he'd first made it! I was the one who pushed him to stick it out, so the bottom line was, regardless of my presence: there was enough internal acrimony going on within the band that Matt would have left either way. He decided he would move down to L.A. full-time to be with me, and put together a new group locally. I thought with his talent, and name recognition from playing with Himsa, he would have no problem and I'm not going to lie and say I wasn't 100% thrilled about things being solidified between us as a couple.

I was still shooting on *Dorm Daze* when he got to L.A., and he was coming with me to the set every day, making arrangements to hook up some of the members of Cradle of Filth — the keyboardist, Martin

Powell, and guitarist James Mc Ilroy. I was excited for him — and quietly relieved — because prior to him hooking up with a new gig, there were a couple weeks early on where he wasn't doing a thing but sitting around my movie trailer or apartment playing his guitar and drawing. He was an amazing artist, and at first he was going to try and get a part-time day gig in animation, but that possibility quickly withered off the vine. Then, he was going to teach guitar for a little while to west L.A. Music, but that went away. I am a work-a-holic, and in my book, actions have always spoken louder than words, so it started to get a little alarming to me when his pattern of maybe jobs that always dried up became regular. I was patient and supportive of his transition, even to the extreme of charging his engagement ring to me on his new credit card…that I was paying off.

As wonderful as that was, the adjustment of learning to live with someone full-time was definitely that, because Matt upon moving in immediately picked back up on his trend of slamming me about my porn past. Most often, he picked on the fact that I had old copies of Playboys and other magazines I'd been the centerfold in or DVDs I sold on eBay to pay ALL OUR bills stored away in the back of a closet. It wasn't like I had these things on display on my living room walls, and this was our livelihood at the time, but still I agreed to move everything related to that era of my career into storage, which I thought was a big concession. I was willing to make it for him, but I definitely didn't appreciate his rubbing my face in it. I had worked hard to get into and out of that business in as short a time as I had, and considered it a real achievement that I was still big enough of a star to be making money off of it six+ years later. Looking back now, I think a lot of the insecurity on his part came at his parent's prodding too, because his mother — who would NEVER speak to me on the phone — talked to him on almost a daily basis. He was a tragic mama's boy, I mean, it bordered on unhealthy, and it was definitely that for us after he'd hang up because routinely, he'd begin bitching at me about my past.

Once he started dictating to me that I had to get rid of my nude photos, and couldn't sell them on eBay any longer, I thought he'd crossed a line because he was fucking with my *bottom line.* I was paying ALL OUR bills with that money, and Matt at that point wasn't lifting a finger to bring any money into the house, so I felt he really had no right to be complaining at all. I kept telling him it shouldn't matter: it was all from my past, and reminded him additionally of the fact that this was our primary income source. In the end, I caved when he threatened to end the engagement and got rid of — NOT SOLD OFF — but literally threw out $15,000 worth of merchandise! That was how deeply I loved him, and how devoted I was to making the relationship work. When I tried to explain to him that even though I was bringing in some money from the Metal hosting, it was still getting off the ground, and between our monthly overhead and my legal fees relative to the 3PW litigation, it wasn't good timing at all. Clearly his pride had made him a zombie in those moments because he persisted, even to the point of next demanding I shut down my website, which I didn't even have control over.

He didn't want anything porn-related being sold to support us, and was doing nothing on his part to replace that revenue. The deeper into the summer we got, the more his jealous, controlling side began to emerge from whatever swamp it had been hiding. As much as I loved him, at times it was almost like a fucking horror movie. He would never raise a hand to me, but he was verbally abusive via his rubbing my nose on a daily basis on my adult-film past. It seemed like I couldn't escape that, no matter who I was with, and it was almost heart breaking at times. I only survived by the same spine I've had to steer my entire adult life with. Whenever any guy let me down and I had to carry both our weight: I'd done it with countless men: from Dick to Earl, and now to Matt, but with him, it definitely hurt the most. I knew he was different from any other man I'd ever been in a serious relationship with, and my heart kept giving him the benefit of a doubt, even when my head would be screaming at me not to. It was maddening at times, because I'd never been so in love and so naturally compelled to keep trying to make the relationship work.

I felt helpless and really didn't know what to do at this point, so I went ahead and did what he'd told me: I called the webmaster of my online site, and got the process started of taking it down. That unfortunately would take a while because they had to recoup some money I'd been advanced from merchandise sales, which of course I got screamed at for. I also had an online diary my fans regularly read that I wanted to keep up, but my jealous hobo-hubby to be had a problem with that too. He was very jealous, and I thought it wasn't ever right, but especially once I found out he'd slept at some bitch's house earlier that spring, while lying to me that he'd been elsewhere. It may seem petty to you now, but at the time it was the straw that broke the back of all the stress I'd been carrying around because of him and his fucked-up possessiveness. I slapped him, threw his ass out to the curb, and broke off the engagement. I felt so betrayed, and once he crawled back to me in tears, I took him back but still had decided to put the wedding on hold. I felt we had some serious, deep-seated issues on his part to work through relative to his jealously and possessiveness.

I am sure many women have been through this, even without an adult-film past, to add on top of the mountain jealous men can build up over the woman they love. It's a universal problem that I'd been through on some much more severe levels in the past where physical abuse had been involved, but what Matt was putting me through in the way of his constant mental and emotional torture was much worse to me. There was nothing wrong with me as a person, and it burned me up inside that he wouldn't accept me for me, in spite of my having taken him into my home and heart with all his faults. Deep down, I had all this animosity for everything he was putting me through — especially in the face of everything I was doing to support him, more than anyone else in his life. I can't lie and say we came to a complete resolution that day, but I agreed to put the engagement back in play. I was too in love with him to let him go at that point, even in spite of the fact that he was living off a credit card I paid the bill on every month!

He backed off for a few days after that on berating me about my past, but then his mother — upon finding out our engagement was back on — persisted in calling him every day with some new piece of my adult film past she'd found online that day. It was a sick little routine she had of playing head games with him, trying to interfere with our life. When I demanded he tell her to stop, he refused, and when I finally got on the phone one day and asked her, 'What is your fucking problem with me, lady? What have I done to your son? I've stood behind him and taken care of him all this time.' She had no reply, and I decided they were almost like mother-and-son Norman Bates, from the movie '*Psycho*' at that point, because it was an unhealthy alliance against me. He was an irretrievable mama's boy, and that was a fact that definitely caused a regular rift throughout our marriage.

I also found it funny that in spite of how *concerned* Matt's mom pretended to be for him where his choice in women was concerned, when it came to her son's health, it was ME who picked up the doctor's tab. He had to cure an acne problem on his back that was causing him to break out horribly. That mattered past personal vanity because onstage as a guitar player, your shirt is off the entire show, and appreciating that from a professional angle, even though I had no health insurance myself at that time, I paid for his operation. The initial visit alone was $200, then there was another $600 in medication costs, all of which I paid for. In spite of his parents knowing this, his mother still said horrible things about me to Matt on a daily basis during their creepy 'mama's boy' phone call routine. Trying in every way she could to cause a rift between us: 'Well, you know where that money probably came from Matt,' all sorts of nasty things of that nature.

As the summer rolled into August, Matt finally got off his ass enough to decide he wanted to relocate temporarily to Europe to record new material with the ex-Cradle of Filth band members toward the end of starting a new group together. I was delighted at the prospect of getting him A) off my sofa and out of the apartment, B) back to work doing something he was absolutely talented at, and C) getting his head into a space where he would be happy. Thus we would be happy as a couple. I LOVED seeing him play music, and once he'd made his wishes known, as excited as I was, I also had to figure out how we were going to pay for it. Once I found out how expensive the trip to England was going to be, I was alarmed because we were running really low on money, but I really believed in Matt and wanted him to do well. And I thought that things might change for the better if I could pull it off, especially knowing his lazy ass wasn't going to lift a finger to help. But in hindsight I should have known I was living in a fantasy of sorts because the truth was: without money coming in from my website at that point, coupled with what he'd made me throw out in the way of merchandise, we had a lot less coming in.

I was desperate to make my marriage work, and driven by the moment of love I felt trapped in, I decided to put it all on the line for my man. The next day I went down to JP Morgan where I had my IRA saving account and liquidated it. At that point, we also needed the money to live on, but I put aside almost $10,000 of it for our forthcoming trip to England. Amazingly, my travel agent was able to find two-first class, round-trip tickets from L.A. to the U.K. for $3000.00, so we had enough money to live on and would at least be traveling into the unknown in style. We were going to be leaving in September and would be staying with his friend James. At least we wouldn't have a hotel bill to deal with on top of all the other expenses for the trip. I can safely admit I was nervous as HELL, because even though Matt was writing with viable industry players that had recently left Cradle of Filth, there was so much we didn't know. I would ask Matt, ' How long is it going to take you to get a record deal?' And he would always say, 'Don't worry, it won't take long.' Plus, he was in litigation with Himsa regarding publishing and his ex-band mates had been trashing him all over the rock media for the lawsuit, so we had a lot riding on the Europe writing trip going well.

Prior to leaving on the trip, we picked up our wedding bands — well in advance of our end-of-year wedding date — and I felt like maybe this trip would be the answer to our problems. It would give us both an opportunity to get a fresh start, away from all the drama of L.A., but I was still very nervous. He'd been displaying different sides of his personality since our engagement that I hadn't seen surface before. From his drinking to his inability to think for himself, which routinely caused him to take the prodding of someone like his mother about my past and re-create a problem even after he and I had settled it. She was waging a campaign to derail our relationship before we got down the aisle, as were all these little groupie/hangers-on that Matt had started hanging around with at the local bar where he'd spent most of the summer running up bar tabs that I had to settle. I loved him in spite of all of the wreckage he'd already caused to my financial well-being, and the sacrifices I made for him in that vein should be all the evidence I need of how committed I was to making things work between us.

He'd gone crazy with it by this point too: demanding I go and have every site on the internet that had ever run a news story about me, or posted a picture, that made any mention whatsoever of my adult film past, be taken down. He was obsessed, to the extreme of wanting me to find some way for eBay to cease the selling of anything of mine — whether I had ownership of it or not. Fans of mine trade my memorabilia all the time on eBay, and I see nothing from it financially, but Matt was so threatened by the existence of any of it that I had to lie to him and promise I'd try. I guess by that point, the emotional abuse he was putting me through had pushed me to a desperate place of trying to do anything to keep us together. He was drunk all the time, and whenever I tried to talk to his mother about it, she would suggest it was because he couldn't handle my past. I'd come home and find him rooting through my personal belongings, ranting on about how he had to know who he was marrying — all based on his mother terrorizing us with phone calls questioning my past on a daily basis. I was VERY alarmed at the psychotic and paranoid way Matt was acting as a result, but I just kept telling myself that once we got to England, away from everything where he could focus on his music with no distractions, that things would improve between us.

In early September, we left for London for Matt to begin his collaboration with Mark Powell, who had played prior thereto in Cradle of Filth and My Dying Brides, and their friend, James McGilroy, who was also formerly of Cradle of Filth. The collaboration looked really promising, and the plan was for the three of them to write and record a demo that we would shop later in the fall after we got back to the States. I had EVERYTHING riding on our relationship at that point, considering I'd liquidated over a hundred thousand dollars total from my IRAs to support us over the next couple years while Matt's music career got back on track. I believed in his talent, and was betting everything on him because I was so madly in love. One thing I found ironic was he had no problem with the gamble I'd taken to finance our bohemian artist lifestyle — even in spite of the fact that I'd earned that money from my adult film years. That made him a total hypocrite in my eyes, but I felt as though when two people commit to one another on the level we had for better or worse means just what it sounds like. Things had already been at their worst for a while, and with this trip, I was investing my life savings in the prospect they would get better once Matt's new band was on their feet. On top of everything else, I was also juggling a litigation battle with my mother over control of the inheritance my father had left to me when he passed.

When we landed in England, Matt was so happy and excited to be making music again that my hopes brightened considerably about our turning things around personally in the same time that they would professionally. We were staying in London, and the band was recording in Sheffield, so we spent our first few days vacationing around London. When we arrived in Sheffield, we were initially booked in to this SHITTY, seedy hotel, so naturally I got us moved — on my dime of course — into a charming Bed & Breakfast that was actually owned by Def Leppard drummer Rick Allen's family. While Matt would spend his days writing with his new group, I would sightsee around the countryside, trying to make it as much of a vacation as I could. Matt and I went to see Stonehenge together, where Led Zeppelin had recorded *When the Levy Breaks*, which was pretty cool. We also got to see one of my favorite metal bands,

Opeth, live while we were over there, which was a lot of fun. So being in England was truly a refuge of sorts for me, in spite of how expensive it was turning out to be.

Matt and his band were making progress, still, as happy as I was for him, not once did he stop to thank me for the amazing level of support I was giving him to make this trip possible. One night it came to bother me so greatly that I called him out on it, and told him: 'It seems like you take this for granted, I'm here standing behind you and took all my money out to support you,' and he still didn't seem to get it. Responsibility always seemed to be lost on him where money was concerned, and toward the end of the trip — in spite of how vocally happy I was about the progress his band was making with their demo — quietly I was beginning to feel I'd been used. That was a horrible feeling to have in my gut, and in the face of my still being very much in love. I dealt with it, but as we headed back to the L.A. from England in early October, my uneasiness continued to grow, even as our wedding date was fast approaching.

In October, my birthday rolled around, and Matt bought me a gift at Tiffany's — using a credit card of course to pay for it. But he really showed his class act a few days after, when he found some old nude slides from some shoot years earlier I'd forgotten I still had buried in my closet. He used that as an excuse to begin bitching at me again about my website, which was out of my hands because of the debt I was in to the web-hosting company. One thing about my husband-to-be that had always bothered me but more recently, had begun to outright alarm me was the fact that he had such a little grasp on the real world in terms of money. His naiveté was STUNNING at times, and I was only able to ignore that concern because of how deeply in love I was with him at that time. He'd even told me he'd rather starve than live off of porn money — which may sound ideal but wasn't realistic at all given his lack of ability to bring in any income whatsoever. The only job he seemed willing to take was as a bartender at the very bar he wasted most of his days getting drunk at, which didn't seem like a smart idea to me given the alcoholic symptoms he was already displaying in our relationship.

It was very confusing at times because here's the love of my life professing he wants to be with me and take care of me for the rest of my life. Can't he man up enough to go out and get a temporary job on his own to bring in any money? On top of that he had the balls to question how

I put a roof over my head. It just seemed CRAZY to me! Still, for better or worse, I was crazy about him, and I was about to take the former vow very literally as our wedding date fast approached. Rather than contribute ANY money toward that union — which I was paying for entirely on my own — Matt threw another monkey wrench in my confidence in him when he bought a brand new guitar in late November. He had just gotten a new credit card, and the last thing he — or WE — needed was a new guitar when he had 8 others, mounting debt, and he had no source of income. I made him return the guitar, which he pouted about, but since I was paying both his and my bills, I felt it was my right.

We went up to Seattle for Thanksgiving. I'm sure you can figure out I wasn't really looking forward to this. We stayed at the W Hotel in downtown Seattle. Naturally I paid for it because his parents hadn't invited us to stay with them, even though Matt said they had plenty of room. On top of that, rather than have us over for any kind of watered down congratulations party/traditional sit-down Thanksgiving turkey dinner, Matt's parents instead met us at some Thai restaurant downtown for lunch. The whole thing was insulting frankly, and they didn't even offer us a ride back to our hotel afterward, they told us to take a TAXI!! I felt like I wasn't wanted, and they had done a very good job of making me feel like absolute shit, which I deduced was part of their strategy of trying to make me so mad that I would call off the wedding. Unfortunately for them, all it did was make me more determined to make my relationship with Matt work. That much harder — I did toward that end.

As our marrying date approached, Matt continued to harass me more and more intensely about my website, almost as if he was becoming obsessed. My hairdresser Debbie — who was my confidant for much of my roller coaster ride with Matt — warned me that between the pressure from his family and the jealousy over my past that was consuming him more and more each day, I would regret going through with the wedding. I was so in love with Matt though that I was willing to forge on, even though she also told me he was also not the man I wanted to have my children with — and she had four. I thought it was cute that Matt and I were always together. Attached at the hip like Siamese Twins, I didn't have a problem with that, but friends of mine tried to point out — correctly in hindsight — that for Matt, that behavior was part of his possessive side come fully to life now that we were engaged. I hadn't been engaged before to anyone, so I had no idea how men were supposed to behave, and

I know my status as a sex symbol caused him some legitimate insecurity around other men. But he'd started to let his paranoia extend as boundlessly as the internet, which I had no control over. I knew this much: he wanted control over me, and at times I was so blindly in love with him that I guess I had no problem giving it to him.

We spent Christmas in L.A., and I'd spoiled him rotten on gifts, but on Christmas morning, Matt had climbed into bed to awake me — not with a kiss — but rather with some new rant about a section of my website he'd been obsessively stalking and prowling around the night before! I saw red and lost it, pushing him to the floor, yelling for him to get out of my house and my life: 'That is not how you start a Christmas morning, get out of this house NOW!' Here I'd gone out of my way to buy all these gifts for him, and this is what I was waking up to Christmas morning? I'm surprised I didn't beat the fuck out of him, because I bet any other woman reading this would have. I just slapped him and kept yelling 'Get out, I can't believe this is Christmas and all you have to say to me is the same old bullshit about a website I don't even control?!' Nothing was ever good enough for him, NOTHING, and I'd at that point given him just about everything I had to give.

He kept telling me he didn't know what he'd done wrong as I pushed him out the door, and it was the saddest thing for me that he'd pushed me to that extreme, but all I wanted was to have a peaceful Christmas with my fiancé, but he'd ruined it. He called me an hour afterward crying about how he'd wanted to make me breakfast-in-bed, and all I could think to say back was 'Yeah, but you probably would have been bitching about where the money to buy the eggs came from!' I was done letting his shit slide, and it was only six days before our wedding date, so part of me was convinced the engagement was off. He came crawling back on his knees to me later that day with roses, crying and apologizing for his behavior, swearing he'd never go on the site again. I took him back because I loved him, but he'd still ruined Christmas, which is one of mine and many peoples' most treasured holidays of the year. Even today, I still feel he deserved my rage, but I felt my hands were tied at that point because I was so in love and would have done anything in the world to keep him.

We were married on the 31st of December 2005, almost a year after we'd first met. It hadn't been a fairytale engagement, but nothing in my life has ever been that easy, and I have always felt any real relationship requires hard work, so it didn't scare me. I wanted to have a nice wedding, but it seemed like too much to plan, so we decided to go to the beach and just keep it simple and beautiful with the ocean as our backdrop. Matt's mom had even surprised us by offering to make a wedding dress for me, but backed out at the last minute, which I should have seen coming. It was a shitty thing to do. Not only did they not bother coming to the wedding, but they didn't even send a card, nothing. When my mother had expressed reservations about my marriage to Matt, I'd done the adult thing and stood by my husband. I said to my mother, 'If you don't want to be part of our life now, maybe you will somewhere down the line,' but he wasn't even standing up to his parents in my defense. I guess I made my peace with it in the moment because he was going through with the wedding in spite of his family's objections, which was the most important thing. Thankfully, I had family and friends on my side, but his were nowhere to be found.

It was definitely a wedding pulled off against the odds: it was pouring rain the day of the nuptials, we had a small ceremony with close friends and no family, but we were still the happiest couple in our little world. Afterward, I heard Matt's mom was crying on the phone when the ceremony was over, but not happy tears and that made me love him even more, knowing he'd gone through with the wedding anyway. I knew I had married a mama's boy, but I never wanted anyone else but him, he's the only person I ever wanted to be with. I was proud to be married to him, in spite of his alcoholism, jealousy and possessiveness; his nutty, overprotective mother, and lack of ability to bring in an income of any sort. I was willing to do anything to make the relationship work because as much as I might be able to fight with him, I couldn't fight the love I felt at the time, so I decided to walk the line, as they say, for both of us. Needless to say, with that decision, my list of New Years resolutions was pretty loaded for bear headed into 2006. Still, the bottom line above anything and everything else was, I was determined to make my marriage work.

PART XX

Married, but still alone in this world...and suicidal

After we married, Matt began to become more possessive than ever before, to the point where he tried to regulate my autograph signings by demanding that I not sign anything 'Jasmin St. Claire!' I felt like asking him, 'Who the HELL are you to be doing any of this?' But then I would remind myself I had taken him as my husband, so in his twisted mind, he probably felt he did have a right. Our marriage was complicated right from the start, and it didn't get any simpler as the year approached its close. He'd throw shit in my face like 'What's more important to you: ME or porn?' as though I were still in a business I'd worked my ass off to get out of as quickly as I did and still remain as popular years later. He had no appreciation for the work involved in getting anywhere near the level of popularity I had, from the sacrifices to the ways in which those sacrifices could continue to pay you back years after they'd passed if you played your cards right. Matt had no idea how to play that game, the only ones he liked to play were with my head, and I was getting sicker and more tired of it with each day that passed.

On top of that, NOTHING was happening with the demo I had financed his trip to Europe to write, and we were steadily sinking further and farther into debt. I kept asking him: 'When are you going to start shopping a record deal?' And he finally explained the band would have to take the demo they'd tracked in England and re-record it into a more proper Label-Quality demo, and enlisted veteran producer Bob Kulick for the task. I was excited for Matt because Bob Kulick's resume included stints as Kiss's unofficial guitarist in the late 70 and early 80s, as well as with such rock legends as Meatloaf and W.A.S.P. Naturally, I was once again the Executive Producer on the project, laying out all the money for

Kulick's studio time upfront, as Matt was still going back and forth with Himsa regarding his settlement check.

That same month, we attended the N.A.M.M. show, which gave Matt a chance to promote his new project while I did my Coffincase and B.C. Rich booth signings, as well as a Coffincase-sponsored Fashion Show. For a change, Matt actually acted like he was proud of me, for the day anyway, but as soon as we were home and away from the public, his jealous side reared its ugly head right back up again. He was still on me about taking down my website, *www.jasminstclaire.com,* which I no longer had control over, and therein no ability to remove it from the web. That only provoked him to make the even creepier suggestion that I sue the site owners or try to buy them out with what was left of my life savings that we were living on at the time.

Matt's jealousy and naiveté were becoming more and more expensive for me by the day. We were in the middle of a lawsuit; he wouldn't work a day job, and from what I could tell, spent most of his days waking up at noon, playing his guitar, talking on the phone for hours at a clip to his mother. When he wasn't doing that, he was bitching at me about his paranoid delusions over my porn past, and I really felt like he was morphing from obsessed into possessed. I felt a real sense of disappointment in the way he was acting, one I'd never quite felt before, likely because I'd never invested so much faith and love in a man before. He was letting me down, one sad notch at a time. Sinking lower and lower with each day's grilling over where I was hiding the rest of my non-existent porn merchandise in our apartment or how much of my professional name, 'Jasmin' vs. 'Jasmin St. Claire' I was signing to a fan's autographed still. He even got so crazy with jealousy one day that he bought a subscription to my website so he could poke around in the members-only section. I had no control over what the webmasters posted there for download, and didn't make any money whatsoever from it. Matt's behavior was costing me money, and in a former life, I would have dragged his ass out into an alley and beat the shit out of him for taking food out of my mouth, but my love for him made me feel helpless. I felt that much more considering the fact that there was NOTHING I could do to change my past and that Matt's obsession with it was slowly costing us our future.

I think the biggest problem had to do with jealousy on Matt's part NOT over my past only, but also over my continued success as a figure within the entertainment business that was in demand where no one was knocking on his door. Yes he had his new project, but he'd walked out of a much more popular and established band, in part to be with me, so that made me more tolerant of his behavior than I might have been with any other guy. I was getting plenty of press from my metal veejaying and modeling — from *Metal Edge* to *Metal Maniacs Magazine*, if I appeared in a two-piece in an ad that would set him off. By the end of February, things had gotten out of hand between us over it: if he'd had it his way, I'd have been dressed like one of those Iranian Muslim Women cloaked from head to toe except for the eye slit. I had gotten so frustrated by that point that whenever we argued, I was just yelling back at him, no longer trying to reason. His jealousy had reached almost the point of insanity, and routinely he would storm off out of the apartment, down the street to his favorite local bar, and proceed to drink it off.

He was a full-blown alcoholic by that point, and it got so bad that night-after-night, I would sleep on the floor of my walk-in closet because I couldn't take another night of his badgering me about my past: *'What was it like when you did it?' 'Why did you sleep with so many guys? 'Aren't you the queen of gang bang? Yes or no, answer me!'* Every day he would ask me that and it just hurt me so bad, worse and worse. It was all he talked about from the time I woke up in the morning till the time I fell to sleep at night, and I know one thing: my marriage DEFINITELY skipped its 'honeymoon' period that spring. I felt like I was on trial, or being put through a trial of some sort to test my heart's deepest depths of resolve. Regardless of how deeply he continued to hurt me, I couldn't bring myself to walk out on him, not so soon after we'd taken the vows to one another we had. I hope it's obvious how seriously I took them in how much I did to support Matt — through EVERYTHING that hell could possibly have thrown at me. Sadly, it would only get worse as the spring wore on.

By Easter, Matt had gotten so paranoid that he suggested I change my professional name, right as I had begun working as a host for a T.V. show in L.A. called *Metal Scene T.V. Show*. He knew that would never fly in reality, and it was becoming clear by such retarded suggestions that he was growing increasingly jealous of not just my past, but my continued celebrity where he wasn't getting any fan attention. He would come with me to shows of the various bands I was profiling for the T.V. show, and I think deep down, when he was at these shows, he was saddened watching all these bands at the place he wanted to be, but wasn't. Sadly, rather than use my position to his advantage in terms of networking, he would sit there drinking all night and usually most of the next day after he awoke from yet another hangover. His whole life was a hangover as far as I was concerned. By that point I couldn't find a way to pull him out of it.

He attended the comic convention with me in New York that April, and I finally think it hit me how deeply out of control his jealousy was spiraling. The first sign of storms to come began at the airport after we landed, when he lost it after watching me sign an autograph for a random fan. In the photo, I was wearing a dress, not even a 2-piece, and after the guy had walked away, Matt lost it with me: 'You can't sell that photo at the convention, if you sell that photo, I'll leave you right now and fly home to Seattle.' How could I feel good about relationship where my sense of security was constantly being shaken, where I couldn't get any shelter? I actually felt shivers run through me at that point, and finally caved, agreeing not to sell that print at the show. Matt went as far as making me throw them in the airport trash, which made me furious because at these conventions, you make your money from autograph signings. Sure enough, I was right to be worried, because once we did get to the convention booth, Matt spent the entire day mad-dogging my fans as they asked for personalized autographs. For instance, I had one fan that drove all the way in from Connecticut, dropped about $300 on my stuff, and wanted me to sign an old nudie magazine, which Matt stepped in and stopped. His reason to the fan: 'She can't sign that, she doesn't endorse that.' I tried to maintain my composure as anger rose through me like a rocket launching, I was that red with fire, but in the calmest, sweetest voice I could muster, I said 'Matt, be nice honey.' And rather than getting my hint, he continued his protest, 'No, she doesn't endorse that.' I lost probably $1000 from his behavior at that show.

He was fucking with my bottom line, and ignoring the fact that I couldn't put on my advertisement in the convention lobby/promo materials that Jasmin St. Claire — sex symbol *international* — 'DOESN'T SIGN NUDE MATERIALS OF ANY SORT.' Could you imagine that? It defeats the whole purpose. It wasn't just on business trips either, at home I dealt with this type of manic jealous misbehavior all the time, and I'd find myself *CRYING* all the time because it was so frustrating. My friends hated seeing what I was going through, and they all tried to help in their own ways: one even sent me $2000 on the sly to help out because things were continually getting worse and worse financially. Matt was putting a stranglehold on my ability to earn a living, and when he wasn't bitching about my inability to support the both of us according to his strict moral standards he spent the rest of his time wining about missing his mommy in Seattle.

By the summer, what life we had left together had become a living hell. He would drink every night away at this neighborhood bar, and stick me with these $250 and $300 bar tabs due at the end of every week. If I threatened not to pay them, he'd counter with a threat to leave me. Even when he would admit he had a problem with alcoholism, he'd blame me, claiming his drinking habit was a coping mechanism for dealing with my adult film past. Then he'd run back off to the bar with his buddy Kaleb, who'd flown down from Seattle. I could tell, in addition to his usual griping about my past, Matt was equally as bothered by the present state of my celebrity. Traction had begun to gain with my new gig hosting the *Metal Scene T.V. Show.* He would HATE it when people recognized me in public, especially when it was a fan that had begun following me during my years in adult film. I couldn't win for losing with him, but couldn't imagine my life without him either. Not yet anyway. I just didn't know where he was going with all of this, but it didn't feel right in my gut, I was just too confused to know what to do at that point.

The only thing I could think to do was support him in his quest to get a new band off the ground, so all through that summer, I drove him back and forth to the Valley while his band was recording with Bob Kulick. In addition to the costs I'd already laid out for the demo — almost $3000 — I paid all the gas, bought and brought lunch to him at the studio every day. This was mainly because the loser didn't know how to drive a car, so I had to chauffer him not just to and from the studio, but EVERYWHERE. That's probably for the better because he was drunk so much of the time he likely would have wrecked my car in a DUI if he had had his license. I was the most supportive person of his music career out of anyone close to him, and its sad thinking back about it now how little his behavior reflected any thanks for that. Looking back, I also see now what a very self-centered guy he was — and many musicians are — but they usually have FANS to validate that egocentricity. On Matt's end, there were none, so I never understood why he felt entitled to act like a prima donna. I was his BIGGEST fan — and arguably only visible one at that point, including his family, so I guess I felt entitled to a little more than what he was giving me in the way of love and appreciation.

Amid the battle I was waging to save my marriage on the West Coast, back home on the East Coast, I was also fighting with my mother in court over inheritance money my father had left me that she wouldn't give up control of. She already didn't approve of my marriage to Matt, but then again, she had never approved of any guy I'd dated since high school so I was trying not to rock that boat as settlement talks between she and I went on. Still, Matt was constantly asking me to meet her, an introduction I DEFINITELY did not intend to make given how uncontrollable his O.C.D. blathering about my adult film past had gotten. I had kept that from my mother entirely, and didn't intend to give dipshit the opportunity to rat me out to her with the litigation still hanging over us. That was just common sense, which Matt clearly had none of.

By the fall, things hadn't improved between my loving, supportive husband and me — *what a shocker!* — But I was doing my best to hang in. I could never understand what I had done wrong as a wife, but Matt still had this talent for mind-fucking me into believing all of his possessive jealousy and verbal abuse was my fault. He was always challenging me to prove how much I loved him, draining me of energy and the funds to keep our life going at the same time. Every day, he would make me feel shittier and shittier about myself, and I kept apologizing, but it never seemed to make a difference. Nothing was ever good enough for him, and it FINALLY sparked a glimmer of light where I'd been blind from love to the question of: Was this guy possibly using me? It sure felt like it at that point, and once that possibility had started dawning on me, it made things like his buying my birthday present that year at Tiffany's on a credit card I eventually paid off, that much harder to ignore. It was a habit on his part that was becoming harder and harder for me to afford as well which made the news that his Himsa settlement check was coming in soon that much more welcome. It was the first money he would be bringing in during the time we'd been married, and no sooner had he gotten the news, in his head he was already spending half of the roughly $8000 he was due, on a new guitar!!!

When I reminded him we had a heavy credit card debt and we needed to put at least half the check toward it, he shot me a dismissive 'of course,' and then launched into me about my 'racy' role in *Dorm Daze II* — it was a movie where he'd sat on the set and watched me film. Still, now, over almost a year of marriage later, it was suddenly too racy for his conservative taste, and since I'd gotten rid of anything 'porn-related' he could complain about, this was the next desperate level he'd sunken too. It was disappointing in ways I can't even fully describe in words, because he was now demeaning the transition I'd worked so hard to make from adult film/wrestling into mainstream T.V. and film gigs. To realize that my own husband would stoop as low as to try and tear down that progress was the equivalent of his spitting in my face, and I finally felt he'd crossed a line that I couldn't forgive. Looking back in hindsight, it was obvious to me that he wasn't ready to be married, I had his back that way, but he clearly didn't have mine. Whenever people in the business would talk shit about him behind his back or online, I was the FIRST to come to his defense, but all he could do in return was talk the same kind of shit to me about my past. At that point in our *marriage*, he had nothing going on with his career and was drinking to cope with it, and instead of admitting THAT was the root of his drinking, he chose to blame it on me and things I'd done almost a decade before.

A lot of our turmoil at that point stemmed from Matt out of desperation to have some hangers-on like he had back in the Himsa days — having hooked up with all these little 19 and 20-year-old equivalents of the cast of the movie *Mallrats*. He spent his days at the bar illegally plying them with drinks, then listening to them build him up about how *Dorm Daze* was my most offensive on-screen appearance ever. Since he'd never watched the movie to begin with and wouldn't because of all the shit his little under-aged rat-pack was telling him would upset him, he never really could be informed. Sitting here now, I can't believe I'm even bothering to give him this much explanatory air-time in MY life story, but he was my husband, and I want my fans to understand why I went to such lengths to try and save my marriage. I felt like there was no way a bunch of kids, who operated on my ex-husband's maturity level, could break up our home. The whole thing seemed silly to me to begin with, but because they fed into his desperate ego, Matt took them seriously, which meant that I had to as well. Accepting the fact that my husband had the emotional maturity of a teenager was difficult to accept, but as time went on, it explained a lot of his naiveté, and made me seriously begin to question whether we could really have a future together.

We were definitely not at a good point in our marriage, and I'd finally begun to quietly accept the possibility that things might not change. I had been the fiercest believer in the opposite notion with Matt for too long, and it had taken so much out of me that letting go of hope was at times the only freedom I felt being with him. Most of the time I felt trapped, but still in spite of a CHORUS of noise from friends of mine that I needed to cut my losses and leave him now before things got any worse for me, for some reason, I couldn't let him go. I spent Thanksgiving that year in L.A. laid up sick in bed, and things weren't looking any brighter heading into the end of the year. Matt's picking and picking at me about the National Lampoon movie got so bad at one point in early December that he actually walked out on me! After a week, he came back on his knees, crying and telling me he loved me, but it didn't give me hope things would really improve. I'd started to lose faith in him as a real man by that point, but tried to give things another shot given it was the holidays, and the little girl in me still believed sometimes miracles could happen at Christmas. That's what I told myself anyway, I just loved him too much to let go of him that easily, even as difficult as things already were.

When Christmas rolled around that year, Mr. Romantic decided to thank me for all these nice presents I'd bought for him by taking me to dinner at the fucking Rainbow Bar and Grill. I love the Rainbow, but it's not exactly Ruth's Chris Steak House, which we probably couldn't have afforded at that point anyway. We were going broke, FAST, and every time I tried to bring up our financial situation, Matt would hit me with a new rant about my past and how he didn't want to live off that money. Still, he wouldn't lift a finger to try and bring in any new revenues, all he kept doing was talking on and on about his forthcoming Himsa settlement check. What he didn't want to hear was the reality that we were so deep in debt at that point that his measly $7000 or $8000 wouldn't begin to cover what we owed. Let alone, what we would owe as time went on and interest rates continued to mount on the credit cards we'd been living off. We spent New Year's Eve at the Terrace Bar and Grill in Marina Del Rey, and I did my best to let my mountain of worries go for the moment, but in truth, I couldn't shake my worries for our future. I just wanted to die. I tried hanging myself finally when Matt had been drinking, but stupidly, I didn't tie the noose tight enough, and my feet were too close to the ground. Besides, who would have taken care of the cats?

PART XXI

Thanksgiving Debacle

2007 began with the receipt of Matt's Himsa check, which was a nice, albeit brief reprieve from our impending financial storm front. Matt was still off living in a fantasyland land that I was bankrolling. In reality, and at this point, my savings had been sucked almost entirely dry — down into Matt's liver via his nasty alcohol addition, which he spent virtually every day up until this point perfecting, rather than focusing on music or making our marriage work. On top of that, there hadn't been any movement with his new band demo, which was truly worrisome. I'd driven him all over L.A. that prior fall to labels to shop it, using all my connections at Metal Blade Records, Century Media Records, and telling all the bands I interviewed for *Metal's Dark Side* and my TV show about his new group. I had been his biggest promoter up to that point, but the bottom line was his music had to stand on its own, and no one had offered a deal thus far. When he did finally receive his settlement check from his ex-band Himsa, it was bittersweet because the money was already spent.

Of the $8000 he received in his settlement, we paid about $3500 off on a credit card I'd been paying for him; then he took another $3000 and bought a new fucking guitar, as if he didn't have enough of those lying around. After the credit card tab and the guitar, and settling with Bob Kulick on the balance we owed for the demo I'd financed 90% of the past summer, we were left with a little under $1000 to look ahead with. Thankfully, the NAAM convention came in later January, which was my first real opportunity that year to make any new money, so I was excited to go and just praying that Matt didn't fuck anything up for me during my signings with his drinking and jealousy. I was signing for Coffin Case, and also covering the convention live for the *L.A. Metal Scene TV Show*, which was a big deal for me, because I got to email Lamb of God, Opeth,

Arch Enemy, Hatebreed among a bad-ass list of others! Sadly, by the end of the first night, even though we'd had a good time hanging out with our friends from Cradle of Filth, Shadows Fall, and Dragonforce, Matt had predictably been drinking and drinking so much that night that even his friends were getting worried.

By 3 in the morning, we were arguing about the fact I had to get up and work the next day. By the time he was done calling me every name in the book in the parking lot of a Taco Bell, I realized his alcoholism was past the point of no return. I had held out hope for so long that he would change, or sober up long enough to realize how much we really had to lose at that point, but he'd let me down every time. My husband had become a joke, a horrible joke, and his drinking problem was far worse than Earl's had been. Earl was an annoying drunk, at worse, Matt was a *DANGEROUS* drunk. He even had the audacity when we woke up arguing the next morning, to suggest we should divorce because I was ruining his career, vs. the alcohol. It was unbelievable, and day two of the convention wasn't much of an improvement: Matt spent the whole day drinking while I was working the convention floor doing band interviews for my T.V. show. He ended that night the same way, which was highly inconsiderate to the next day I had before me, which included another signing, interviews for the T.V. show, and a fashion show, all of which I had to fit into one day.

After the fashion show, we headed home and I found out Matt had blown $500 of the $1000 he had left out of his settlement check on a bar tab! I was livid, but tried to keep things on an even keel while I figured out whether to stay in the marriage or not. I felt at that point as though I'd spent my entire adult life taking care of the men in my life, and felt it was time the one I'd chosen to be my husband stepped up for me for a change. Still, when I broached the subject of his getting a job of ANY sort, his solution — as usual — was to berate me about my adult film past and suggest I was somehow holding him back as a musician. It was laughable, and honestly, by that point, Matt could have been one of those clowns on that A&E show *Intervention.* He was that sad of an addict and his concept of reality rested entirely in whatever bottle of Jack Daniels he was pounding that day.

That February, for his birthday, we were so broke I could barely afford to buy him a present, and by March, things looked the bleakest they had at any point in our relationship. Matt had become so controlling by that point that he wouldn't allow me to even do booth signings at conventions! That was my bread and butter, and the fact that Matt was jealous of any fan of mine because he attributed ALL their adulation to my adult film past was ludicrous! It was also bringing us to the literal edge of financial ruin. To put that reality in perspective for my readers — even though Matt still didn't seem to get it — by that April, for the first time in my adult life, I had problems paying the rent. Not surprisingly, my deadbeat husband — as usual — was doing **NOTHING** to contribute to our living expenses, and had put such a choke-hold on my ability to cover those costs that I was beginning to feel suffocated, and even panicked in a way I never had before in my life. I even felt so desperate about Matt's drinking problem that I resorted to calling his mother to speak to her about it, but she basically blew me off.

When our eviction notice arrived later that month, I was heart-broken. I'd lived in that apartment for a decade, it was my home, where all my memories had been built, and were now being torn to shreds — along with what was left of my dignity, heart and marriage. I was at a true low point, and the fact that Matt wouldn't even swallow his pride to call his parents and borrow a month's rent just made my heart sink even lower. Everything was on me at that point, and I didn't know if I had the strength to pull through this time. We got a Notice to Appear re our eviction about 10 days later, and I'd hoped at the very least that would be a wake-up call of sorts for Matt to see how desperate things had gotten, but it seemed lost on him. I wound up selling furniture trying to come up with the outstanding rent, precious keepsakes like the first dresser-set I'd ever bought after moving to L.A., our living room couch that I'd had for years, gone. I was watching the pieces of my personal life being removed one by one, and didn't know how much more I could take, or have taken from me.

By June, we were formally being evicted, and our plan was to move to Seattle to live in Matt's parents' basement while we re-grouped, with my cats being left out back in the cold in some chicken coup. It was rock-bottom, and it was the first time in my life — even with everything I'd already been through — that I felt I'd really hit that point. No matter what emotional issues I might have been working through in the course of my adult film career, that pain was at least compensated for by the stardom and financial stability I'd worked so hard to accrue. From there, working my way out of that business, out of those fucking strip clubs and into wrestling performance/promotion- it had all been a climb upward. Then graduating into the world of Metal as a model and Veejay personality, for every sacrifice I'd made along that way, there had been a reward, which to me had offered at least some sense of it being worth it. Now, having watched all of that slowly slip away over the past year into the avalanche that was now bearing down on us, I felt completely helpless for the first time in my life.

On top of everything else, I could tell his parents HATED the idea of my moving in with them, and was desperate to avoid us having to take that route. I knew it would be the ultimate death of our relationship, and after losing everything else in my personal life, it was the only thing I had left to fight for. Thankfully, my then-best friend Sickie came to the rescue and offered that we could move temporarily to New York to live with him until we got back on our feet. It was the first lifeline anyone had thrown us that I really welcomed, and was truly relieved we didn't have to lower ourselves to living in my husband's parents' basement. Still, it was perhaps the only silver lining to an otherwise very dark set of clouds hanging over us. When we finally were evicted, we had to leave my bedroom set because we didn't have room in storage. We had to leave my six cats in L.A. with friends of Matt's, and sell my beautiful yellow Mustang that had been my dream car for many years and that I'd worked my ass off to buy. A dear friend of mine paid for our plane tickets to fly to New York, and when we landed, I was just relieved to be away from the shame of everything that had just gone down back in L.A.

Thankfully, later that June, I signed at a comic convention in New York and made a few thousand dollars, which helped get us back in our feet in the very short term, but we were still living very much day to day. Matt had also landed a gig with Warrel Dane's solo band, and was writing a lot of material for that while I helped Sickie run his eBay business, so I just focused on making sure I didn't lose my career like we had everything else. As happy as I was for Matt finding a potentially viable music project, it hurt me deeply that his parents were willing to shell out $1500 to help him buy a 4th guitar when they wouldn't lend us that same money to keep from being evicted back in L.A. I felt our marriage at that point was definitely in a probationary period of sorts, and so I tried to be supportive and not make an issue of it, but quietly, it stung me deeply. I knew that even if things got better between Matt and me by some miracle that his parents would never accept me into their family, and I found an entire new struggle trying to make peace with that.

In later July, we decided to move back to L.A. to rebuild our life, and were crashing on my friends' Bobby and Shelia's couch while I waited on some royalty money from Australia to get moved into a new apartment. While things had been temporarily peaceful in New York, as soon as we landed back in L.A., Matt was back at it with me again, picking fights over nothing and drinking himself under the table on a daily basis — when we could least afford it. We finally found a cute studio apartment in West Hollywood that I felt I could live with, and even though we had a roof over our heads again, we had no car and no money coming in on Matt's end, so again I became our sole provider. At this point, I had stopped giving a shit about the fact that my husband was a deadbeat; I was in survival mode, trying to make sure the rent stayed paid and that I could afford payments on the little car I'd managed to get my hands on. More importantly, I had to quickly re-establish my presence back in L.A., and began working again on my *L.A. Metal Scene T.V. Show* in August, focused on the future and picking up the pieces of my career, and maybe in time, the rest of my shattered life. Little did I know that the worst was yet to come.

As the fall blew along, things were beginning to look up because Matt was going to be heading to Nashville in later October to begin work with Warrel Dane of Nevermore on his solo project from the record label for his songwriting on the album. I was happy for the most part because I felt maybe Matt had finally found something that might actually encourage him to do something with himself professionally. For almost the entire duration of our relationship up to that point, he hadn't done anything once his stint in Himsa had ended. Many of his friends had let me know that there had been musical opportunities that had come his way in the interim, but he'd been happy to mooch off of me, and really hadn't ever carried his weight financially in the marriage. So this was great news it was a chance for him to do something to contribute, because I'd been so busy paying for everything, putting a roof over our heads that we were running out of money. I'd loss the income from my website since he made me take it down and though I had some money coming from a 3PW licensing deal for Australia, I was really looking forward to my trip there to further shore things up. I had a really big signing lined up with wrestlers Rob Van Dam and Sabu for the Armageddon Festival in

Australia, and I'd decided to bring Matt with me so we could get away together. Naturally, I paid for his ticket because he had no money of his own, and we stayed in a really nice hotel, were taken out to dinner that night by my friends, so everything was comped for him, thanks to me. Nonetheless, he still saw fit to act like a dick throughout the entire trip, and was drinking heavier than ever. By the time it was over, I'd thankfully made about $4500, most of which I put into an IRA I wanted to replace and keep safe from Matt's alcoholic clutches.

One night I got us into Motorhead's show through my relationship with Lemmy, who let us all backstage, and it gave Lemmy and me a chance to catch-up. Lemmy is someone I've always thought really highly of, and he has to be one of the nicest people I've ever met in L.A. People see him as a God, but to me, he's always been Lemmy — this really kind-hearted person. He's better than Dr. Phil when it comes to advice! Matt was busy wandering off backstage, throwing back Jack Daniels and Coke one after another, and after a while, was acting like a total dope in front of my friends. I'd dealt with this once before with Earl Slate, who was also an alcoholic and drug addict, and it had just kept getting worse and worse with my husband. I'd even called his mom earlier in that year to alert her to the fact that I thought he had a drinking problem, and of course, she blew me off, which I thought was sad given it was his own mother. I've always been a very loyal and loving person, the type of person who puts my significant other first when I love them, and makes them my priority, which meant I was putting Matt's problems before my own happiness. Though that should have been his # 1 priority, I wanted him to get well. Even though he acted like a drunken ass all week, I tolerated it in the hopes things would change. Still, in another part of my heart, I knew the end of Matt and I was getting near. It wasn't a matter of if, it was matter of when.

When we got back to L.A., we were in the midst of a drama with my landlord over this old toxic heater they wouldn't fix. Thankfully, we were leaving town right after we got back to go to Nashville for Matt to record his guitar parts for Nevermore singer Warrel Dane's solo album. Matt and Warrel were working with this songwriter Peter Wichers and I was excited for Matt to finally be recording new music. He and I stayed at this horrible Days Inn because Warrel — also a raging alcoholic — was staying at the band's apartment, and I didn't want him and Matt together drinking it up all night when Matt was there to work. In an odd way, I felt inside as though this was our last chance to get on our feet again as a couple, namely by Matt starting to take some kind of aim professionally toward being a real man and pulling his weight financially. While he was recording, I'd bring Matt down food to the studio because he had low blood sugar, and our money was starting to run low. One night Warrel offered to take me out to Applebee's for lunch while Matt was working, and we ended up getting thrown out because Warrel was being drunk and louder than the staff apparently would tolerate. It shows you how these two were evil twins, and in an example of how much worse things got once they were together, on one of our last nights in town, Warrel took us out to Ruth's Chris Steakhouse for dinner. Naturally, he and Matt got wrecked throughout the meal to the point where Warrel excused himself at one point in mid-conversation, turned away from us and vomited underneath the table before returning to the meal/convo as if nothing had happened. We stayed with Warrel for the last few days in the band's apartment, and after tripping over empty Vodka bottle after empty Vodka bottle, I decided it was just a really unhealthy environment for me to be around. Thankfully, I was able to move us to the album producer, Peter Wichers' house, which was a cleaner environment for everyone involved.

The next time we touched back down in L.A., things only got worse when I was greeted walking in my door to an eviction notice. Amazingly, Matt's check from Century Media Records arrived within the next couple days, and he wouldn't use any of the money toward fighting it. I finally begged $300 out of him but saw from that action among many others how arrogant he was becoming, walking around with a rooster chest like a big rock star. It finally began to occur to me that I might be too good for him, which love had blinded me too up to that point. I was always a very smart woman until I fell in love...I never learned my lesson. Still, just as I had begun to feel like I was starting to see things clearly, everything went into a sudden blur. I had had what I thought was our final fight one night in early November, shortly before heading out to the Rainbow Bar and Grill on Sunset with some friends to blow off steam. Someone wound up drugging my drink that night, and while thankfully no one took advantage of the situation, I wound up barely making it home. After my ride dropped me off, I started losing consciousness as soon as I walked into the apartment, knocking over a lamp, slamming into a dresser on my way to the floor in a blackout. When I woke up the next morning on the kitchen floor, I saw I'd knocked right into Matt's laptop and knocked over one of his guitars. I felt horrible, even though it was a total accident, knowing he wouldn't understand. Sure enough, when I'd woken up, he'd already been home, packing his things, and greeted me with ' I'm leaving you, don't want anything to do with you anymore, don't touch my shit, I want a divorce, you fucking cunt.' When I tried to explain what had happened, he blew me off and left me instead.

When we finally spoke a couple days after, he said he'd decided to move back to Seattle, and left me to deal with the eviction alone. Strangely, he called a couple days later from San Francisco, told me he loved me, had always felt I was his partner, knew he was wrong, and to come up to join him in Seattle. As soon as I felt we were finally getting somewhere in the relationship, just as Thanksgiving Day arrived, he pulled a complete 180 and dumped me by email. I'm sure that move was partly his parents' doing, but to have led me on like that was cruel, and my heart was broken. I spent Thanksgiving at my friend's house, and felt just horrible and confused and completely depressed about everything. Back home, things were worse with the Eviction court date approaching on December 3rd.

I was broke with no where to live, and even though the apartment management company eventually settled with me out of court, I had to move all our belongings into storage at the last minute and couldn't even afford a hotel to stay in till things were settled. I'd never been at a bleaker point in my life heading into the holidays. I know how good an actress I am though by the front I put up for everyone during that December. To start with, I had no car because I'd had to sell it to get Matt out of debt the year prior, so I had to rent a mini-van, where I and my four cats wound up LIVING for a few weeks. I would go into work every day at Fuse TV to film a special I was hosting for them, and would shower every morning at my work-out gym without anyone realizing I was essentially homeless. It was the scariest moment of my life; I had no sense of security because Matt had essentially taken care of me. I was lost, and remember driving up the 5 freeway toward Seattle on Christmas Eve, not knowing exactly what I was doing, but thinking there might be one more chance for us. I also bided my time transcribing an interview I'd done with King Diamond, which was the month's only highlight. He was really cool to talk to, and it was a cover story for *Rock Brigade Magazine*, and actually ended up selling it to two other magazines as well, so it gave me some small sense of meaning during that dark, dark time. I remember I was at an internet café I worked out of a lot, one day I happened in the course of checking my MySpace email to see Matt's page, where he'd already changed his status from married to single. Just like that, it was over. I don't remember driving as I processed all of this, just that I wound up by the ocean in Santa Monica, and spent Christmas alone in my cold, rented van with my four cats. I also spent New Years that way, it was the dreariest ever, because it also fell on mine and Matt's wedding anniversary of all days! I felt like my life was going nowhere, and actually thought about killing myself again, but decided I wouldn't give Matt the satisfaction of knowing he'd gotten the best of me.

PART XXII

2008: The Year of New Beginnings (and the 42-Year Old Virgin!!!)

I resolved heading into 2008 to get my life back on track without Matt, beginning with the good news that my Australia licensing advance was finally showing up, which allowed me to take a sublet in the Marina. I couldn't rent an apartment on my own at that point because my credit was so FUCKED (Thank You, Matt), but I didn't care, I was just grateful to be living with a roof over my head again. I had the NAMM Convention coming up later that month. I was nervous because I knew I'd invariably run into Matt for the first time since our pre-holidays split, and heard he'd been spreading lies all over town about me to our friends, claiming I'd cheated on him, playing the victim as he always did.

By the time the NAMM show arrived, I felt I'd made my case, and felt a lot better showing my face, which I was contractually obligated to do anyway, at the convention. I had interviews to do for the *Metal Scene TV Show*, and had started working for Stay Heavy TV in Brazil, as well as writing for *Rock Brigade Magazine*, in addition to my usual signings for Coffin Case, etc. So things were looking up professionally, free of the weight of Matt to drag me down. I could sign my name however I liked to, or talk to whoever I wanted to on a professional basis at the convention without worrying about his jealousy flaring up. When I finally did run into him, it surprised me both at how bad he looked which was like total shit — and at how little I cared. I just shot him the coldest stare anyone could conjure up in that moment of freedom, and could tell he felt it. He wouldn't even look at me, let alone speak to me. It was really good for my ego, and I celebrated by going out and partying my ass off every night of the convention. I worked as hard as I partied too, making a bunch of new connections, and feeling pretty confident I'd made the right move by letting go of such a heavy monkey on my back.

Matt responded by serving me with divorce papers at the end of January, by some fat chick that I used to help get into shows and help her pathetic ass out socially, no less. I found out Matt had been staying at her house, using her, no doubt, for a place to crash, and who knows what else. She was a fucking pig, and she had no business sticking her snout in my business. The impending divorce made life a little harder emotionally throughout February, which featured both Matt's birthday and Valentine's Day, and the reality of our leading separate lives hit me once and for all. There were days I was heartbroken, but there were more days when I was determined to remain resilient and rise above the lows I'd traveled with that scumbag. I knew I was better off without him, and decided to focus over the rest of the spring on getting my life back on track. I still had all sorts of legal madness to get through, and began sorting through it all by hiring a lawyer to represent me in the course of my divorce. Matt was trying to dump all our debt off on me, just as I was working through trying to let him go. I knew this time in my life was a wake-up call for me to realize the relationship was done and over with, and I knew for the first time in my heart it was time to move on.

As the spring wore on, I began the formal process of legally untangling myself from both Matt in the courts, as well as from YET ANOTHER lease, because my rental turned out to be a sublet of a sublet that was ending soon. The latter was affected by the former because my credit had been so fucked up in the course of our marriage that I couldn't get a lease anywhere in my own name. This was such a far step down from where I thought I'd be at that point when I'd married Matt 3 years earlier. It wasn't the first time I was cleaning up an ex-boyfriend's messes, but I was determined this time would be the last. Word by this point had gotten out among our friends in the Hollywood social scene that we had split. So in the course of re-entering that world, my friend had flown in from Florida to see her boyfriend, Paige, lead singer/guitarist from a band, and was staying with also as for moral support while I got back on my feet. She was a stripper name Angie, and though she would later turn out to be a back stabbing bitch, or as I like to call her type: a professional groupie-in-training, initially it was nice to have the company. After she had a falling out with Paige, he ended up dropping her things off at the Marina, and we wound up being one another's shoulder for the last 10 days of her stay. She called herself ***Angie Disas on her MySpace page, and as time went on, I found it to be an appropriate name. I found out after she left that she had been trolling through my computer contacts and business cards looking for numbers to steal. It was a very vulnerable time in my life, and I guess that reflected in my ability to see people's true colors at that point, but was trying to keep the faith.

With my court date in April fast approaching, I'd hired a lawyer to handle the appearance for me. I was sad to learn my hopes for recovering some of the money Matt owed me through the course of debts he'd run up during our marriage, were dashed with the news that the State of Washington tends to favor the husband financially in these types of actions. Heading into the court hearing, I had this nervous feeling in my stomach that reflected the general way I'd been feeling around then — constantly anxious, emotionally empty, and unsure of whom to trust. The break I needed came when the divorce was finalized and the judge reverted all decisions regarding the settlement of financial issues to be decided in the State of California, which I found to be a huge relief. I was actually surprisingly upbeat given the added bonus that Matt had shown up to court without an attorney and his mommy and daddy acting as his lawyer instead. I burst out laughing when I'd heard that Matt's father was actually squabbling with the judge, wining about various financial issues I guess he'd assumed would be settled in Washington instead of California. It was a potentially huge legal victory for me, and I decided to use it as a motivation to keep the faith, and look to the future. I felt like I was engaged in a game of chess, and that Matt had just lost a big piece on his side of the board.

As April neared its end, I was busy packing to move out of my Marina sublet when the original owner of the lease actually came back into town early and walked in on us! She had no idea I had been living there, and it wasn't until I'd explained everything that she agreed not to call the police! I grabbed up another sublet in West Hollywood, which returned me to Matt and my old stomping ground, but I looked at it in a way as glorified storage since I was leaving for Brazil in early May. I loved Brazil, and felt it would truly hold my best prospects for a new beginning, especially since things professionally were looking very promising. Brazil has a huge metal market but not a lot of celebrity veejays, and I had a pretty good following there to build on, so I'd started writing for *Rock Brigade Magazine* and vee-jaying for *Stay Heavy* Metal *TV Show*, the premier metal show in South America. I posted somewhat of a thank you on MySpace when I left the states, to those who had stuck by me on my divorce from Matt which read: 'I just wanted to say thank you to all of my fans and loved ones for their support through my divorce and the crap that also went with it. Thanks for understanding and keeping me strong. Without the love of my fans, I seriously would have hung myself. Without the love of my friends such as Amy, Angie, Tommy H. & Sickie, I never would have made it as far as I have. It is nice to know that when I was homeless & almost penniless because of Matt Wicklund (yes, the guy that dumped me after he had my unconditional love & support for years. No, I never cheated on him like he is lying to everyone to save face. Ultimately, he was just jealous that I had people who love me and admire me & stood by my side. So many great things have happened since & I will never shut my heart down to anyone. I know that many of you were concerned that this bad situation jaded me, but it has not & it never will. I hope that one day my story may inspire someone to follow their dreams and be strong. I also hope that one day my story of when my ex left me for dead & penniless & the fact that I was living in a van with our 4 cats & pulled myself up by my bra-straps to better myself will inspire someone one day. I am going forward and doing an autobiography. My story needs to be told by me, not some stupid internet website that has their facts wrong. There is a reason why Rhea became Jasmin St Claire. I need to tell my story for the sole reason of hopefully changing someone's life for the better.'

I stopped off in Miami on my way to Brazil to film some interviews for *Stay Heavy TV*, and got to spend some with my friend Mustis, the keyboardist in Dimmu Borgir, who I also saw while I was down in Florida. When I arrived in San Paulo, Brazil I felt like I'd finally escaped the craziness of L.A. and all the drama surrounding my divorce with Matt. It had been a dark cloud following me around for too long now, but here there were only blue skies, and I really felt like I was going to be given a clean slate personally. Professionally, I was focused on expanding my fan base even further with my work for Brazilian TV and *Rock Brigade Magazine*, but I also had taken work as a celebrity promoter for a booking agency, working to get Metal bands to tour Brazil. The position wasn't a token position. I got it because of the network of contacts in the Metal world I'd built up from my work on *Metal's Dark Side* over the years. Through my contacts with the folks at Metal Blade Records, as one example, I was successful in bringing down a number of the band's marquee metal acts to Brazil, as well as getting their catalogs distributed in the country for the first time. Through that deal, we secured the release of the Cannibal Corpse catalog in Brazil, and in another distribution pact I brokered, we got Koch Entertainment to license Hatebreed's catalog for release. I had first been flown there to emcee a big Metal festival, but I found myself feeling so at home I decided following a brief June trip back to L.A. to start looking for a permanent place to live in Brazil.

Once I touched down back in California summer was in full swing in West Hollywood, which as far as I'm concerned is the bottom-feeder capital of L.A. Being single among a flood of men on the prowl, I found that while I didn't miss Matt, I actually did miss being married to someone in terms of dealing with the formerly mentioned assholes. While I'd just been in paradise, I was now in a place filled with fake, pretentious wanna-bes who drain your energy, and find out who you are and what you do and how you can help them. It's not my type of scene, because they are not constructive people doing anything positive. It's like a big rat race of people who couldn't be shit except the dirt below my shoe trying to compete with me — whether professionally or personally, when women would pretend to be my friend to go after my husband. I had rescued my position at the *Metal Scene TV* show back from that bitch and former friend of mine when I resumed my veejay post with Ron Estrada. I continued working with *Stay Heavy TV* covering concerts for them around L.A. Shortly after arriving back in town, I ran into the aforementioned bottom-feeder at the Rainbow Bar & Grill, one of MY longtime local hangouts, and decided to confront her once and for all on the subject. I can't fully describe the thrill I received from shoving her face in the bowl of clam chowder, but the laughter that erupted around me was enough validation that she had it coming. Another downer came in July when my brand new Ford Escape SUV was stolen out of my parking lot while I'd been out of town for a few days. I didn't have full insurance on the car as I was just getting back on my feet, so I had to eat the loss, which I could NOT afford! I hadn't had that fucking car six months. I ended up driving fucking rental cars after that when I was home in L.A., and because I traveled a lot, it wasn't as bad as it could have been I guess, but still sucked ass — just like the trick who stole my truck!

As the summer rolled on, I was staying extremely busy, filming 4 or 5 times a week covering shows for *Metal Scene TV*, but my heart was still set on Brazil. I went back down in July to do some work for *Stay Heavy TV*, and decided while I was in town to begin my formal search for an apartment. I had to return to L.A. in August but had an agent on the hunt for me in San Paulo. Back in the States, I managed to find a lease in Marina Del Rey, which was important for me personally because it made me feel like I'd come full-circle in a way from the bottom I'd hit in my relationship with Matt. It had always been home to me since I'd first moved out to L.A., and I'd lived there for almost a decade before I'd lost my apartment during my marriage. Reclaiming that part of my life meant something to me because it was the first I'd ever attained after moving to this city as a nobody, almost 15 years earlier, but it wasn't just materialistic. It was just a beautiful place, it was quiet and calm, and didn't have that whole Hollywood crowd mentality, and I'd always felt drawn to it.

With my personal and professional life getting back on track, I picked up another writing gig that summer working for *Cover Guitarra*, the biggest guitar magazine in Brazil, reviewing the metal scene in the States and writing a column. I also began working for Poland's Hard Rocker Magazine, which also had a huge following throughout Eastern Europe. It made me feel good to know my fan base was alive and well throughout both Europe and South America, where I'd really worked over the years through all of my various professional paths to expand and grow. Still, I hadn't attained anywhere near the popularity I had with those markets in adult film or wrestling, it had come primarily from my work as a metal veejay for *Metal's Dark Side* and my other metal-themed gigs. I had always loved the music as a fan, so it was that much cooler to be getting paid to work in a field I loved. I had had that experience in wrestling, but not as much because I had had to be the business brains as well as a performer. I was still my own best ambassador in the world of metal, but fans supported my transition from the wrestling to metal world because they knew I had a genuine love for both, and put equal heart into both pursuits! That popularity translated into my being approached at the end of August to appear on South America's version of *Dancing with the Stars*, which I turned down at the time, along with an offer for a Latin version of *Big Brother*. Both felt wrong at the time in context of my desire to stay fully-focused in becoming the South America's biggest Metal Veejay, which I felt required 100% of my attention. Also, on a personal level, I felt that the way they performed DWTS in South America was a little sleazier than I wished to be associated with at that point in my career, having worked as hard as I did to move out of and away from that world. It felt like participating might have been the equivalent of doing soft-core porn as far as my credibility would have been concerned.

I still wished Matt dead when I closed my eyes, so while time had been good to me, I knew I would need a lot more of it to go by before I was fully over the end of my marriage. The fall was an exciting time because heading into October I was invited by *Stay Heavy TV* to work at the Music Expo in Brazil, which was that country's equivalent of the NAMM convention in the States. In addition to doing interviews with all the major Metal stars attending the convention, I also was doing a big signing of my own at their booth, as well as a separate signing that had been lined up for me at the *Rock Brigade Magazine* booth. I knew it would be a great opportunity to network and expand my presence in the Latin metal world, which was a constantly growing market. I got to hang out with my friends in Sepultura and met Paul Diano from Iron Maiden. I also saw a lot of other cool international metal bands that had followings in South America, so the whole conference just had a really cool vibe, and I just felt overall there was a lot less drama in the Brazilian metal business — less bullshit, less wanna-bes. While at the convention, I also met a blonde-haired, blue-eyed German named Gerard who worked at LASER, which was the label I'd negotiated the deals with Metal Blade and other labels for among others, and we started hanging out. We went out on a couple of dates and I really liked him and he seemed to really like me, but for whatever reason, he didn't want to take it further. I thought maybe he was just a little more old-fashioned, so I raised the idea of staying a few extra days, and most men would jump at that, but he didn't for reasons I'd find out later. I still liked him though, and knew I'd be coming back down the next month, so we left it at that for the moment.

Back in L.A., all I could think about was Brazil. It was the place I definitely wanted to be. I was happier there and less stressed out, and I felt like there were far more professional opportunities available to me. To that end, I made my visit back to So Cal short and by early November was back down in San Paulo, and had even rented my own flat. I hooked back up with Gerard and while we felt like we definitely had chemistry things continued to heat up as we started dating. They would never quite explode the way my body wanted them to. Even with a full pack of Viagra and a penis injection, this guy could NOT get an erection! It had me instantly curious: was he secretly married? Had he been in a relationship previously where sex had been a big issue so he didn't want to rush into that? Did my past reputation as an adult film star make him nervous in bed? Whatever the case, millions of men have successfully celebrated plenty of fantasies about me over the years. Whether alone or with their girlfriend (or girlfriends) from some of the fan mail I've received — here is the one man I want to have sex with and he couldn't get his dick up to save either of our sex lives! I'd dealt with that on set before with fellow porn stars that had to inject themselves in the jimmy to keep it hard; that's the extreme they were willing to go to, in order to stay hard with me. And for all Matt's faults, that was never one of the problem areas in our marriage. Then I started to wonder if he was maybe gay?

A couple of nights later we had a big fight back at the hotel in Rio over his acting like a drunk Matt-type asshole down in the hotel bar. When we took it back up to the room, naturally, we continued to argue as he had no other plans for me. In hindsight, I was happy we did because he was thankfully drunk enough to reveal that the real reason for his impotence had little to do with me, or any woman for that matter, since it turned out he'd never been with one!!! And he was 42 years old!!! Yes, I was officially dating the '42 YEAR OLD VIRGIN!' I remember looking at him in stunned disbelief when he told me, and he started crying, begging me to be patient with him. I guess I felt bad for him in the moment, but thankfully was leaving for the holidays back to the States the next day and knew I had a lot to think about. I thought maybe his parents had emotionally — castrated him, but I was already over it. The bottom line is you can't be in a relationship with someone and not have a sex life; it never works, especially long-distance! As you can imagine, once I was back stateside, things slowed down dramatically with Gerard, but thankfully they were busy in L.A. I spent the early part of December doing a new round of interviews for *Stay Heavy TV* which was really cool because by this point, I was beginning to carve out a reputation as The Brazilian Metal Veejay around L.A. In addition to my work for *The Metal Scene TV Show*, the latter distinction is important because around L.A., one of the new trends I'd grown SO tired of among the West Hollywood wanna-bes were these little groupie bitches who had MySpace or YouTube Metal Shows. No one would legitimately hire them for that kind of work, so they 'self-published' so to speak, not understanding that after the first gig or so, you're only a legitimate Veejay if you get paid for your time. It just got more and more on my nerves because every time I'd return from Brazil, there were more and more of them popping up everywhere. Showing up at concerts I was covering for a legitimate television show with a real camera crew while they stood outside with a little camcorder or video cell phone pretending to do my job. Some of them would even follow my MySpace calendar of upcoming shows and show up there, it was stalker-ish and creepy, and something I looked forward to permanently escaping (along with L.A. altogether) in the new year.

In the course of filming those interviews, I covered a show by Dimmu Borgir, one of my favorite metal bands, and ran into my friend Mustis (a.k.a. Øyvind Johan Mustaparta,) Dimmu's keyboardist. We really had a blast catching up and among the other good bits of news I got from him during our meet-up was 1) he had just gotten out of a relationship (which I won't lie and say wasn't music to my ears), and 2) he would be back in the States for NAMM in January. That was an early Christmas present, and I wound up spending the holiday that year in the Marina, in a very different place in my life than I'd been a year earlier. I was grateful for all life's turn-around(s) that year, and I remained focused on 2009 and a future free of L.A. for good. I headed back to Brazil for a few weeks shortly before the New Year. I have to say I found it delightfully ironic that while I had spent the previous New Year's Eve in a van with my four cats, a year later I was looking out over the ocean from the balcony deck of a beautiful mansion in Rio de Janeiro sipping champagne. I remember making a toast/promise to myself for 2009: that entering into 2008, I'd had no idea where my life was heading, and wouldn't begin the New Year that way. I had refocused myself personally and professionally, and thought I was making great progress in moving with my life.

To sum the year up, I posted a very personal thank you on my MySpace blog to: 'Everyone who had stood by me in my turn-around, beginning my ode to you all with the very real acknowledgement of the fact that as all of you know at this time last year I was homeless, thanks to an ungrateful, selfish ex husband ('Cretino' is the word we use in Portuguese) who swindled me for my money. But I am SOOOOOOOOOOOOOOOOOOOOOOOO HAPPY that it happened. I wanted to thank ALL of you who gave me courage to live and see that I would be better off without him. I never saw it then, but I sure as hell see it now. It was a rough ride to get back on my feet. Last Thanksgiving was the worse, but then, we fast forward a year & here I am living in Sao Paulo like a total princess, at a BBQ in a mansion in Rio, doing really well. Getting the Rock City Music Award for best metal TV show (*The Metal Scene TV Show*); having the privilege of living in the USA, as well, and working here — working on Sao Paulo's premiere metal TV show. More magazines, a South American *Playboy* layout (yes, I took my clothes off one last time...I think many of you will be happy,) my own calendar, and sooooooooo much more. Who would have ever figured this would have happened? I know it sounds cheesy, but everyone's words meant more to me than anything else at that time. Thanks again... all of you were right!!! I am beyond thankful for all of the years I have had wonderful people who stood by me and, of course, those of you who have made fond memories for me that will be with me forever. I hope that all of you have a wonderful New Year and thanks again for the wonderful thoughts and words. Beijos, Jasmin.'

PART XXIII

2009 & Beyond...

I started off the New Year by formally breaking it off with Gerard for obvious reasons, as well as some unknown to him. Mainly having to do with the fact that I'd hooked up with Mustis from Dimmu Borgir, back in December, and we'd been talking on almost a daily basis via Skype, from Norway ever since. Knowing we were going to be together again at NAMM near the end of January had only fueled our fire, which I'd already confirmed he could stoke so to speak (*wink wink.*) By the time NAMM arrived, I was excited to see him, which was important because the rest of the convention proved to be something of a drag. It was the same old crowd, and I didn't even feel like going out to party my ass off like I had in 2008, it just felt different. I had really had it with L.A., by that point, and the convention felt to me like something of a sad circus. It wasn't the bands who made it suck either, it was all these stupid fucking wanna-be groupie YouTube/MySpace metal show Veejays wandering around the floor trying to blow the bassist from whatever metal band would give them the time of day. I did the Coffin Case Fashion Show, and my usual booth signings, as well, with a real camera crew — my interviews for *Stay Heavy TV* and the *Metal Scene TV Show* — but it felt like work for the first time. Not that I didn't love my work, but in terms of the people who didn't really belong there, in my opinion because they hadn't earned it, were flooding the floor that year. So NAMM was really an opportunity more than anything else for me to observe the people and all the bullshit that was around that I didn't want to be involved with. The Brazilian conference had been a much fresher experience. Not really due to the bands because I saw many of the same groups there that I did at NAMM, but because of the difference in attitude among the staff working the booths, etc., at the Music Expo. It just further validated my instinct that my future laid in Brazil.

Before I could leave, I had to deal with packing, which was a bitch, because I felt like I'd just moved into the Marina. I was planning to keep the apartment and sublet it out so I had a place to stay when I was in L.A., but I had set my mind to moving down to Brazil for real this trip. I'd sold all my furniture right before NAMM and aside from packing my belongings, there was also the issue of my cats to consider. At first, I'd explored my options for taking them down to South America with me, but they would have had to stay quarantined for 6 months among a variety of other issues. In the end I decided to find a good home for them back in L.A. which turned out to be a debacle all on its own. The people who I had lined up to take them — even though they came very highly recommended — wound up being mad reefer heads — lets call them Stems and Sticks. That would have been fine had I not worried about them eating all my cat treats, and more importantly, getting my money's worth since I was paying them to take cats that had been with me through thick and thin. Before I dropped them off, I'd bought them over $800 in supplies (food, litter, etc), and paid them some money to take care of the cats. Even though when I got to the house, it was wharfing with the smell of marijuana. My cats took to them right away, which was reassuring at first, but the alarms started sounding a couple days after that when she called to hit me up for even more money to 'bathe' the cats at the vet's. My reply was signature Jasmin, 'They just had baths 3 or 4 days ago, maybe it's you that smells?' She didn't really reply, and I left it alone, because I think she just wanted more money for weed. I was paying them $200 a week already, so we eventually decided to leave the original deal intact.

I headed back down to my lovely new home-to-be in South America the second week of February. I'd been invited to be part of the biggest festival in San Paulo, Brazil, by the largest Samba school 'Vai Vai' as part of their annual parade called CANIVALE, which is a really prestigious thing. I was their very first 'metal' celebrity invite to be part of a float. In the context of my local popularity there, was a really big deal professionally for me, and personally, because of the fans who helped make that happen. I posted this thank you to them in my online blog, which should help better explain how overwhelmed with pride I felt at the opportunity, explaining, 'This is kind of weird for some of you to understand, but it's actually a pretty cool thing. As a lot of you know, Carnival is one the most treasured events in Brazilian culture. It is a huge part of the culture here & quite a major deal to be invited. It is not just about shaking your ass or tits; it is a whole big deal and very hard to learn. I was invited by the biggest samba school in Brazil to be on their 'superstar' float at Carniva. I am also the first person in metal that has been invited (Matthew McConaughey was invited, and many other stars). Nobody from Sepultura was ever involved. I have to say that I am very proud, especially since my family is Brazilian as well. They judge the schools as they parade (the school that has invited me, won last year, so we are the last ones to parade. Trust me it's an hour long to pass thru the whole of Sambadrome.) They judge each school on the samba skills, outfits (yes, I have a very sexy gold outfit & will post pictures if you ask nicely,) their singing of the song and looks. It feels great to know that metal has now made it into the biggest, most traditional and very mainstream part of Brazilian culture and I feel honored to be chosen to represent the metal community. I am totally stoked to have accomplished this. There will be an extreme amount of press there as well. This is where the super model in me comes out. This is a very non-metal, but extremely glamorous thing and a great way to bring metal to an even higher mainstream level here. Expose more metal heads to the TV show (we already get over 9 million viewers here) I do here and get more attention to the bands whose videos we play on the show. I hope that those of you who get the Brazilian stations, and those of you in South America, watch me & cheer on!! Metal will always get bigger & bigger, Stay Brutal!!'

Ahead of the parade beginning, I had a video shoot lined up with a Latin boy band (no, NOT Menudo,) which was one of many fabulous new opportunities my press agent Marsha had helped to land for me. I also had a bunch of shows to cover for *Stay Heavy TV*. It felt like paradise, and from the second I got off the plane, I had a ton of shit to do. There was always a lot of pre-press before the big carnival, and in addition to that, I had to go to the Samba School who was sponsoring our parade float, Sambadrom, to pick up my outfit. In Brazil, in preparation for this annual festival, there are people who spend half the year just making the costumes outfits. You have to pick that out in advance, and how the procession generally works is that whoever won last year goes last, sort of like the headliner, and my school — which is the oldest and most prestigious in San Paulo — had won in 2008. Though it's a celebration, it's not a party the way you'd think because it's a big, big production people take a lot of pride in readying. I remember I was running back and forth between Samba rehearsals for the parade and the boy-band video shoot, which they shot around my schedule. We didn't get through till 3 or 4 in the morning and I was drained and so slap-happy, that what should have taken a half hour to wrap took a couple hours heading into the day of the festival. The day of the parade, I remember I went out to lunch with my publicist Marsha and the 42 Year Old Virgin texted me, desperate to hang out. When I turned him down, he replied by text with the question: 'Why do you have to make this so hard?' To which I answered: 'It's not like that's a subject you know anything about anyway, so let's just drop it.' The day of the parade, we were still in rehearsals as we had been the past few days prior. I was placed on the top-tier of the float, so had we not trained, we could have gotten really hurt. The parade was held in a town called San Paulo, and it is huge, it takes a whole hour to get through the whole thing, and the streets are lined with thousands and thousands of people, packed like a stadium. I remember before getting there that night, me and the other girls on the float had started drinking champagne, and then kept getting fucked up on whiskey with the rest of the half-naked float girls on the whole way over on the bus. They said to be there at 8 that night, which meant 9 or 10, so we were pretty ripped by the time we arrived even though they'd told us 'No more drinking, no more snorting coke, etc.' That was funny to me because our school preached this philosophy of living healthy, and the anthem we were singing on the float, in Portuguese, is all about health and well being. Nevertheless, our float turned out to be a big success at the parade. I was shown on Globo TV at least 30 times throughout the night. The same night the carnival happened, I posted the following blog entry on my MySpace site, beginning with the fact that after standing for so many hours, 'My feet are tired as hell. I was featured numerous times on the largest TV Station called Globo last night during the coverage for Sao Paulo Carnaval. I was placed on the first car float for Vai Vai in the front & we didn't parade until 4 a.m. The beats of the drum for our 'Bateria' really got my adrenaline pumping, so I danced my ass off for an hour. We waited for 5 hours before we could go.' We didn't go on till 2 in the morning, and the parade didn't wrap till the sun was coming up. We kept partying, went out to breakfast, and then home to bed. It was one of the truly most surreal and beautiful experiences I've ever had.

As the spring bloomed on, so too did my relationship with Mistus, we were getting closer and closer, and I couldn't wait to see him again at the end of February. I'd never communicated that well with any of my past boyfriends (and definitely not with my husband), so that was refreshing, as was the fact that we were getting along really well, and he turned out to be a lot different than I thought he was upon first impression. He had a 6-year old daughter and was a wonderful father, and as the weeks went by after our NY visit — with me back in Brazil and him in Norway — I couldn't wait to see him again. I had some shows to shoot for *Stay Heavy TV* at the end of March in Brazil, but in early April, planned to fly to Norway for the first time to visit him on his home turf. Over Easter, I met Mustis's daughter, parents, sister, and other family, and got on really well with everyone. It was entirely the opposite of my experience meeting Matt's family for the first time, because his family was actually nice and welcoming to me as his girlfriend. He was really grounded, as they were, so it was cool to see the stock he came from, and know he had been raised in a good home, and that his family supported his profession as an artist. I'd been in close quarters with the opposite, so as our relationship progressed, that was reassuring for me.

I headed back to the States in middle April and then to Brazil for work, with the plan to meet back up with Mustis in May in Norway, to join him on the road with his band for some summer tour dates. That's when the only downside of dating him appeared in the form of his band's jealous, shit-talking, super-bitch horns-and-micro-Manager who was constantly jocking me whenever I was around the band during rehearsals for home shows. My first encounter with her was during a late-May date the band had to play in Trondheim, Norway. I found out she yanked my pass to cover the show as a media member, and had been doing that for other festival dates I had been slated to cover for *Stay Heavy TV* that Dimmu Borgir happened to be playing. Mustis and I'd started planning out our summer, coordinating between his touring schedule and my shooting schedule for some shows throughout Europe that his band dates happened to be overlapping. Apparently, she'd gotten wind of his plan to have me out on the bus with the band, and told him I wasn't allowed to come out on the road. She put it in the guise of insurance restrictions, but we both knew the real reason for her not wanting me around was rooted in her jealousy. I flew home briefly to Brazil, and then met him in Germany, as the band's tour continued into June. Mustis actually rented a car separately so we could follow the bus and travel together between his dates. We slept in the car a couple nights when the band was sleeping in bunks on the bus on the road, but we stuck it out together in spite of the manager-with-horns-and-hooves' attempts to keep us apart.

At one point, I shared with fans my thoughts on the she-devil in the moment on my MySpace site in a blog that began with the colorful title,

'Love Hog Gone Wild.' Before you read this blog, let me explain to you what a love hog is. It is nothing to do with swine flu or Valentine's Day. It is a term generally reserved to describe a female that is particularly, but not always, unattractive and overweight. You can imagine how scared I must be when it has come to my attention that a particularly rabid love hog named Yvette has had me in her cross hairs and has been stalking me relentlessly for a while. She has yanked my passes when needed to cover concerts, had me banned on the van or bus that my boyfriend is traveling on (she also did this to another guy's girlfriend) and spread vicious rumors about me having diseases, including to people I do business with! I have done NOTHING wrong to this woman. I have never bothered her. In fact, if she wasn't saying all of these vicious things about me, I wouldn't even know that she existed. Maybe that is the problem. As we speak, I am lawyering up with my cousin's boyfriend who is one of the partners at Skadden Arps *(www.skadden.com)*, and forwarding all of the information that backs this up. Unfortunately, all of the money that I would get by winning a lawsuit against this 'love hog gone wild' would not compensate for the aggravation and heartache she is trying to impose on me. While I sympathize how hard it must be for a groupie trying to be legitimate by managing a huge band, there is no need for her to act the way she smells. Her attitude stinks as much as she does. She obviously does not want any other women around so she can be the only one and use the band's success to gain her own 'fame.' She has given me no choice but to fight back and stand up for myself. I would never do this to someone's manager, but I don't consider this woman professional. Any true manager would be insulted that this glorified groupie runs around calling herself a manager. I am not looking to pick a fight, but I am not running away either. This is a result of her starting with me. I am not the only person she has picked a war with; she did this to another woman as well. I have dealt with many cockblockers in my time, but never on this level. This is my first and last warning to her that I will fight fire with fire. Roast pig is one of my favorite dishes!!'

It was good we were in such a great place in our relationship because after his Munich concert we arrived at another of the tour's dates, where I ran into my ex-husband Matt for the first time since NAAM of 2008, after we'd first split up. I wasn't nervous about seeing him because I knew in my heart I was WELL over him, but it still presented the prospect of being awkward. Thankfully, Matt — though not surprisingly drunk and touring with a band called God Forbid — didn't want it that way either, and even helped me get backstage after Mustis's bitch manager stripped me of my V.I.P. pass. Not only did he get me backstage, but he also made sure I was able to stand on the side of the stage and watch Dimmu Borgir. Amazingly, even he and Mustis got along, which naturally was a huge relief for me instead of having tension in the air, which I'm sure has happened to every woman reading this before. This happened at another show where both bands happened to be on the same bill, and that time, Matt took me up to the soundboard to watch the band after that she-devil had had my backstage pass yanked. Unfortunately, this divisiveness continued throughout the dates, which only worked to bring Mustis and me closer together. When we were in Sweden for the last of that series of shows, I remember I was shooting some footage for *Stay Heavy TV* and the bitch tried to pull another backstage pass — thinking I was with Dimmu. I was able to tell her to fuck off because my access had come from working with another band. That felt like an awesome way to tell her goodbye with a middle finger!

I split the rest of the summer between Brazil and Norway, and looking to the future, I felt like I was looking out on really clear horizons for the first time in a LONG time. I have come full circle several times in my life — beginning with my induction into and graduation out of adult film, and everything thereafter I did as a pioneer for female promoters in the world of wrestling. I have carved out a niche for myself as the female face of death metal in both the U.S. and worldwide — given my show *Stay Heavy TV*'s continual expansion in popularity throughout South America, at 9 million viewers strong and growing. It's ironic to me that when I started out my career in adult film, my being multi-lingual made me seem exotic as it still does — only now, I literally am as a Veejay — I speak Portuguese when hosting *Metal TV* locally in Brazil. I have been amazed at the number of cultures I've had the opportunity to experience locally throughout my global travels over the past two decades, and have found Brazilians to be among the warmest. I feel blessed to call San Paulo home, and to have found the peace I have in my heart today living there. Sometimes when walking against the sunset along the beach near my home in Brazil — typically a time for reflection in most movies, greeting cards, or ballad music videos — that I really am like one of those few characters who escaped to paradise. When I look back on everything I've been through in my life leading up to now, I feel I've gotten a lot of closure, but at the same time I feel my life is still a very open-ended affair with the unknown. I find a great deal of comfort in that fact too because more than anything else I love the adventure of life. While I wouldn't encourage anyone to go down many of the roads I've traveled, I would also very honestly say I don't regret the consequences of my journey, as it was a means to the end of finding myself again...

CONCLUSION

In Order for Rhea to live… Jasmin must die…

To whom this may concern,

Writing this book has been an exhausting once in a lifetime cathartic experience. It has completely drained me. I feel emotionally flat-lined. In giving you my life story, I feel like I have given you a piece of my life & my soul.

Where do I go from here? Who the hell knows? I guess that after writing this book, I have realized how much of my life I have lived in denial. Looking back at it objectively, to say the least, is overwhelming.

Decisions that I have made, people that I have trusted & loved, have constantly let me down to the point where I no longer expect anything positive in this lifetime.

When I really get sad, I try to tell myself that life begins from this moment on and the past is as relevant as yesterday's newspaper. But unfortunately, the world is filled with people (you know who they are…Matt Wicklund) that will never let you forget the mistakes you have made and throw them in your face with a venom that would extinguish the spirit of the most optimistic and happy person. I still have nightmares about being shaken awake from a dead sleep with Matt's eyes bulging out of his head (I swear he had smoke coming from his ears) when he was berating me by serenading me, 'are you the gangbang queen or not?'

I guess it's not that hard to see why he reacted that way, given my former manager Charlie Fry's conclusionary assertion that: 'Even today — a decade later — in 2010, Jasmin is still in the top 10 in terms of brand name recognition.

Now particularly with the internet, there are thousands and thousands of girls, and back in her heyday, there were hundreds and hundreds of girls who did lots more movies than Jasmin ever did, and you couldn't name me one of them. But at the end of the day, people will always remember Jasmin St. Claire.'

I have never been the strongest person, any amateur psychologist, or anyone who has read this book, can tell you that. So, between being cursed with a fragile soul and a bruised ego, all of the snide remarks, all of the judgmental comments, all the sarcastic jokes about my past have taken a cumulative toll on my feelings and self worth. I cannot tell you how many times in the past decade I have attempted, or just thought about ending my life. Rationalizing that I would be doing my critics (my ex husband and ex boyfriends from hell) and the hypocritical charter members of the moral majority a favor...You know who you are...We have crossed paths many times on my turf. For example, the first boyfriend from hell, Dick, whose abusive ways were chronicled earlier in this entire book, is now a successful lawyer for a prestigious NYC firm. He parades around in a clown outfit he calls an Armani suit. Underneath his cheesy phony Australian accent and freshly groomed slimy fingers, is the same low life that not only beat the living crap out of me, but was able to convince me that I deserved it. I could never fight the Dicks of the world back with my fists, but I can fight them with the words more powerful than any punch to the head...the truth.

There is an expression that the truth will set you free. In my case, I want the truth to just let me rest in peace.

I am tired, burnt out, saddened, disgusted and my feelings are numb. I honestly don't know how much more of this I can take.

This chapter started out being an introspective reflection of my life, but I fear it is transforming into my own self-written obituary.

Before I do, or did, anything really drastic, I had to write this book and get my side of the story out to the masses. It is too late for me to save my own life, but hopefully my experiences can prevent others from suffering a cycle of abuse and attempted suicides like I have experienced.

I am also known as the mistress of extreme metal. So, at this point, I must defend the music I listened to. It was the only thing that stopped me from doing something drastic to myself or to the people who abused me.

The advent of the 'world wide web' and the process of how information is infinitely stored in a collective memory bank called the internet — caused several heartaches for me — and for my loved ones. My name is forever linked to one or more acts that I committed when I was a naive kid. I never dreamed that when I entered the world of porn that I would be taunted and haunted on a daily basis about a few acts where nobody or nothing was hurt or killed, except for my own self worth. Society has treated me like a pariah.

The only way I can escape the stigma of my past is to disappear off the face of the earth. At that point, nobody can whisper, 'isn't that the girl who?' or threaten to expose my past to my loved ones. I cannot tell you how many times I have met people who really liked me and were charmed by me and then after putting my name in a Google search, they would not even talk to me.

There are a million ways to die in this world such as overdosing on sleeping pills, pain killers, hanging myself, blowing my brains out, slicing my wrists up, jumping from a building or even drowning myself. Believe me, I think of them in alphabetical order on a daily basis.

I think my mark in this world is going to be that I will be the first person to die of unnatural causes. The coroner will state that Jasmin St. Claire did not die of any illness or injuries...she simply stopped breathing from being googled to death...

MARDI GRAS

ABOUT THE AUTHOR

Nashville-based music biographer Jake Brown has published twenty-five books, including the authorized memoir of founding Guns N Roses guitarist *Tracii Guns, Motorhead: In the Studio* (co-written with Lemmy Kilmister), *Jane's Addiction: In the Studio, Heart: in the Studio* (co-written with Ann and Nancy Wilson), *Rick Rubin: In the Studio, Dr. Dre: In the Studio, Suge Knight: The Rise, Fall and Rise of Death Row Records, 50 Cent: No Holds Barred, Biggie Smalls: Ready to Die, Tupac: In the Studio* (authorized by the estate), as well as titles on Kanye West, R. Kelly, Jay-Z, the Black Eyed Peas, and non-hip hop titles including *An Education in Rebellion: The Biography of Nikki Sixx, Red Hot Chili Peppers: In the Studio, Alice in Chains: In the Studio, Meat Puppets: In the Studio* (co-written with Curt and Cris Kirkwood), and the Behind the Boards Rock Producers Anthology Series. Brown is also a featured author in Rick James' autobiography, *Memoirs of Rick James: Confessions of a Super Freak,* and is the author of *'AC/DC in the Studio, Tom Waits: in the Studio,* and *Iron Maiden: in the Studio,* all due in the late spring of 2011. In February 2008, Brown appeared as the official biographer of record on Fuse TV's *Live Through This: Nikki Sixx* TV special and Bloomberg TV's forthcoming Jay Z special. Brown has received additional press in national publications including *USA TODAY,* MTV.com, *The New York Post, Vibe,* NPR, *Billboard, Revolver,* and *Publishers Weekly.* Brown was recently nominated alongside Lemmy Kilmister for the 2010 Association for Recorded Sound Collections Awards in the category of Excellence in Historical Recorded Sound Research. Brown is also owner of the hard rock label Versailles Records, distributed nationally by Big Daddy Music/MVD Distribution and celebrating its 10th anniversary in business.

Project Thanks: First to Jasmin for the amazing journey that has been writing this opus, I am happy we're finally heading to stores, congrats!; to Harry Slash for hooking Jasmin and I up in the first place; our literary agent, Albert Longden for your tirelessly hard work getting this book to the finish line; our publisher Ben Ohmart and BearManor Media for taking the chance you did on this memoir; Robin Perine for the AMAZING cover photo; Lemmy Kilmister, Ron Jeremy, George Fisher, Dominic Accara and Charlie Fry for the fantastic interviews; and lastly to my friends and family for your continued support of all the dreams I live to chase and chase to live!

Dangerous Curves atop Hollywood Heels
The Lives, Careers, and Misfortunes of 14 Hard-Luck Girls of the Silent Screen

VERNON DENT
STOOGE HEAVY
SECOND BANANA TO THE THREE STOOGES AND OTHER FILM COMEDY GREATS
BY BILL CASSARA

SEXBOMBS, SIRENS, BAD GIRLS AND TEEN QUEENS
50s
Fifties Blondes
RICHARD KOPER

Burlesque:
A LIVING HISTORY

by Jane Briggeman

FOXY LADY
The Authorized Biography of Lynn Bari

Yabba Dabba Doo! ...or Never A Star
The Alan Reed Story
by Alan Reed and Ben Ohmart

GEORGE RAFT
THE MAN WHO WOULD BE BOGART
BY STONE WALLACE

Just Joan
A Joan Crawford Appreciation
DONNA MARIE NOWAK

CPSIA information can be obtained at www.ICGtesting.com
Printed in the USA
267426BV00003B/88/P

9 781593 936044